CHINA UNDER REFORM

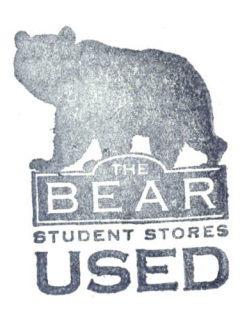

POLITICS IN ASIA AND THE PACIFIC
Interdisciplinary Perspectives

Haruhiro Fukui
Series Editor

China Under Reform, Lowell Dittmer

Global Television and the Politics of the Seoul Olympics,
James F. Larson and Heung-Soo Park

Japan's Foreign Aid: Power and Policy in a New Era,
edited by Bruce M. Koppel and Robert M. Orr, Jr.

Popular Protest and Political Culture in Modern China: Learning from 1989,
edited by Jeffrey N. Wasserstrom and Elizabeth J. Perry

Southeast Asia in the New International Era, Clark D. Neher

FORTHCOMING

Japan's Land Policy and Its Global Impact, Shigeko N. Fukai

Mass Politics in the PRC: State and Society in Contemporary China,
Alan P.L. Liu

Nationalism in Contemporary Japan, Bruce Stronach

Comparative Politics of Asia, Sue Ellen M. Charlton

Popular Protest and Political Culture in Modern China,
Second Edition, edited by Jeffrey N. Wasserstrom
and Elizabeth J. Perry

Southeast Asia in the New International Era, Second Edition,
Clark D. Neher

*This Volume Is Sponsored by
The Center for Chinese Studies,
University of California, Berkeley*

CHINA UNDER REFORM

Lowell Dittmer
UNIVERSITY OF CALIFORNIA, BERKELEY

Westview Press
BOULDER • SAN FRANCISCO • OXFORD

Politics in Asia and the Pacific: Interdisciplinary Perspectives

All rights reserved. No part of this publication may be reproduced or transmitted in any form or by any means, electronic or mechanical, including photocopy, recording, or any information storage and retrieval system, without permission in writing from the publisher.

Copyright © 1994 by Westview Press, Inc.

Published in 1994 in the United States of America by Westview Press, Inc., 5500 Central Avenue, Boulder, Colorado 80301-2877, and in the United Kingdom by Westview Press, 36 Lonsdale Road, Summertown, Oxford OX2 7EW

Library of Congress Cataloging-in-Publication Data
Dittmer, Lowell.
    China under reform / Lowell Dittmer.
      p. cm. — (Politics in Asia and the Pacific :
interdisciplinary perspectives)
    Includes bibliographical references and index.
    ISBN 0-8133-1119-5. — ISBN 0-8133-1120-9 (pbk.)
    1. China—Politics and government—1976– . I. Title. II. Series:
Politics in Asia and the Pacific.
DS799.26.D58   1994
320.951—dc20   93-23584
                                                                                      CIP

Printed and bound in the United States of America

∞ The paper used in this publication meets the requirements
    of the American National Standard for Permanence of Paper
    for Printed Library Materials Z39.48-1984.

10   9   8   7   6   5   4   3   2   1

To the Memory of My Mother

Contents

Acknowledgments		xi
1	From Revolution to Reform	1
2	The Lineage of Reform Socialism	9
	The Golden 1950s, 10	
	The Revisionist Interregnum, 13	
	A Cultural Revolution? 24	
	The Inauguration of Reform, 31	
	Genealogy of Reform, 36	
	Conclusions, 45	
3	Political Leadership and Succession	49
	Mao Zedong, 55	
	Deng Xiaoping, 80	
	Conclusions, 104	
4	Emergence of a Public Sphere?	109
	Conceptual Background, 110	
	The Structure of Political Publication, 116	
	The Impact of Reform, 125	
	Spontaneous Political Activism, 131	
	Conclusions, 153	

5	Domestic Reform and International Adaptation	159
	Transnational Relations, 160	
	International Relations, 181	
	Conclusions, 196	
6	The Future of Socialist Reform	199

List of Acronyms and Abbreviations 211
About the Book and Author 213
Index 215

Acknowledgments

This is a study of the political consequences of economic reform in the People's Republic of China, a process that has been so successful that (barring an economic calamity) it can no longer be reversed, although it can still be steered in different directions. Having unleashed this economic dynamo, politics appears at this point on the verge of losing command. This may, of course, be only temporary—for the world's last major Communist Party-state now awaits its third generation of leadership. Heir to a sterling economic performance, that leadership is apt to be haunted by rising expectations and perplexed about how to reconcile continued growth with its own political interests. Realistically considered, its options are limited. Either the leadership will grasp the tendencies that have been loosed and shape them creatively in the national interest, or a less edifying recent trend will resume: stagnation amid orthodoxy at the center, as the more dynamic regions become integrated with Hong Kong, Taiwan, and the surging Pacific Rim economies.

Although, of course, the blame is entirely mine for any flaws that remain in this study, I am indebted to many for any conceivable virtues. I am grateful to Elizabeth J. Perry and to Chin-chuan Lee for reading and criticizing an earlier version of Chapter 4. I wish to thank Susan Sherman for acquainting me with the gerontological literature cited in Chapter 3. Kenneth Lieberthal made useful comments on a much earlier draft of Chapter 2. An anonymous reader read the entire manuscript and made many helpful comments. I am grateful to Haru Fukui for including me in his series. I am indebted to Westview's Susan McEachern for the book's title and for the tireless prodding without which the book would probably never have been written. The Center for Chinese Studies at the University of California at Berkeley sponsored the project and helped subsidize my research, for which I am thankful. For serendipitous suggestions and intellectual stimulation I wish to thank my students and my family. Guoliang Zhang did a fine job on the index and helped with the jacket design. Finally, having published on some of these topics before, I have taken the liberty to plagiarize myself liberally, often without sufficient attribution: Thanks!

Lowell Dittmer

1

From Revolution to Reform

The American image of China has fluctuated throughout the twentieth century but perhaps never more dramatically than at the end of the 1980s, when the Chinese regime's well-publicized massacre of student protesters at Tiananmen Square electrified American public opinion and dissipated much of the goodwill that had been built up during a decade of highly successful economic reform. The protesters had caught the imagination and sympathy of the American media and public as nothing in Chinese politics had since the Cultural Revolution, and the bloody terminus of their protests when negotiations and leadership appeals failed to disperse them only sanctified that support. Thus the American love affair with China seemed to reach its simultaneous apotheosis and eclipse in the flames that gutted hundreds of abandoned military vehicles littering the streets of Beijing on June 4, 1989.

Yet despite the temporary pause in reform momentum that followed the crackdown, reform has henceforth resumed with apparently undiminished vigor: China's gross domestic product (GDP), already the third largest in the world, according to new World Bank calculations, surged in 1992 by 12.8 percent (the fastest in the world); per capita GDP jumped by nearly 20 percent; and China attracted U.S.$11.6 billion-worth (all dollars are U.S. dollars unless otherwise noted) of foreign investment—nearly as much as was lured by the United States, the world's biggest economy.[1]

---

1. *Economist* (London), December 4, 1992, and January 23, 1993. This was clearly China's best performance in three years: GDP growth was recorded at 4 percent in 1989, and at 4 to 7 percent in 1990 and 1991. China's trade performance, up 22 percent to $165 billion, allowed it to surpass Taiwan, South Korea, and Singapore, taking eleventh place among the world's trading powers. More joint ventures were registered in 1992 than in the whole previous decade (47,000, vs. 37,000). By 1994, China's economy is almost sure to be four times bigger than

At the same time, despite the regime's best efforts to put worries to rest through a rotation of elites at the Fourteenth Party Congress (October 1992) and the Eighth National People's Congress (NPC) (March 1993), the structure of the political system has remained essentially Leninist, leaving it still susceptible to factional splits, purges, succession crises, mass movements, and other forms of politically driven instability. Although China's unique synthesis of economic reform and political dictatorship has thus far spared it the fate of the former Soviet Union, how well can such a patchwork of contradictions be expected to survive the storms yet to come?

This book reconsiders the progress and pitfalls of Chinese reform socialism at a crucial turning point, as the regime stands poised between the fatal discrediting of its revolutionary leadership and the succession of a new generation. Our purpose is to assess the politics of the reform decade—in the light of its historical antecedents, its authors' intentions, its consequences. At a pivotal juncture, when so many different contingencies and options are still open, it goes without saying that any such assessment must be preliminary and schematic.

In analyzing a topic of such complexity, it is necessary to be somewhat selective; and to select, it is necessary to have some basis for deciding which aspects of political reality are most important. The basis for such a selection is first to locate the central overriding feature of a given epoch, making it possible to consider the various secondary and tertiary features in terms of their relevance to this central feature. Accordingly, our premise is that *the most significant single development in China since the death of Mao has been the shift from revolution to reform.* Revolution consists of the attempt to smash the structure of legitimacy through a violent, all-or-nothing, apparently spontaneous breakthrough. Reform attempts to effect change through an incremental, sequential process of compromise. In the course of the post-Liberation era, the Chinese Communist Party (CCP) leadership has experimented with both modes of political change. It is a useful simplification to label the period from 1949 to 1978 one of "continuing revolution under the dictatorship of the proletariat" and the period from 1978 to the present one of structural reform (though the transition did not become official until June 1981, when the CCP consecrated it with a central document[2]).

---

it was in 1978, exceeding Hua Guofeng's 1978 projections (then scorned as overambitious) by six years; if the Chinese economy continues to grow at an annual average rate of 7 percent, by 2002 it will be eight times bigger than it was in 1978. By that time. China would have matched the performance of Japan, Taiwan, and South Korea during their fastest quarter-centuries of economic growth.

2. See "Resolution on Certain Questions in the History of Our Party Since the Founding of the People's Republic of China," as adopted by the Sixth Plenum of the Eleventh Central Committee on June 27, 1981, translated in *Resolution on CPC History* (Beijing: Foreign

During the era of continuous revolution, the chief vehicle of revolutionary change was the mass movement, steered by charismatic leadership. The leadership mobilized the masses in repeated reenactments of the revolution against a series of "human targets" authoritatively selected to symbolize "bourgeois reactionary," "feudal," "revisionist," or any of a host of other "counterrevolutionary" values and interests.[3] China's continuous revolution was thought to have international significance, and Chinese foreign policy was designed to pursue not conventional national interests but universal revolutionary values (although national interests, of course, also had to be protected, because in the international jungle only the nation-state could serve as host and redoubt of the revolution).

During the early and mid-1950s, this combination reached its acme in terms of synthesizing revolutionary and conventionally defined economic objectives. The goals of revolutionary Marxism-Leninism were realized via "socialization of the means of production," i.e., the country's most productive agricultural and industrial property was seized to be operated in the public interest (as defined by the Party vanguard) in a series of mass campaigns. At the same time, impressive levels of economic growth were achieved, particularly in terms of industrialization. China's revolutionary foreign policy broadened its scope, moving beyond the Communist bloc to embrace a number of sympathetic new regimes in the Third World, making China a power to reckon with in both Washington and Moscow.

Only toward the end of the decade did this so-called revolutionary approach to modernization seem to run amok. The Three Red Flags of 1958–1959 (Great Leap Forward, People's Commune, and General Line), an initiative that boldly threw off the trammels of the Stalinist model in favor of a distinctively Chinese (Maoist) approach to development, made further ideological gains at the expense of what appear in retrospect to have been appalling economic and human costs and had to be rescinded in 1961–1962.[4] China's revolutionary foreign policy was abandoned by

---

Languages Press, 1981). For insights on its formulation, see Deng Xiaoping, "Remarks on Successive Drafts of the 'Resolution on Certain Questions . . .'" (March 1980–June 1981), in *Selected Works of Deng Xiaoping* (Beijing: Foreign Languages Press, 1984), pp. 276–297.

3. For a more fully elaborated discussion of this era, see Lowell Dittmer, *China's Continuous Revolution: The Post-Liberation Epoch, 1949–1981* (Berkeley: University of California Press, 1987).

4. Chinese sources since Mao's death have revealed that perhaps the greatest famine in the world occurred in China in the three years following the Great Leap Forward, causing the deaths of an estimated 20 to 30 million people. See Judith Bannister, "Population Policy and Trends in China, 1978–83," *China Quarterly*, no. 100 (December 1984), pp. 717–742. The famine was more specifically examined in Thomas P. Bernstein, "Stalinism, Famine, and Chinese Peasants: Grain Procurements during the Great Leap Forward," *Theory and Society*, 13:3 (May 1984), pp. 339–377.

more prudent leftists in the Third World in favor of Moscow or the Nonaligned Movement. Beijing found itself on the ideological margins of the international arena, in serious danger of being caught in a pincers movement between the two superpowers.

Yet the "contradiction" between economic and revolutionary objectives that was exposed in its most acute form by the Great Leap Forward was destined to be neither resolved nor abandoned in the next two decades. One of the most serious dysfunctions of charismatic leadership, as it turns out, is that the supreme leader is in a position—if sufficiently daring and politically adroit—to overrule a majority and bend the whole system to his will. Having invested in a zero-sum outcome, CCP Chairman Mao Zedong persisted in the simultaneous pursuit of both heroic economic growth and progress toward the communist utopia, purging any colleagues who dared take issue with him. During the later phase of the Cultural Revolution (1971–1976), the increasingly obvious functional incompatibility of revolution and production resulted in an oscillation between campaign high tides, on the one hand, and a focus on economic production and political consolidation, on the other. The radical vanguard of the campaign waves was the so-called Gang of Four, led by Mao's wife, Jiang Qing; the leaders of the moderate forces who tended the economy were Premier Zhou Enlai and (after his rehabilitation in 1973) former "capitalist-roader" Deng Xiaoping. Only in foreign affairs was a certain equilibrium achieved, as China—although continuing to pay lip service to national liberation wars in the Third World and terrorism in the developed countries—opened to the West in order to protect vital national security interests.

Upon Mao's death, the "contradiction" between the two ideological positions sharpened, culminating in a showdown in which Jiang Qing and her fellow radicals were arrested and publicly repudiated. The first attempt to modulate Maoist radicalism by Hua Guofeng ran aground due to a combination of its intrinsic programmatic flaws (e.g., too much deficit spending and reliance on foreign loans) and skilled political opposition from the Deng Xiaoping group. The latter proceeded to replace Hua's followers and to implement its own program, which departed rather sharply from the Maoist paradigm while continuing to maintain a face-saving semblance of political continuity.

If the shift from revolution to reform is the dominant feature of contemporary China's political landscape, our task must be not merely to chronicle the reforms but also to show how reform flows from the politics of revolution. Despite the sharp contrast between ideal types, reality weaves between them in a rather convoluted dialectic. In Chapter 2 we trace the reform juggernaut of the 1980s back to the radical initiatives and subsequent pragmatic adaptations to those initiatives of the three previous decades. Unsurprisingly, we find the greatest kinship between reform and the "revisionist" line, but we can also discern certain interesting lines of continuity with past radical impulses. In Chapters 3 through 5 these continuities and changes are more closely examined as they manifest themselves in three key political arenas: central leadership, the mass public, and foreign policy. In each of these arenas we see a vivid contrast between the universalistic revolutionary impulses with which the regime first set forth and the reform line later undertaken to reconcile momentum with control.

In the leadership arena, synthesis has essentially involved an effort to routinize charisma. Thus we begin Chapter 3 by reviewing the tempestuous career of Mao Zedong, who personifies charisma as few others have, before turning to his erstwhile favorite and posthumous nemesis, Deng Xiaoping. Although each man was to some extent the beneficiary of revolutionary charisma, both leaders seem to have been aware of its great drawback: its inherent instability. An overreliance on an inspiring but mortal and all-too-human individual leader carries the seeds of instability, particularly during that leader's inevitable passage from the scene. Both men undertook efforts to correct that drawback by preparing the way for leadership succession. Mao's solution was sweeping and poetic, changing China's political landscape in vast but unlikely ways. Deng's solution was no less ambitious and much more systematic. Yet it, too, fell frequent prey to weaknesses inherent in its autocratic origins—the tendency of the process to be superseded by the personal interests of the actors involved. Deng thus leaves an oddly unfinished legacy: leadership that has made considerable progress toward institutionalization, yet remains highly personalized, a sort of institutionalized personalism.

The reform leadership upon its debut seemed to have completely forsworn mass activism of the sort that characterized the Maoist era, but the reality has turned out to be somewhat more complicated. Mass movements under CCP sponsorship have indeed been increasingly self-frustrating and infrequent. However, the public arena has therefore been left open to voluntary political entrepreneurs. Albeit forbidden by the reform regime, spontaneous mobilization has continued to recur since Mao first legitimated it. Its chief drawbacks have been (1) its iconoclastic, anarchic, "breakthrough" mentality, deriving from its Cultural Revolutionary origins, and (2) its dependency on the existing leadership (or a faction thereof). We find that considerable progress has been made in the course of the reform era in checking the grass-roots movement's propensity for incivility, but that its inability to develop autonomous leadership has continued to inhibit the emergence of true "civil society." Yet clearly it is overstated to say that China lacks a "public sphere," an idealized entity that is inherently polymorphous and contested, even in the Western context.

In the international arena, we have witnessed a tug-of-war between the desire, on the one hand, to make the Chinese revolutionary experience conceptually meaningful and valid to the rest of the world, and the need to satisfy the specific national and material interests of the Chinese state, on the other. During the People's Republic of China's (PRC) first two decades, promoting revolutionary ideology assumed pride of place in Chinese foreign policy. Only at the end of the 1960s—and only when threatened by the possibility of a preemptive nuclear strike in the context of anti-Chinese collusion by both superpowers—did Beijing subordinate concern for ideological principles to the imperatives of national interest. With this compromise, Chinese foreign policy took a first step toward reform. This pragmatic trend has continued through the 1980s with increasingly successful results, expanding Beijing's ambit for diplomatic maneuver and multiplying its international options.

Again, Tiananmen has marked the onset of new challenges for Chinese foreign policy. On the one hand, Soviet-American détente and the termination of the Cold War (not to mention the dissolution of the Soviet Union) have, at least for the time being, dissolved the Strategic Triangle, thereby depriving China of the leverage it once had as an indispensable strategic counterweight to the Soviet Union. On the other hand, the Communist bloc has disintegrated, and the Third World has lost whatever cohesive identity it once had in the wake of the collapse of bipolarity. As in many other countries at this historical juncture, China's foreign policy establishment thus finds itself challenged to redefine its international mission (in a nation that has always needed a mission) without guidelines from familiar international reference groups or an obvious triangular game plan.

One of the implications of the mushrooming Tiananmen demonstrations and the regime's tragic overreaction to them is that the shift from revolution to reform was less complete than it at first appeared to be. Although Deng has accelerated his efforts in the twilight of his reign, he is likely to leave his country still only "half-reformed." Whether China will execute the other "half" of its domestic reform (and if so, precisely how) remains to be seen, but in any case it should hardly surprise anyone even slightly acquainted with history to predict that the post-Mao era will continue to bear the stigmata of its revolutionary origins. Despite the collapse of communism nearly everywhere else, it may continue to survive here for some time to come—certainly that is the strong preference of a strategically positioned and highly motivated segment of the Party-state.[5] After all, in spite of its reservations about the "errors" Mao is said

---

5. On this point, see Brantly Womack, "Asian Communism: Enigma Variations" (Unpublished paper presented at the Conference on Comparative Socialist Reforms, Royal Institute of International Affairs, Chatham House, London, November 19–22, 1991). Also see Joseph Fewsmith, "Chen Yuan and the Economic Agenda of Neoconservatism" (Unpublished paper presented at the Forty-fifth Annual Meeting of the Association for Asian Studies, Los Angeles, Calif., March 25–28, 1993).

to have committed during his later years, the Deng Xiaoping regime has by no means repudiated its revolutionary heritage. Unlike Mao, Deng has not sought to draw a sharp "line of demarcation" between himself and his predecessor in order to create a brave new world, but has sought to craft a working synthesis between a "feudal-colonial" past and a "modernized" future. Mao Zedong and his Thought are still reaffirmed, and since Tiananmen, tributes to his memory have made a noteworthy resurgence. The challenge for the future is likely to remain one of integrating the (currently quiescent) revolutionary impulse for social justice with the unleashed dynamism of a marketizing economy.

2

The Lineage of Reform Socialism

Amid the accumulating body of, on the whole, highly perceptive writings analyzing China's post-Mao reform movement[1] or speculating about its prospects,[2] there have hitherto been few efforts to trace the ancestry of reform through the complex "family tree" of pre-1976 political cleavages.[3] Such a search for "pedigree," however, is second in importance only to a firm empirical grasp of the reforms themselves in trying to project the movement's future direction. In fact, the current reforms are the confluence of often contradictory ideas and social forces, and their future is correspondingly more uncertain than if they stemmed from an established ideological "line"—as did, for example, the Great Leap Forward and the Cultural Revolution. China's reform movement is more clearly defined by recent historical errors it is trying to refute than by any

---

1. E.g., see Richard Baum, ed., *China's Four Modernizations* (Boulder: Westview Press, 1979); Elizabeth J. Perry and Christine Wong, eds., *The Political Economy of Reform in Post-Mao China* (Cambridge: Harvard University Press, 1985); Jack Gray and Gordon White, eds., *China's New Developmental Strategy* (London: Academic Press, 1982); Stephen Feuchtwang and Athan Hussain, eds., *The Chinese Economic Reforms* (London: Croom Helm, 1983); Harry Harding, *China's Second Revolution* (Washington, D.C.: Brookings, 1987); Hsi-sheng Ch'i, *Politics of Disillusionment: The Chinese Communist Party Under Deng Xiaoping, 1978–1989* (Armonk, N.Y.: M. E. Sharpe, 1991); Kenneth Lieberthal and Michel Oksenberg, *Policy Making in China* (Princeton: Princeton University Press, 1988); Hong Yung Lee, *From Revolutionary Cadres to Party Technocrats in Socialist China* (Berkeley: University of California Press, 1991); and many more.
2. See especially Hong Yung Lee, ed., *The Limits of Reform in China* (Washington, D.C.: East Asia Program, Wilson Center, Smithsonian Institution, 1982).
3. See, however, Stuart Schram, "To Utopia and Back: A Cycle in the History of the CCP," *China Quarterly (CQ)*, no. 87 (September 1981), p. 420. Also see Tang Tsou, "The Historic Change in Direction and Continuity with the Past," *CQ*, no. 98 (June 1984), pp. 320–347.

self-conscious vision of the future. By examining how the antecedents of the current reforms fared—what difficulties arose in the course of their implementation, what opposing arguments or adverse consequences precipitated their eventual suspension—we should become able to make a more clear-headed assessment of the current movement.

The thesis of this chapter is that the Chinese reform movement can be traced back to at least three different pedigrees: the period of the First Five-Year Plan (1953–1957), the period of recovery from the Great Leap Forward (1962–1965), and the Great Proletarian Cultural Revolution (1966–1976). For members of the reform coalition who claim ancestry in the 1950s, the reform movement represents a restoration of the noble achievements of the founding fathers, who brought the revolution to fruition and established the legitimacy of Party and state; for those who trace their roots to the Cultural Revolution, the movement represents the antithesis of a chaotic, misconceived crusade and a deliverance from chronic squalor. Those features of the reform movement that derive from the early 1960s remain fatherless in a sense, for although Liu Shaoqi, Deng Xiaoping, and most other principals of that period have since had their verdicts reversed (if sometimes posthumously), that rehabilitation seems to have been somewhat controversial at the time, and the "revisionist" episode in CCP history remains ideologically tainted. Yet the revisionists were successful in capturing the strategic heights of the Party-state apparatus and in removing all who voiced serious misgivings, whereupon they pushed through a set of policies bearing a more than passing family resemblance to those first experimented with in the early 1960s. Although riven by schism since then, the reform grouping is still the major source of new political ideas in China.

Among the most momentous consequences of Tiananmen has been to put the future of China's reform movement at issue and to reopen the whole decade of achievements to question. By defining the tradition from which this apparently open-ended movement derives, we hope to grasp the historical dialectic foretelling its future. We begin by looking at each of its conceptual birthplaces a bit more closely.

The Golden 1950s

For those who experienced the 1950s, that decade is still a golden age.[4] After nearly a century of civil war and foreign invasion, the country was once again fully united and at peace, enjoyed the protection of what seemed at the time a benign and powerful socialist motherland, and

---

4. Of course, we are speaking here of the CCP leadership, whose members have monopolized the right to define the history of their movement, not of their victims, who remain voiceless in China.

could boast a young, unified, and relatively vigorous leadership. The CCP inaugurated not a proletarian dictatorship but a New Democracy, which promised a useful role to all patriotic classes in implementing a progressive but relatively moderate social program. The First Five-Year Plan was an outstanding success, revitalizing agriculture while forging ahead with industrialization to achieve overall economic growth rates (particularly in industry) without precedent. At the same time, socialization of the means of production was achieved in both agriculture and industry, expediting the transition to socialism in unexpectedly short order. The regime thus seemed to have combined radical redistribution with economic growth at no perceptible cost to either goal.

The 1950s were indeed euphoric times in many respects, but because they telescoped together so many divergent tendencies it has proved difficult for reformers to find a meaningful "home" for their policies here. Many of the more ambitious liberal reformers have been fascinated with New Democracy, for instance, and with the promise it seemed to hold for a democracy of the whole people (i.e., including the "bourgeois democratic parties"), within an economy containing a sizable private sector. This interest has been implicit, for example, in critiques of the land reform and collectivization experiences as being too precipitous and forced. It became more explicit in the theoretical reclassification of China as being in the "primary stage of socialism" at the Thirteenth Party Congress (November 1987). For Party veterans, the symbolic centerpiece of the 1950s is the Eighth Party Congress, during which Mao Zedong Thought was deleted from the CCP Constitution in the name of collective leadership, and an accord was reached confirming that class struggle had ended with socialization of the means of production. This left the leadership free to concentrate henceforth on rapid economic growth, thereby resolving the principal remaining "contradiction" between advanced productive relations and underdeveloped productive forces. For Party veterans, the Eighth Congress represented "rectification according to the norms" and the other attributes of wholesome "Party life" before it was poisoned by Lushan and the purge of Peng Dehuai, events that first signaled the accession of Mao Zedong to an arbitrary, unilateral decision-making mode.

> Twenty years later, looking back on the turmoil of the Cultural Revolution, most people felt nostalgic for 1956 and regarded it as the best period in the history of the People's Republic, calling it "the golden year." Some thought if it had not been for the antirightist campaign in the following year, Chinese society would have developed in a far more humane way.[5]

---

5. Liu Binyan, *A Higher Kind of Loyalty: A Memoir by China's Foremost Journalist*, trans. Zhu Hong (New York: Pantheon, 1990), p. 61.

Yet there are problems with tracing the reform program back to this heroic age. There is no question that certain specific forerunners of important reform policies first appeared then. For example, the first prototype of the responsibility field system seems to have been introduced by Deng Zihui in the mid-1950s.[6] Yet it is doubtful that Deng was presenting a conscious alternative to the Party line; it is far more likely that he was simply improvising a temporary fallback expedient for households not yet prepared for full collectivization.[7] The case illustrates the difficulty of conducting history by analogy: There really was considerable ideological consensus at the time about the need for a transition to socialism, despite admitted quibbles about speed and tactics of consummation. Contrast that with the willingness of Deng's reformers to defer such questions indefinitely, promising that the stage of primitive socialism would last at least fifty—and later, a hundred—years.

Even the more leftist members of the reform leadership might not feel fully at home with 1950s policies. Although there does seem to have been greater leadership consensus during this period, we might question whether that was really because everyone played by the rules of collective leadership, or whether it was simply because Mao's handpicked crew of trusted subordinates continued to follow orders—why should they not: A rising tide raises all boats—and were dumped when they did not, like Deng Zihui or Peng Dehuai? In this connection the reformers have conceded that many of the failings that culminated in the Cultural Revolution—blind-sided utopianism, intense personal commitment to an omniscient hero-leader, an intolerance of criticism that let the Party lurch

---

6. By virtue of his efforts to resist hasty collectivization and his pioneering advocacy of the responsibility system, Deng Zihui has emerged as something of a hero before his time in several articles by younger Chinese historians. See Editorial Board, "Shenqie huainian Deng Zihui tongzhi" (Deeply cherish comrade Deng Zihui's memory), *Nongcong gongzuo tongxun* (Agricultural Work Bulletin), no. 5 (May 5, 1981), pp. 7–9; also Qiang Yuangan and Lin Bangguang, "Wo guo nongye jitihua de zhuoyue zuzhizhe Deng Zihui" (Our country's outstanding organizer of agricultural collectivization), *Xinhua wenzhai* (New China Documentation), no. 7 (1981), pp. 187–190, as cited in Thomas Bernstein, "Reforming China's Agriculture" (Paper presented at the conference To Reform the Chinese Political Order, Harwichport, Mass., June 1984). Gao Gang and Rao Shushi, however, seem to bear no political kinship to later reformers; it has even been plausibly argued that they were overzealous Maoists. See Roy Grow, "Soviet Models in China: Kao Kang and the Politics of Economic Development" (Unpublished ms., Waltham, Mass., n.d.); see also Lawrence R. Sullivan, "Leadership and Authority in the Chinese Communist Party," in David Goodman and Gerald Segal, eds., *China at Forty: Mid-Life Crisis?* (Oxford: Clarendon Press, 1989).

7. There was no indication that the dissidents of the 1950s were aware they were presenting a programmatic alternative to the orthodox "line." However, this is not a decisive disqualification, for I would argue that the evidence that the revisionists of the early 1960s were consciously articulating a coherent line does not hold up very well either.

from one extreme to another before any flaw could be corrected—were already implicit on a smaller scale in the "Golden" Fifties (e.g., the overzealous "antirightist movement" that Deng led in 1957).

The Revisionist Interregnum

"Revisionism" was the epithet used during the Cultural Revolution to characterize the policy platform that was introduced by Liu Shaoqi, Deng Xiaoping, and their followers during the early 1960s to facilitate recovery from the economic problems precipitated by the Great Leap Forward. This set of policies, like those sometimes resorted to in the 1950s, seemed at the time to have emerged as no more than an ad hoc assemblage of pragmatic responses to the problems of the day. It was not until the Cultural Revolution that revisionism was synthesized into a fully coherent "line," "road," and "headquarters"—and then at the hands of radical polemicists. Yet there is a grain of truth in the polemics. Due to the systemic character of the crisis precipitated by the Leap, the policies adopted in incremental response were, taken cumulatively, relatively comprehensive. Thus it is not inappropriate to group them under the common rubric of "revisionism"—without necessarily adopting the term's pejorative connotations.

There are actually several reasons for the more systematic character of the post-Leap experiments. During the first decade, all members of the elite seem to have been drawn together, at least to some extent, by the consciousness that they were part of an international movement pursuing the same transcendental vision.[8] Differences over speed or tactics of implementation were easily subsumed under this conceptual umbrella. Moreover, the almost uninterrupted series of successes that greeted implementation of new policies made losers more willing to repent, winners more willing to forgive; objective success crowned ideological unity. After Khrushchev's repudiation of Stalin in 1956 dispelled the illusion of a universally applicable socialist truth (there were "many roads to socialism"), the leadership began to depart from the Soviet model, first with the Hundred Flowers experiment, then with the Great Leap Forward. Mao Zedong initiated such departures, but he brought the rest of his leadership with him. He was able to do so for reasons having to do not only with the Party's unbroken string of policy successes (and Mao's personal successes interceding to accelerate "socialization of the means of production") but also with the elite consensus that

---

8. See Benjamin Schwartz's preface to the second edition of his *Chinese Communism and the Rise of Mao* (Cambridge: Harvard University Press, 1979), p. vii.

this was but an early stage of a "continuing revolution" in which revolutionary transformation was generally considered the Party's mandate. This meant that those espousing decisive changes or "breakthroughs" held an intrinsic theoretical advantage over those advocating more modest adjustments of the status quo.

However, this new, "Maoist" consensus was more fragile than the one it succeeded, partly because it now lacked the blessing of a superior outside patron, and partly because of the inherent risks of a unilateral decisionmaking style. That Mao's early efforts at theoretical innovation proved so unfortunate in their objective consequences was to destroy the leadership consensus and precipitate a crisis of confidence. A world in which some twenty million people could starve to death only months after the leadership had been convinced that the economy was on the threshhold of material abundance and Communist utopia inspired a rethinking of its conceptual foundations.[9]

In retrospect it now seems clear that not one but two policy lines emerged in the wake of the CCP rejection of the Soviet model: a radical and a revisionist line. Notwithstanding later polemical allegations to the effect that radicalism represented a departure from the Soviet line whereas revisionism continued to adhere to it, in fact *both* rejected the Soviet model. The radical line was articulated first in order to justify the Great Leap Forward. In rationalizing its failure, Mao Zedong introduced such theoretical innovations as the reversibility of historical progress (i.e., the "capitalist road" as a theoretically conceivable alternative), the absoluteness of imbalance and the relativity of equilibrium, the primacy of superstructural factors in the progress from one historical stage to the next, and the historical inevitability of "struggle," even in the Communist utopia. Using such assumptions as a basis, he first launched the Socialist Education Movement and then, when that seemed to have bogged down, the more organizationally heterodox Cultural Revolution.

The revisionist line emerged in pragmatic response to the difficulties that radicalism had inadvertently precipitated; although less iconoclastic, revisionist experiments with privatization and marketization represented a no-less-significant departure from the Stalinist model than the

---

9. The impact of the famine was so great that it was reflected in Chinese demographic statistics, according to which the average death rate rose from 11 per thousand in 1957 to 17 per thousand in 1958–61, while the birth rate declined from 34 per thousand in 1957 to 23 per thousand in 1958–1961. In Judith Bannister, "Population Policy and Trends in China, 1978–83," *CQ*, no. 100 (December 1984), pp. 717–742. The Chinese famine literature is examined in Thomas P. Bernstein, "Stalinism, Famine, and the Chinese Peasants: Grain Procurements during the Great Leap Forward," *Theory and Society*, 13:3 (May 1984), pp. 339–377.

Maoist linkage of central planning with the "mass line."[10] Indeed, innovation proved to be the revisionists' Achilles' heel (e.g., in 1962, Mao, an economic Stalinist in many respects, unilaterally reversed many revisionist initiatives by implying that they were ideologically deviant). The radicals were, in contrast, able to legitimate their innovations by turning Mao into China's ideological fountainhead, cutting off contact with anyone in the outside world who might contradict them and transforming the nation into a "schoolhouse" of "Mao Zedong Thought."

Liu Shaoqi, as the major theoretical innovator and symbolic bellwether of revisionism, deserves pride of place in any reconsideration. Documentation concerning Liu's career is by now quite comprehensive, deriving from three distinct time periods and political perspectives: contemporaneous materials, Cultural Revolution polemics, and materials gathered for the posthumous reversal of verdicts.

Liu's worldview was characterized by a certain moral elitism, as his Red Guard critics claimed—a belief that the political elite, specifically the CCP leadership, was morally superior to the masses. This accusation can be most readily corroborated by a reading of such classics as *How to Be a Good Communist*.[11] Whether the criticism is altogether fair is another question, for Liu's elitist tendencies were not merely an invasion of inadequately repressed Confucianism but a Sinification of Lenin's doctrine of the "leading role" of the Party vanguard, to which Mao also subscribed.[12] Be that as it may, nowhere else in the canon of Chinese Communist classics is the Party's claim to moral superiority so elaborately rationalized. In contrast, Mao's writings do not frequently address themselves to the elite per se or define its sacred mission. Mao preferred to think in terms of an elite that was in principle indistinguishable from the masses it led. For Mao, the "broad masses" were the ultimate source of Truth; "only the

---

10. For example, it was during the revisionist aftermath of the Leap and not during the Leap itself that the shift was made from the Stalinist emphasis on heavy industry to a more balanced emphasis among heavy industry, light industry, and agriculture. See Kjeld Erik Brodsgaard, "Paradigmatic Change: Readjustment and Reform in the Chinese Economy, 1953–1981, Part I," *Modern China*, 9:1 (January 1983), pp. 37–83.

11. Liu Shao-ch'i, *How to Be a Good Communist* (New York: New Century, 1952).

12. Indeed, the evidence is convincing that Mao originally endorsed *On Cultivation* itself. Liu gave a long lecture to the students of the College of Marxism-Leninism on July 8 and 12, 1939; Mao read it and promptly wrote a letter saying that it was quite well written and could "promote righteousness and oppose evil winds" and that it should be published as soon as possible. The lecture was then published in *Liberation*, a weekly journal, and issued in book form; the Party Central Committee subsequently selected it as one of the study materials for the Yanan *Zhengfeng* (rectification) movement in 1942. Wu Liping, "Before and After the Publication of *On the Cultivation of Communist Party Members*," in *Huainian Liu Shaoqi tongzhi* (In memory of Liu Shaoqi) (Changsha: Hunan, 1980), p. 271.

masses" made world history, and the tendency of the "bureaucratic class" to "divorce" itself from the masses and luxuriate self-importantly amid the perquisites of office threatened to sap leadership of all vitality and make it an exploitative burden on those it should serve.[13] Mao was essentially a populist, whose populism for various reasons radicalized with age. Mao never shrank from iconoclasm, from his 1927 reminder that "revolution is not a dinner party" to his Cultural Revolution injunction to "smash" all the "frames" dividing the elite from the mass.

To Liu, the touchstone of the Party's superiority was its synoptic vision. Ordinary people might be able to discern and pursue their individual or group interests, but only the Party elite was capable of grasping the interests of the people as a whole. Only the Party elite had the theoretical ability to reason at such a high level of abstraction; only the Party elite had the moral self-discipline to renounce all personal perquisites on behalf of the public interest. These qualities were learned, or "cultivated," not ethnically inborn or even intrinsic to a particular class. The Party could be conceived as a vast hierarchy of moral efficiency, in which those best able to serve the interests of the whole and abnegate self-interest would provide leadership and cultivation to those who had not yet reached the "level" of consciousness achieved within the Party. Thus, moral efficiency and synoptic vision would inevitably also result in upward career mobility. By the time the efficiently altruistic official had reached the top of this pyramid, personal and general interests would have become identical; that is, they "merged":

> It must be understood that the interests of the Party are identical with the interests of the people. Whatever benefits the people also benefits the Party and must be carried out by every Party member with heart and soul. Likewise, whatever injures the people also injures the Party. . . . The Party has no special interests of its own beyond the people's interests.[14]

One of the most significant implications of Liu's elitism is that it led him to embrace a dichotomous conception of Truth (similar in this respect to the ethos Max Weber ascribed to medieval Jews, Indian Parsis, and other pariah groups). Virtue is concentrated in the Party. Even within the Party, Truth is not equally distributed but is defined via correct orga-

---

13. In a characteristic aside when discussing the problems of reforming medical service delivery, he caustically noted: "When making an examination, the doctor always puts on a gauze mask, regardless of what kind of patient he is dealing with. . . . I think that the main reason is that he is afraid of being infected by other people." From "Instruction on Health Work" (June 26, 1965), as trans. in *Current Background*, no. 892 (October 21, 1969), p. 20.

14. Liu Shao-ch'i, "On the Party," as trans. in *Collected Works of Liu Shao-ch'i*, 3 vols. (Hong Kong: Union Research Institute, 1969), vol. 2, p. 41 (hereinafter *Collected Works*).

nizational procedures, and, given the way such procedures as "democratic centralism" have always worked out in practice, by the Politburo. Freedom and necessity, theory and practice merge within the Party. But outside its purview other criteria might apply. There, pragmatism was the rule—at best this implied a situation ethic, at worst *Realpolitik*.

This double standard—"value rationality" within, "purpose rationality" without—proved quite useful in facilitating underground operations in enemy-occupied, or "White," areas during the first and second civil wars and the Sino-Japanese war, legitimating alliances of convenience, the adaptation of slogans to fit the audience, the systematic infiltration and manipulation of "front" organizations, and so forth. For example, in 1936 when the CCP entered into a truce with former Shanxi warlord Yan Xishan, Liu saw to it that key positions in Yan's military organization were staffed by nominally penitent "former" Communists (who had signed public confessions as a price for release from Kuomintang [KMT] prisons). Thus when Yan broke with the CCP in 1940, the latter emerged with some forty of his regular regiments. In another context, Liu noted with satisfaction that:

> In a few regions, fairy tales can play a very useful role among the underground societies. In a certain locality, it is widely said that Zhu De is the descendant of the first emperor of the Ming Dynasty, and the underground societies in the locality have maintained particularly good relations with the Eighth Route Army.[15]

Liu was quite prepared to fulfill the demands of client groups he in no way condoned as well as demands of those he sanctioned. If an indigenous guerrilla group demanded booty as a price for collaboration in an expedition against Japan (or the KMT), the group should get it.[16] Similarly, Liu was prepared "actively and energetically" to lead the labor unions he had helped organize in strikes for higher wages even when he deemed their demands unwise, or even "doomed to failure" under prevailing economic conditions, hoping thereby to rouse the engaged workers to an awareness of their common interests.[17] Mao, in contrast, seems to have had a more absolute and monolithic conception of Truth—certainly this was true during the Cultural Revolution, when his moral standards were superimposed on all of Chinese Communist history, but

---

15. Liu, *Collected Works*, vol. 1, p. 74.
16. Liu, "Work Experiences in the North China War Zone" (1938), in Henry G. Schwarz, *Liu Shao-ch'i and "People's War": A Report on the Creation of Base Areas in 1938* (Lawrence: Center for East Asian Studies, University of Kansas, 1969), pp. 33–34.
17. Liu, "Training in Organization and Discipline," in *Collected Works*, vol. 1, p. 400.

the tendency was discernible before that. For Mao, the Party's claim to Truth was contingent upon embodying the masses' interests—not merely representing the masses, but being physically *among* the masses—to a far greater extent than was the case for Liu Shaoqi.

Whereas Liu recognized as legitimate the pursuit of plural values, two seemed more basic than the others: politics and economics. Economics was essentially concerned with production to improve living standards. Improving living standards was by no means demeaning; it was "absolutely necessary." Altruism was not endemic to the masses, whereas egoism was; yet the pursuit of egoistic desires was not illegitimate and in fact at least moderate satisfaction of material needs was necesssary before it would be realistic to propose anything transcending them. As Liu put it in Shandong in 1942, "Only after the masses have become enthusiastic about protecting their personal interests, would and could they become equally enthusiastic about safeguarding their country."[18] Economic desires were "universal," and also most "important" for human existence; after all, people everywhere, and always, need to eat, sleep, and clothe themselves. Yet political questions are "higher" than economic questions, because they must embrace a wide range of discrete economic interests. In Liu's view the satisfaction of economic interests had no intrinsic moral significance unless people were thereby brought to understand the broader political ramifications of such satisfaction. Thus, "all the economic demands of the masses must be integrated with political or cultural demands. When the masses begin to take action on one simple demand, we must lead the masses in fields related to their action on this simple demand so that they can better understand a series of problems and further push their actions to a still higher stage." By thereby "raising the economic demands to political demands, raising local demands to state and national demands," the masses are brought to a "higher" conception of their interests. Only the Party is fully qualified to handle "political" questions, because only the Party has the combination of synoptic vision necessary to aggregate diverse particular interests and the moral self-discipline to renounce personal self-interest on behalf of the public interest. Contrary to Red Guard accusations to the effect that Liu placed "economics in command," Liu was no less inclined than Mao to endorse the primacy of politics; although the two men's conceptions of politics differed, there were significant parallels.[19]

---

18. See Lu Zhenyu and Jiang Ming article in *Zhongguo qingnian* (China Youth), 290:27 (September 16, 1960).

19. See Graham Young, "Liu Shaoqi on Party Leadership" (Unpublished seminar paper, Australian National University Contemporary China Centre, May 8, 1979).

Liu's distinction between politics and economics contained two more far-reaching implications. First, his essentially favorable attitude toward the division of labor inclined him to grant considerable autonomy to the economy (and to other functional subsystems) on that basis. A "line of demarcation" *(nei wai you bie)* had to be maintained between the Party and other functional subsystems, creating an insulated elite subculture known as "Party life." Outside that line, instrumentalism held sway; Deng Xiaoping's famous adage that "it doesn't matter whether a cat is black or white, so long as it catches mice" is a not misleading paraphrase of the revisionist position. Provided secular interests were not permitted to penetrate the Party's sacred boundaries and thereby distort its synoptic vision of the whole, wide latitude could be extended for the pursuit of economic or professional interests in institutions established for that purpose.

After all, although politics was of superior value, it was ultimately dependent on an economic base; therefore, if the economy threatened to founder, practically any expedient necessary for recovery was acceptable. To try to run the economy on the basis of political principles, Liu once exclaimed, was a form of "feudalism." The economy should be run on the basis of sound economic principles, the press on the basis of professional journalistic principles (bylines for meritorious reporters, investigative journalism, feature articles), scientists and artists should have ample range to function creatively within their respective spheres on the basis of principles appropriate to those subsystems.[20] Such principles were assumed to be universal to artists, journalists, or surgeons in all class structures, so learning from the experience of colleagues in other systems might be permitted or even encouraged. (Liu seems to have been particularly interested in the possible applicability of managerial techniques from capitalist monopolies or "trusts" to socialist enterprises.) In the name of subsystem autonomy, he at one time or another also endorsed merit-based wage differentials, preservation of a private sector in

---

20. Liu's distinction between economics and other vocational subfields assumed the legitimacy of a functional division of labor, which has been persistently controversial in Marxist thinking. Marx himself was ambivalent, marveling at its impact on productivity but deploring its segmentation of the soul—and he prophesied that the division would be superseded in the Communist utopia. Mao took a starkly adversarial position on the issue and in the later stages of his career determined to move toward its abrogation in the *hic et nunc*—the People's Communes took a step in this direction, as did the Paris Communes and the Revolutionary Committees. Within the Marxist tradition, Liu ranks (with Bukharin) among those most sympathetic to the division of labor. Liu seldom discussed utopia (like Confucius), and he clearly appreciated the advantages of a division of labor during the intervening Socialist transition.

industry, a lease-back arrangement similar to the later "household responsibility system" in agriculture, the expansion of markets, advertising and market research to promote retail sales, and even restoration of the stock market. Should any conflict emerge between the requirements of subsystem autonomy and universal system needs (as determined by the Party), it went without saying that the latter took priority.

Second, tolerance outside the Party implied discipline within it in order to preserve dedication to the public interest and unimpeachable personal morality. In fact, the more relaxed the Party's socioeconomic regulation, the more rigorous must be the Party's self-cultivation. This accounts for the paradoxical contrast between the relatively liberal economic and cultural policies pursued during the post-Leap recovery period and the draconian enforcement of cadre discipline during that time. The most authoritative studies of Party implementation of the Socialist Education Movement (or "Four Cleans") find Liu Shaoqi to have consistently pursued a very hard line indeed (later categorized as "apparently 'left' but actually right").[21] The sanctions Liu endorsed did not include mass criticism or purge (which would have violated the line of demarcation between Party and masses), but were nevertheless very severe. Based on his own field investigations[22] and on the more intensive involvement of his wife, Wang Guangmei, at Taoyuan (Peach Garden) Brigade, which led him to conclude that two-thirds of the country had fallen under the sway of "bad people," he advocated infiltration by outside work teams on a clandestine basis, confidential interviews with informants hostile to the local leadership, intensive grilling of suspects, and stern disciplinary sanctions (including heavy fines) against those found to be corrupt—all within a long-term time frame that anticipated continual pressure upon sequential components of the Party's organizational apparatus for many years to come. The movement was, however, brought to a premature halt by Mao's unilateral decision in 1965 to relieve pressure on lower-level cadres and turn the movement against the "faction in power" (*dang quan pai*)—including Liu Shaoqi himself—

---

21. See Richard Baum and Frederick C. Teiwes, *Ssu-ch'ing: The Socialist Education Movement of 1962–1966* (Berkeley: University of California, Center for Chinese Studies, 1968), as well as Baum, *Prelude to Revolution* (New York: Columbia University Press, 1975). See also Deng Liqun's reminiscences of Liu's role in the Four Cleans in *Huainian Liu Shaoqi tongzhi*, p. 37: "In the second half of 1964, his [Liu's] estimation of the situation of class struggle in the countryside was more serious. Comrade Mao Zedong criticized him, and he accepted the criticism."

22. From April 1 to May 15, 1961, Liu made investigations for forty-four days, thirty-two of which he spent in the countryside. Zhang Pinghua, "Xuexi Liu Shaoqi tongzhi" (Learn from comrade Liu Shaoqi), in *Huainian Liu Shaoqi tongzhi*, p. 57.

marking the onset of the radical critique of revisionism that emerged during the Cultural Revolution.[23]

The Cultural Revolution will be dealt with on its own terms below, but it deserves consideration here as an indigenous backlash against revisionism. If the revisionist response to the disasters of radicalism was economically successful, why, after all, did the Cultural Revolution erupt? First of all, there is no question now that although mass mobilization attained unprecedented spontaneity in the course of the movement, it took several months to set the stage for the upheaval, and this preparation involved conspiracy, deception, and entrapment. In retrospect it would seem that at least two leading Politburo figures, Peng Zhen and Liu Shaoqi, were prefabricated targets. Other casualties, such as Lu Dingyi and Deng Xiaoping, seem to have fallen because they were closely associated with primary targets (with Peng and Liu, respectively). Still others, including Zhou Enlai, Li Xiannian, Zhu De, Chen Yi, Tan Zhenlin, Bo Yibo, and perhaps the vast majority of cadres, were within target range, but were simply kept in the dark about Mao's plans and left to sink or swim in the "cauldron" of revolutionary criticism.

If the "rebellion" that erupted during the "fifty days" when Liu and Deng led the movement in June–July 1966 was thus not exactly spontaneous (or necessarily a reflection of inherent flaws in revisionism), neither can a spark start a fire without fuel. After all, Mao had been attempting since publication of the October 1965 critique of Wu Han to find "a method, starting from below and mobilizing the broad masses, of exposing our dark side openly and completely,"[24] but not until the spring of 1966 did he hit upon a successful formula. He was able to do so by exploiting cleavages in Chinese society running counter to the Maoist focus on egalitarianism and mass solidarity. True, China had in the past seventeen years attained a level of equality impressive by either historical or comparative standards, but there were marked discrepancies between

---

23. When Mao proposed that "the emphasis of this movement should be placed on punishing the *dang quan pai* who take the capitalist road within the Party," Liu expressed disagreement: "We'd better not use *'pai'* [faction], because it would harm a great number of people . . . we'd better use *fenzi* [elements, i.e.], elements who take the capitalist road. It is comparatively proper and also closer to the reality." But Mao insisted. Again, when Mao asserted that "the contradiction now in the countryside between *dang quan pai* taking the capitalist road and the majority of the masses is . . . an antagonistic contradiction," Liu disagreed; there were "various kinds of contradictions crisscrossing each other; antagonistic, within and without the Party." Hei Yannan, ed., *Shi nian dong luan* (Ten years of chaos) (Hong Kong: Xing Chen, 1988), pp. 53 ff.

24. *Renmin ribao* (RR) (People's Daily) January 14, 1976, p. 2; see also Mao's talk with two Albanian officials on February 3, 1967, as quoted in *Mao Zedong sixiang wansui!* (Long live Mao Zedong thought) (Hong Kong: n.p., 1969), part 2, p. 664.

the emancipatory language of the revolution and a heavily regimented cultural and intellectual life, and between an egalitarian distribution of wealth and a steeply hierarchical distribution of power. Perhaps even more divisive than these horizontal cleavages were vertical cleavages between work units, geographical regions, and administrative hierarchies, which were sometimes perceived invidiously. When the work teams were sent, their modus operandi tended to exacerbate these cleavages by segregating the host population into various categories and trying to interdict communication among them, ostracizing deviants for mass criticism, dividing movement participants against each other on the basis of ascribed characteristics such as bad class background (variously execrated as the *hei wu lei* [five black classes] and *hei qi lei* [seven black classes]), and otherwise compartmentalizing the movement.

Both the cleavages themselves and the Party's inadvertent reinforcement of them in the course of implementing the Cultural Revolution were attributed to "revisionism" by Maoist polemicists—and not without a certain plausibility. Liu had always emphasized inner-Party mechanisms of self-cultivation, with a clear line of demarcation between a truth-seeking elite and the money-grubbing masses. When the Party was still an outlaw band, its claim to monopolize Truth was in a sense vindicated by the Party's lack of power or wealth, but in the post-Liberation period the Party acquired monopoly control over the distribution of budgetary resources, employment, political power, status, and, indeed, all social values, placing it in a hegemonic position. The Party's emphasis on maintaining its purity behind a line of demarcation gave rise to its complacency and isolation from the masses, leading (in the context of mass mobilization) to polarization. Though the critique of revisionism was sanctioned and to some extent orchestrated by the Maoist leadership, it was largely articulated by members of the "revolutionary masses" (via wall posters and uncensored tabloid newspapers). Clearly these themes tapped an enormous ground swell of popular support, resulting in the greatest mass mobilization (and most sweeping purge of the CCP) since Liberation. This was impressive in view of the fact that these young critics of authority still had to reckon with the possibility of a "reversal of verdicts after the autumn harvest" (i.e., cadre retaliation). In sum, regardless of its fairness or empirical accuracy as an indictment of Liu Shaoqi, the critique seems to have bespoken a widespread and probably genuine sense of discontent with the power structure as it had become constituted during the first seventeen years of CCP rule.

The relevance of this depiction of revisionism to a discussion of the origins of reform is fairly obvious. The reform regime, was after all, inaugurated by Deng Xiaoping, erstwhile "number two Party person in authority taking the capitalist road," with the help of many other cadres who had been purged because they had been associated with Liu Shaoqi and the revisionist platform. Liu's name disappeared from the Chinese media (where he had been a target since 1967) immediately after Deng Xiaoping was restored to all previous posts in July 1977. Other revisionists followed: Peng Zhen was rehabilitated in 1979, followed by Wu Han (and his play), Deng Tuo and Liao Mosha (of *Evening Chats at Yanshan* fame). Deng's comeback trail was indeed paved with a quotation from Liu (*shi shi qiu shi*—seek truth from facts—from *On Cultivation*).[25] Despite clear evidence of high-level opposition, the reformers took the trouble to rehabilitate Liu posthumously (at the Fifth Plenum of the Eleventh Central Committee (CC), in February 1980).[26] He was said to have endured "the biggest frame-up the CCP has ever known in its history ... created out of thin air by fabricating materials, forging evidence, extorting confessions, and withholding testimony."[27] Three of Liu's classic works—*On Inner-Party Struggle, How to Be a Good Communist,* and *Be a Good Party Member and Build a Good Party*—were declared "Marxist works of great significance" and republished; excerpts from these and other writings and speeches got front-page coverage in the national news media. A major campaign was launched to popularize *How to Be a Good Communist* as a teaching manual for Party cadres. Three eulogistic anthologies were published memorializing Liu, in one of which Xu Xiangqian wrote the inscription: "The glorious achievements of Liu Shaoqi remain a model for everyone to learn from."[28] Liu's *Selected Works* were compiled (with particular emphasis on his discussions of Party rectification)[29] and published, in two volumes.

---

25. Authorship is ambiguous, as the same slogan is cited in Mao's "Where Do Correct Ideas Come From?" Liu's work was, however, clearly published first (July 8, 1939, vs. May 1963).

26. The meeting that approved his rehabilitation was so heated that the session had to be extended three days (February 23–29, rather than 23–26). An unusually long period passed before Liu's memorial meeting was finally held on May 17, and Ye Jianying and Li Xiannian were both conspicuously absent from the ceremonies. And although the communique of the Fifth Plenum cleared Liu without qualification, both Deng's memorial speech and the concurrent *Renmin ribao* editorial delicately referred to his "mistakes"—the only memorial statement of the many delivered in the preceding three years to do so. See Lowell Dittmer, "Death and Transfiguration: Liu Shaoqi's Rehabilitation and Contemporary Chinese Politics," *Journal of Asian Studies*, 40:3 (May 1981), pp. 455–480.

27. Xinhua News Agency, March 12, 1980, as trans. in *Foreign Broadcast Information Service-China* (*FBIS-China*), March 22, 1980, p. L1.

28. Xinhua, April 22, 1980, in *FBIS-China*, April 23, 1980, pp. L2–L3.

29. Liu's works on the Party were included without exception in his two-volume *Selected Works*. One article, *Lun fayang minzhu* (On developing democracy), first published in February 1948, was not republished, probably because Deng's line on democracy was harder than Liu's—perhaps due to the Cultural Revolution experience. And in the rehabilitated image of Liu, the moderate and controlled aspects of his notion of inner-Party struggle were emphasized even more than in the original, whereas discussion of struggle was toned down. The "struggle against leftist deviation" got even more attention than in the original, although the struggle against rightist deviation was soft-pedaled. Unity and resolve, not contradictions, stand in center stage. Siegfried Klaschka, *Die Rehabilitierung Liu Shaoqis in der chinesischen Presse* (Munich: Minerva, 1987), pp. 65–66.

Of course the possibility cannot be dismissed that this was a sentimental gesture rather than a calculated political move—Chinese are traditionally quite sentimental about the deceased, and in view of Liu's centrality in the previous careers of these men, such a gesture would not be surprising. But rational and emotional motives are not mutually exclusive: If the sentiment is sincere, one might expect Liu's characteristic approach to politics to survive in the policies of those who restored his reputation. As we shall see, it has.

A Cultural Revolution?

As an event that has been compared to the Holocaust in its traumatic impact, the Chinese Great Proletarian Cultural Revolution has continued to preoccupy the minds of those involved, giving a retrospective, reflexive character to the reforms introduced in its wake.[30] Like the policies introduced during the iconoclastic heyday of the Cultural Revolution, many of the reforms seemed to need no justification other than the fact that they reversed the policies of the last ten years. But the wholly negative official depiction of the Cultural Revolution in post-Mao China belies the complexity of its impact on the reform era. That impact may be seen on at least two levels. On the more obvious level, it provided a springboard for policies reversing Cultural Revolution programs of scant intrinsic popularity or that had been pushed too far. On a more implicit level, those relatively few Cultural Revolution policies that had successfully tapped a wellspring of popular support tended to be co-opted into the reforms.

At the time Hua Guofeng came to power as Mao's personally designated successor in September 1976, there was every expectation, among both his supporters and his future political adversaries, that his tenure was secure and was likely to be long. Deng himself said in a congratulatory letter that he looked forward to a long period of stability because of Hua's relative youth. As the first to occupy all three strategic positions in the Party-state leadership (viz., chairman of the Party, premier of the State Council, and chief of the Central Military Commission [CMC]), Hua's position seemed unassailable. Yet within about two years he had been pushed into a politically passive position, and within five he had been dismissed from the leadership altogether. The chief beneficiary of Hua's political downfall was Deng Xiaoping, who had helped engineer

---

30. "Many people in West Germany in the 1960s once asked their parents: 'What were you doing during the Nazi years?' We, who experienced the 'Cultural Revolution,' may well ask ourselves, 'What were we doing then?'" "'Cultural Revolution' Has Lessons for All," *China Daily* (Beijing), August 29, 1986, in *FBIS-China*, August 29, 1986, p. K5.

it, as Hua himself had correctly anticipated. This was the first time in CCP history that a sitting leader had been divested of power in the absence of some disabling political catastrophe. The way Deng performed this feat of political legerdemain was subtle: He used slight nuances to differentiate himself from Hua on several key issues, thereby appealing to unattached political constituencies (both cadre and mass) for their support.

The first of these issues concerned the role of the leader. Mao Zedong had encouraged a personality cult to develop around his own public persona and role as an ideological oracle; then exploited that cult to purge any political actor who disagreed with him and to raise high any whose services he deemed useful (e.g., the Gang of Four), regardless of whether his colleagues concurred. During the Cultural Revolution, his Thoughts were encapsulated in a small book of epigraphs, and the sole criterion for political legitimacy became whether a given policy or set of political arrangements agreed with Mao's Thought as expressed in his writings or in his "latest instructions." Hua Guofeng agreed with that criterion, as he publicly indicated in his February 1977 "two whatevers" formula ("Whatever decisions made by Chairman Mao, we must resolutely uphold; [and] whatever directives were issued by Chairman Mao, we must follow without fail")—with which Deng Xiaoping explicitly (albeit not publicly) disagreed at the time.[31] In one of his first decisions upon seizing power from the Gang of Four, Hua also opted to build a large public mausoleum to house Mao's sarcophagus in the center of Tiananmen Square and placed himself in charge of the committee to edit the remainder of Mao's *Selected Works*. That Hua had a sincere personal devotion to the dead Chairman should not be gainsaid, but he also expected to profit politically from such posthumous expressions of respect. By closely associating himself with Mao, in dozens of public portraits depicting the two chairmen together, in visits to places associated with Mao's legendary career, he made a clear bid to become the keeper of the sacred flame and high priest of the cult—the authorized exegete of Mao's Thought. Not only was the fifth volume of Mao's *Selected Works* published in record time (with a proprietary foreword by Hua), but a large number of selections appeared in the press, with a boldface quotation on the front page of every *People's Daily*.

Deng managed to identify himself as an opponent of the cult while avoiding any Khrushchev-like explicit criticism of Mao or his Thought. He did so by quoting Mao's own words in support of a pragmatic rather

---

31. See Deng Xiaoping, "The 'Two Whatevers' Do Not Accord with Marxism" (May 24, 1977), in *Selected Works of Deng Xiaoping (1975–1982)* (Beijing: Foreign Languages Press, 1984), pp. 51–52 (hereinafter *Selected*).

than a dogmatic interpretation of Maoist doctrine and by explicitly confronting the supposition that Mao's Thoughts were infallible with reasoned counterarguments—Mao's Thoughts were relevant essentially to the time and place of their genesis but should not be overgeneralized, and so forth. At the Third Plenum Mao's fallibility was for the first time officially conceded, albeit by implication: "It would not be Marxist to demand that a revolutionary leader be free of all shortcomings and errors." Henceforth, "no personal view by a Party member in a position of responsibility, including several leading members, is to be called an instruction."[32] These tactics succeeded in generating strong support from cadres once tyrannized by rigid dogma.

At the same time, Deng made his own disinterest in either a Mao-style cult or a hegemonic position clear, and although the latter disclaimer may not have been entirely sincere, Deng has at least assiduously avoided the trappings of the cult (much to the disappointment of the villagers in Paifangcun, Sichuan, who yearn to turn his birthplace into a tourist trap). Indeed, he made the restoration of collective leadership one of the top political priorities of the reforms. The institutions of collective leadership have revived, as indicated by the increased regularity with which the Party Congress, the NPC, the Chinese People's Political Consultative Conference (CPPCC), and their various standing committees (the Central Committee, the NPC Standing Committee, and so forth) meet. New agencies of collective leadership—the Central Advisory Commission (CAC), and the Central Disciplinary Inspection Commission (CDIC)—were created and staffed, and although the idea of introducing a check-and-balance relationship between them went nowhere, their creation has perhaps resulted in a wider dispersal of power. Executive power was also disseminated more broadly (at least formally), with Deng replacing Hua as chair of the CMC, Hu Yaobang as secretary general of the restored Party Secretariat, Zhao Ziyang as premier of the State Council, Li Xiannian as chief of state, Peng Zhen as chairman of the Standing Committee of the NPC, and so forth. It must be conceded that a continuing discrepancy between formal position and informal power (about which more later) has meant that the dispersion of power has been more nominal than actual, but in time informal power may more closely mesh with formal structure.

A second issue on which there was a clear reversal of Cultural Revolution policy involves the Party's attitude toward intellectuals, formal

---

32. "The Whole Party Shifts to Socialist Modernization," in "Communiqué of the Third Plenum of the Eleventh Central Committee" (December 18–22, 1978), trans. in *FBIS-China*, December 26, 1978, pp. E5–E12.

education, and the cultural sector. All ruling Communist parties have perhaps harbored suspicions, at the least, toward this stratum, which characteristically threatens to challenge the Party's claim to a monopoly on Truth. But in China that suspicion carried over to persecution that was particularly severe, reaching its acme during the Cultural Revolution. Partly because intellectuals composed a traditional elite during a period of emphasis on egalitarianism and mass conformity, and partly because they were more likely than most to challenge Mao's infallibility claims, they were subjected to mass "struggle" and typically sent down to the countryside to do manual labor or in some cases even sent to prison. In parallel speeches to a National Science Conference in the spring of 1978, Hua Guofeng expressed in milder form a continuation of Maoist suspicions of the intellectual community, whereas Deng Xiaoping implicitly called for emancipation of the intellectuals, making the then novel claim that those who worked with their minds were also working and hence were members of the proletariat. During the so-called Beijing Spring period from 1978 through much of 1979, the reformers voiced the slogan Emancipation of the Mind, and called for a revival of the Double Hundred policy ("Let a hundred flowers bloom, let a hundred schools of thought contend").

It must be conceded that the reformers have not remained altogether consistent in their attitudes toward the intellectual community.[33] In fact, a cleavage soon opened in the reform movement between those who place top priority on the Double Hundred and those who stress the Four Cardinal Principles. The more ideologically orthodox group within the reform leadership continues to draw a direct causal connection between wayward intellectual discussion and spontaneous mass movements deemed threatening to the established order—as became particularly clear during the December 1986 student protest movement and the CCP backlash toward it (which included the purge of several prominent intellectuals) in the first three months of 1987. Despite such indications of continuing ambivalence toward the intellectual community, science and technology have been given higher priority in the reform program than before, and formal schooling has been acknowledged as the necessary means to that end; educational credentials are being gradually incorporated into the recruitment criteria of Party and state cadres. This represents a reversal of Cultural Revolution priorities and a recourse to the prerevolution pattern in which political upward mobility tends to correlate with educational achievement.

A third important reversal of Cultural Revolution policies involves

---

33. See Ch'i, *Politics of Disillusionment*, pp. 123–141.

the renunciation (with qualification) of class struggle and the mass movement. During the Cultural Revolution, which was the great mother of all mass movements, class struggle was construed in a freehand way that legitimated factional warfare, economic disruption, and even assaults upon the Party-state apparatus, all of which was extremely damaging to the interests (even the lives) of both cadres and masses. The communique of the Third Plenum of the Eleventh CC (December 1978), widely celebrated as the inauguration of reform, stated that "large-scale, turbulent class struggles of mass character have, *in the main*, come to an end (emphasis added)."[34] Class struggle has been retained as an option (and, since the Tiananmen demonstrations, a live option) to justify the suppression of "enemies of the people" (i.e., political dissidents); and mass mobilization has occasionally been revived (as in the 1981 campaign against bourgeois liberalization, the brief 1982–1983 campaign against spiritual pollution, or the 1987 and 1989 campaigns against bourgeois liberalism) in order to repress certain social trends for which the regime has discovered no better antidote (although mass mobilization has not proved to be particularly effective either). Yet these reversions to class struggle and mass mobilization are perceptibly milder than previously, probably because they clash with the revisionist economic policies officially sanctioned by the regime.

The surviving political animus of the Cultural Revolution includes those elements of the movement that did succeed in tapping a reservoir of unmet needs, for which there is continuing popular demand. According to subsequent interviews I conducted in Hong Kong with former participants, the main such element was a vague but real yearning for greater personal freedom, deriving essentially from chronic deprivation. The only positive experience with such freedom came in the decidedly uncivil context of the Cultural Revolution, but the appetite has since been kept alive by a series of spontaneous protest movements that inherit some of the Cultural Revolution's spirit and tactics, such as Democracy Wall, the fall 1985 demonstrations against the Japanese commercial invasion, and the protest movement in favor of democracy and reform that swept China's major cities and campuses in the fall of 1986 (to be considered at greater length in Chapter 4). The reaction of the leadership to this legacy has been to forbid (with imperfect success) the most disruptive features of such movements (e.g., big-character posters, unofficial publications, and the notion that there are "people in the Party taking the capitalist road"), to co-opt other aspects (e.g., the antibureaucratic animus seems to have been integrated into the campaign against cadre corruption), and to respond in good faith to still others (e.g., the clampdown on Democracy Wall was immediately followed by the introduction of multi-

---

34. "Communiqué," pp. E5–E12.

ple-candidacy elections to local people's congresses, and there has been a quite massive effort to retire aging veterans and replace them with younger cadres).[35] Yet popular demand for the freedom once euphorically experienced in the chaotic melee of the Cultural Revolution has not been sated by the official response.

The adoption of the Cultural Revolution as bête noir, a negative compass point from which to take bearings for the journey to reform, has thus proved uneasy. The regime has found the "ten years of catastrophe" story useful to justify a departure from economically irrational commitments and reorient China's economic development strategy and to break free from the mental toils of ideological dogmatism and adapt to problems somewhat more flexibly. Yet it could not permit the heady allure of "breakthrough" democracy to reemerge. In order to preserve the Cultural Revolution experience as myth qua horror story, at once justifying the taboo against certain types of political behavior without allowing the experience to exert its undeniable anarchic appeal, the regime has subtly shifted its interpretation over time. In the early post-Mao years the image of the Cultural Revolution was negative but ambiguous, on the one hand, symbolizing the nightmare of factional anarchy and "chaos" (*luan*) when the forces of order are overthrown, but, on the other hand, also depicting the tyranny of ideological dogmatism, which is mass-enforced, but ultimately emanates from faith in a supreme fount of wisdom.[36] Aiming criticism at these two images had quite different policy implications: The

---

35. For a perceptive review and analysis of this policy, see Ch'i, *Politics of Disillusionment*, pp. 43–114.

36. The ideological terror theme was emphasized during the early post-Mao period, particularly after Deng was placed in charge. Account after graphic account of the wounds inflicted by the Gang of Four was articulated, and the models selected for emulation during this period were usually martyrs who died in opposition to the Four—such as Zhang Zhixin, a Party member whose throat was cut prior to execution to prevent her from shouting her loyalty to the revolution, or Chen Xinwen, the pilot allegedly shot by Lin Biao for insubordination in the course of the latter's abortive escape attempt. E.g., compare Xi Chen, "A Great Struggle to Defend Party Principles—Revealing the True Nature of a Major Political Incident: The 'February Adverse Current' Concocted by Lin Biao and the 'Gang of Four,'" *RR*, February 26, 1979, trans. in *FBIS-China*, February 28, 1979, p. E19. Then, as the struggle with Hua moved toward a climax, Mao and the "cult" came into focus. See Editorial, "Restore the True Qualities of Mao Zedong Thought," *RR*, May 14, 1980, in *FBIS-China*, May 15, 1980, pp. L3–6; Contributing Commentator, "Correctly Understand the Role of the Individual in History," *RR*, July 4, 1980, in *FBIS-China*, July 7, 1980, pp. L4–7; Liu Maoying, "A New Interpretation of the Story of the 'Foolish Old Man Who Moved Mountains,'" *Wen Hui Bao*, August 13, 1980, in *FBIS-China*, September 22, 1980, pp. L1–9; Wang Zikai, "Commenting on Kang Sheng's Theory of 'The Supreme and Ultimate Criterion,'" *Beijing ribao* (Beijing Daily), August 8, 1980, in *FBIS-China*, August 22, 1980, pp. L9–14; Ruan Ming, "An Important Task on the Ideological Front," *RR*, August 28, 1980, excerpted from *Lilu yu shiyan* (Theory and practice) (Liaoning), no. 9; Contributing Commentator, "Power Must Not Be Overconcentrated in the Hands of Individuals," *Hongqi*, no. 17 (September 1, 1980), in *FBIS-China*, September 17, 1980, pp. L24–26.

"chaos" myth justified political institutionalization and rationalization, whereas the "cult" myth was emancipatory, implying a need for pragmatism, the Hundred Flowers, and Emancipation of the Mind.

After the post-Mao succession crisis was resolved, the "cult" myth seemed to lose its political utility: The intellectuals had been drawn into the reform camp, the Democracy Wall protesters had been mobilized to help reverse verdicts on the first "Tiananmen Incident" in Deng's favor, and most important, Hua Guofeng and his followers (the "small gang of four")—the last possible beneficiaries of the "cult" myth—had been driven from the political stage. The "crimes" of the Gang of Four, previously damned as "apparently 'left' but actually right," were reclassified as "ultraleftist and idealist" (and damned as such in their 1981 trial), reflexively pushing the ideological center rightward.[37] Meanwhile, continued sporadic outbursts of spontaneous mobilization, during the introduction of multicandidate district elections in 1980–1981 and on other occasions, reinforced elite apprehensions about mass indiscipline.

Thus in the period of reform consolidation the image of the Cultural Revolution became more univocal, standing simply for the chaos and anarchy that would surely follow any breakdown of authority.[38] It was this

---

37. Compare these two critiques, written before and after the Third Plenum, respectively: "On Reversing the Verdict of Tiananmen: The 'Gang' Is Seen as 'Counterrevolutionaries Who Could Never Hide Their Rightist Features by Disguising Themselves as 'Leftists,'" *Hongqi* (Red Flag), no. 12 (December 2, 1978), p. 77; and Jin Wen, "Thoroughly Criticize the 'Left' Deviationist Line Viciously Pursued by Lin Biao and the Gang of Four," *Guangming ribao*, (Enlightenment Daily) (Beijing) January 23, 1979, in *FBIS-China*, February 2, 1979, p. E11. On the occasion of the rehabilitation of Liu Shaoqi, the leadership declared, "It is now clear that the danger of so-called right revisionism did not actually appear in our Party before 1966." Contributing Commentator, "The Distinction Between Marxism and Revisionism Should Not Be Blurred," *RR*, April 3, 1980, in *FBIS-China*, April 4, 1980, pp. L1–5; also Huang Nanshen, Zhang Yixing, Zhao Jiaxiang, and Chen Zhannian, "The Relations of Revisionism, Dogmatism, and Empiricism to the Political Line," *Hongqi*, no. 6 (March 16, 1980), in *FBIS-China*, April 15, 1980, pp. L13–14.

38. This was particularly evident during the last concerted public discussion of the radical experience, the 1984–1985 campaign to "totally negate" the Cultural Revolution, which attempted to discredit all factionalism, all leftist radicalism (even the "three supports and two militaries" that justified People's Liberation Army (PLA) intervention), all "extensive democracy," and "mass criticism." See Commentator, "We Must Precisely Totally Negate the Cultural Revolution," *RR*, April 23, 1984, in *FBIS-China*, April 23, 1984, p. K1; "Questions and Answers about Thoroughly Negating the 'Cultural Revolution,' Eliminating Factionalism, and Strengthening Party Spirit," *RR*, as reprinted in *Guangming ribao*, July 28, 1984, pp. 1–2; Commentator, "It Is Essential to Conduct Profound Education in Totally Negating the 'Great Cultural Revolution' for the Broad Party Members and Cadres," *Hongqi*, no. 14 (July 16, 1984), in Joint Publications Research Service (*JPRS*) (September 19, 1984), p. 17; Commentator, "Completely Negate 'Extensive Democracy,'" *RR*, August 15, 1984, in *FBIS-China*, August 16, 1984; "First Phase Party Rectification Units in PLA Uphold Principle of Self-Education, Score Fine Results in Totally Negating the 'Cultural Revolution' from Theory to Practice," *RR*, December 5, 1984, in *FBIS-China*, December 10, 1984, pp. K1–3, and so on.

antinomian image that the hard-liners conjured up (and perhaps even believed) to rationalize their crackdown at Tiananmen—despite the best efforts of the demonstrators to avoid that stereotype by singing "The Internationale," generally steering clear of violence or vandalism, and taking other precautions. Ironically, this left the regime with no alternative but a revival of Mao Zedong Thought to legitimize its brutality—that is, revival of a symbol system inextricably linked to the Cultural Revolution and Mao's troubling role as its driving spirit. After all, in principle Mao endorsed criticism of authority: His May 1966 comment that only northern warlords repress student demonstrations has not been forgotten.[39]

The Inauguration of Reform

The reform era began with the rise of Deng Xiaoping to a position of de facto leadership within the Politburo at the Third Plenum of the Eleventh Central Committee in December 1978. In the ensuing months he and his followers introduced a comprehensive series of reforms in rapid succession, beginning with agriculture and then proceeding with industrial, intellectual, and political reforms. In addition to the revival of the market reforms he and Liu had initiated in the aftermath of the Great Leap, the commune was dissolved, small markets were allowed to proliferate in both rural and urban venues, and financial controls devolved from central to local or factory levels. Although the focus of reform has shifted appreciably over time, the overall pattern includes three facets:

1. The "responsibility system," though still sailing under the socialist slogan "from each according to his abilities, to each according to his work," nonetheless entails a significant shift from the Maoist calculus of payment according to labor *input* to payment according to labor *output*–this is one meaning of "responsibility."[40] It entails precise measurement of ouput and precise specification of the responsible work units (in the countryside, the effective unit is the family, now termed a "brigade"), as well as increasingly differentiated mate-

---

39. Beginning in 1990, the CCP launched a new campaign to revive the cult of Mao. A book entitled *A Recollection of Mao Zedong's Talks on the Prevention of Peaceful Evolution* was published, and Bo Yibo called on the nation to "study and propagandize the Thought of Mao Zedong." *RR*, December 26, 1990, p. 1, as cited in Alan P. L. Liu, "Communications and Development in Post-Mao Mainland China," *Issues and Studies*, 27:12 (December 1991), p. 95, n. 54.

40. See Louis Putterman, "The Restoration of the Peasant Household as Farm Production Unit in China: Some Incentive Theoretic Analysis," in Perry and Wong, *Political Economy of Reform*, pp. 63–83.

rial incentive scales.⁴¹ The net effect has been that households work harder to produce more in order to earn more; because they work more productively, fewer people are needed to work the land, and surplus labor is siphoned off to rural industries or to commercial ventures ("specialized households," or *geti hu*). In industry, responsibility has been allocated through a number of schemes (e.g., higher profit remission rates, tax-for-profits, profit contracting), all of which involve greater emphasis on enterprise self-management and market autonomy and more extensive use of bonuses and other output-based incentives. For the economy as a whole, the responsibility system implies greater reliance on the market mechanism, which promises an automatic correlation of value and price, of incremental output and incremental reward.

2. With regard to the relationship between political leadership and social structure, reform seems to imply an apolitical form of *meritocratic pluralism*. This means that outside the political sphere, each functional subsystem comprises a hierarchy designed to maximize the values orienting that particular subsystem: cost-benefit efficiency in production, service in commerce and retailing; specialized competence in the various scientific, professional, and cultural subsystems. Even the political system is vertically divided into various subsystems, apparently based on some notion of functional specialization: the CDIC was commissioned for the enforcement of Party norms and the CAC for the implementation of orderly retirement, the NPC has introduced specialized standing committees, and there has been increasing emphasis on the elimination of overlapping roles and functional duplication at all levels.⁴² Just before Tiananmen, an independent civil service was proposed that in principle would be completely autonomous from the Party. Each subsystem is hierarchically organized and enforces discipline within its ranks through selective allocation of promotions and other perquisites and the imposition of organizational sanctions. Each subsystem has (limited) ambit to pursue the values on which its autonomy is premised, and there is increasing freedom (in the form of horizontal vocational mobility) to choose the value system the individual aspires to adopt.

---

41. Deng's concern with "responsibility" is a long-standing one. See "Some Comments on Industrial Development" (August 18, 1975), in *Selected*, p. 45; and "Report on the Revision of the Constitution of the CPC" (September 16, 1956), in *Deng Xiaoping: Speeches and Writings*, 2nd expanded ed. (New York: Pergamon Press, 1987) (hereinafter *Deng Xiaoping*), p. 20: "Without a division of labor and individual responsibility we would not be able to carry out any complicated work and would find ourselves in the woeful predicament of no one taking responsibility for any particular task."

42. See Sullivan, "Leadership and Authority," pp. 49–65. This is quantitatively documented with respect to the military in Monte R. Bullard, *China's Political-Military Evolution: The Party and the Military in the PRC, 1960–1984* (Boulder: Westview Press, 1985).

3. There is a general policy of *opening*. Intellectually, this implies an encouragement of open-mindedness, pragmatism, and flexibility, and opposition to dogmatism or "superstition." This opening policy, as expressed in the slogans, Seek Truth Through Facts, Practice as the Sole Criterion of Truth, Let a Hundred Flowers Bloom, and Emancipation of the Mind, made its first appearance in the more enlightened policy toward intellectuals first inaugurated in 1979. Repression of intellectuals was replaced by a (qualified) revival of the Hundred Flowers motto Deng had originally opposed: Intellectual "blooming" began in the summer of 1986 and, after a hiatus following the crackdown on "bourgeois liberalization" in early 1987, resumed with élan in 1988–1989.

Economically, opening has resulted in the so-called "open-door policy" (*kaifang zhengzi*), which has essentially reversed Mao's "self-reliance" in favor of opening to the outside world.[43] This has entailed a rapid increase in external trade,[44] and the encouragement of foreign private investment,[45] as well as relaxed emigration policies and an encouragement of tourism and cultural exchanges. One controversial implication has been that Chinese students are allowed to study abroad, resulting in an exodus (from 1978 to mid-1992) of some 160,000 of China's brightest young people (the majority of whom are still overseas at this writing). It

---

43. See Kenny Chin, "China's Open Door to Foreign Investment, 1978–1984" (Ph.D. diss., Political Science Department, University of California at Berkeley, December 1985); also see Samuel P. S. Ho and Ralph W. Huenemann, *China's Open Door: The Quest for Foreign Technology and Capital* (Boulder: Westview Press, 1984); Nicholas Lardy, *China's Entry into the World Economy* (Lanham, Md.: University Press of America, 1987); Robert Kleinberg, *China's "Opening" to the Outside World* (Boulder: Westview Press, 1990); and Yue-man Yeung and Xu-wei Hu, eds., *China's Coastal Cities* (Honolulu: University of Hawaii Press, 1992).

44. From 1978 through 1988, the PRC's share in world trade more than doubled (from 0.8 percent in 1978 to 1.7 percent in 1988); China's total trade as a percentage of gross national product (GNP) rose from an average of 2.62 percent for the 1950–1976 period to 8.31 percent for the 1982–1984 period. From 1982 to 1984 the average rate of growth for total trade was 18.7 percent, compared to an average GNP growth rate of 10.6 percent. He Xinhao, "Exploit the Role of Foreign Trade and Accelerate the Rate of China's Economic Development," *Guoji maoyi* (International Trade), no. 5 (1982), as trans. in *Chinese Economic Studies*, 16:4 (Summer 1983), pp. 37–50. China's Seventh Five-Year Plan, presented by Zhao Ziyang to the annual session of the NPC in March 1986, called for trade to reach $83 billion by 1990, up 40 percent from 1985 (at a slightly lower annual growth rate of 8 percent). *Wall Street Journal*, March 26, 1986.

45. Direct investments made their most noteworthy increase since the 1984 reforms and the earlier relaxation of restrictions. Joint equity ventures formed during the first half of 1985 totaled 687, nearly four times the total for the first half of 1984. "Decision of the Central Committee of the Communist Party on Reform of the Economic Structure," *Beijing Review*, 44: (October 29, 1984), pp. iii–iv. From 1979 through 1987, China received roughly $8.47 billion from direct foreign investment in more than 4,000 joint ventures of various kinds. *Beijing Review*: (February 8, 1989), p. 30.

has also resulted in the creation of a number of Special Administrative Regions (SARs), in each of which greater leeway is to be given to experimentation and innovation than in the rest of the country.[46] The planned incorporation of Hong Kong into China in 1997 is conceived to fit into this policy and even to extend it, facilitating "one country, two systems," as the 1982 State Constitution puts it (the other SARs remain fully socialist; only Hong Kong will retain capitalist relations of production).

To be sure, there are limits to opening, spelled out in the intellectual realm in Deng Xiaoping's Four Cardinal Principles (whose range of application has been vague and elastic) and underlined in recurrent campaigns against "bourgeois liberalization," "spiritual pollution," and so forth. Yet in view of the recent experience with precipitate transformation, Chinese caution is understandable. As Deng himself put it in criticism of his predecessor, "We went too fast before and thus made a series of mistakes—left mistakes, as we say."[47]

The general consensus is that these economic reforms have been highly effective. The nation experienced a vigorous economic revival, as national output (GNP) growth averaged 10.3 percent per annum in the 1980–1988 period, giving China the second-highest growth rate (after Botswana, whose economy is essentially extractive)[48] in the world—compared to a rate of about 5.1 percent from 1955 to 1977 (less than 5 percent if the more realistic prices of the late 1970s are used to measure national product). Per capita national product during the 1977–1985 period grew at over 6 percent per year, or 75 percent overall. Agriculture, the sector that was first and most radically reformed, was also the sector that grew most rapidly: The rate of growth in the gross value of agricultural output from 1978 to 1984 was 9.4 percent per year, compared to 2.9

---

46. See Kuan-yin Wong and David K. Y. Chu, eds., *Modernization in China: The Case of the Shanghai Special Economic Zone* (Hong Kong: Oxford University Press, 1985).
47. Deng Xiaoping, "Conversation with the Liberian Chief of State" (May 6, 1982), as trans. in Helmut Martin, ed., *Die Reform der Revolution: Eine Milliarde Menschen auf dem Weg* (Berlin: Siedler Verlag, 1988), p. 36.
48. According to the World Bank World Development Report 1990, as reported by Myron J. Gordon, *Globe and Mail* (Toronto), January 18, 1992. China's annual growth rate for farm output was 2.1 percent in the 1970s and 6.2 percent in the 1980s; at the same time, employment in rural township enterprises grew from 22 million in 1978 to 93 million in 1988, meaning that roughly half of China's farm families had income from nonagricultural work supplementing their farm income by this time. And, for the first time since the early post-Liberation years, economic growth was translated into impressive increases in living standards: The 1991 United Nations Human Development Report placed China among the medium human development countries, with a real (not exchange rate) per capita GNP of $2,470 in 1988.

percent per year over the previous two decades.[49] China has become the world's largest grain producer, with the highest grain yield per unit of arable land—with less arable land than the United States, China grows enough grain to feed one-fifth of the world population. Rural industry has absorbed the agricultural surplus and boomed, contributing (at this writing) more than half of rural production, or over one-third of China's total industrial production.

Whereas growth during the Maoist period had been achieved largely by the high rate of growth in inputs of capital and labor (extensive growth), most of the growth in the post-Mao period can be accounted for in terms of productivity growth[50]—the rate of capital formation has actually fallen slightly, whereas the share of the budget going to consumption has increased.[51] This suggests that the reforms have played a major (to be sure, not exclusive) role in the improved economic performance, though it is still uncertain whether their beneficial impact will turn out to be temporary or capable of stimulating a self-sustaining boom analogous to that achieved by Japan between 1950 and 1980. In this context it should be noted that the rate of growth in the gross value of industrial output over the same period has declined, amounting to only two-thirds of the long-term growth rate. Industrial growth has also been relatively inefficient, especially in the large, state-run urban factories, at least one-third of which operate at a loss.[52] This inefficiency is due to constraints on personnel policy (the "iron rice bowl"), infrastructure bottlenecks (especially energy), and bureaucratically fixed prices.

The political consequences have been unsettling and less successfully dealt with. One result has been looser CCP control in the rural areas, as indicated, for example, by difficulty in collecting taxes or by the inability to enforce birth control as effectively there. Laxer control implies greater lateral mobility, as surplus labor migrates to cities (or to more prosperous rural areas) to improve living standards. Urban state industries have been seriously challenged by rural township and village enterprises, which achieve cost reductions by paying lower wages and offering few benefits; in a market context, urban industries would lay off workers to

---

49. If agriculture (including rural industry) had continued to grow at its previous rate through 1984, the rate of Chinese GNP growth in 1977–1985 would have been no more than 6 percent instead of 8 percent per year.

50. Dwight H. Perkins, *China, Asia's Next Economic Giant?* (Seattle: University of Washington Press, 1986).

51. This is particularly apparent in agriculture, where there has been a 20 percent reduction in the amount of land plowed by mechanical means. There has also been a 50 percent reduction in state investment for agriculture, a 60 percent reduction in state investment for water projects, and a significant reduction in the share of land that is cultivated.

52. Ann Scott Tyson and James L. Tyson, in *Christian Science Monitor*, June 2, 1992.

achieve greater productivity or go bankrupt, but that would mean unemployment, a larger "floating population," and urban unrest. To unplug the infrastructure bottleneck price reform is needed, letting energy and raw material prices rise to their supply and demand equilibrium, but complete price reform would trigger an outburst of inflation that would infuriate the regime's urban political base, as was illustrated in the summer of 1988. Thus the regime adopted the expedient of a "dual price structure," in which various commodities have one planned price and one (or more than one) market price. This compromise, however, stimulated an illegal arbitrage known as *guan dao*, in which those with access to commodities at the planned price (usually cadres or their relatives) buy them for resale at higher market prices. This and other analogous shortcuts have made distributive inequalities more severe—inequalities many feel are based less on productive efficiency or marketing skills than on political "connections." Finally, the relaxation of central control over the economy seems to have exacerbated an investment cycle in which the political fortunes of reformers and antireformers rise with each boom or bust, respectively. Thus, after a decade of reform and economic growth, "Tiananmen" is the anticlimax.

Genealogy of Reform

China's post-Mao reform movement, moving cautiously ahead "groping for stones to cross the river" without a clear notion of what is on the other side, may look back at three foundings or "homes" for guidelines: the "Golden" Fifties, when ideological and economic objectives seemed happily to coincide; the post-Leap revisionist period, when China began to experiment with its own eclectic blend of socialism; and the Cultural Revolution, which sounded the death knell for radical socialism and opened the way to much bolder experimentation than ever before. In the absence of elite consensus or an explicit blueprint for the future, a sense of where the movement is coming from offers some insight into where it is going, whereas simply waiting for the next act of the drama to unfold offers none. And each line of descent offers different clues about the odyssey's ultimate destination.

The 1950s seemed to prove that socialism could work—socializing the means of production, redistributing income and services at no perceptible cost to vigorous growth or enthusiastic mass support. In retrospect it seems a golden age, symbolizing above all the sense of revolutionary solidarity, youth, and optimism (e.g., the old man who could move mountains), that many nostalgic Party veterans (particularly those associated with Chen Yun) would like to recover after "ten years of catastrophe" followed by the "three crises" of faith. Whether this is a realistic aspiration is, however, another question. True, Mao Zedong was able to recapture that revolutionary spirit in 1966, but only at a cost his aging ideological legatees would find intolerable and that he himself was never again able to apply constructively. The wish to turn back the clock to New Democracy misses the point that this was a brief transitional period between capitalism and socialism, whereas the stage theory adopted at the Thirteenth Party Congress plans a century-long holding pattern at the "primary stage of socialism"—and remains mute about what will succeed it. The 1950s held a sense of teleological momentum, since lost amid pragmatism; the credibility of the ideological component of the early Maoist agenda not only legitimated the redistributive policies but helped to attract the idealists now losing interest. Without this consensus on a political direction, the various elite opinion groupings are left free to tug and haul in different directions, and even the support of the masses, a full generation after land reform, is no longer unconditional.

The Cultural Revolution aroused intense, mostly negative feelings and thereby provided a powerful springboard for the reform era. Whereas both the revisionist experiments and the post-Mao reforms were introduced in the wake of major radical policy disasters (the Great Leap in the case of the former, the Cultural Revolution in the latter), it would seem from conversations with Chinese informants that the latter left deeper scars on the Chinese psyche than the former.[53] Why this is so is not entirely clear—the extent and intensity of damage inflicted by the Leap would seem to have been objectively greater than that suffered during the Cultural Revolution—but perhaps not to the urban middle and working classes that have become the regime's core political constituency. In any case, the Cultural Revolution created a cadre of elite "struggle" veterans who may have learned something of the plight of the common people from having been "sent down" to work among them; nevertheless, they regard the experience as a nightmare they are determined to ensure should never recur. To use a slightly different analogy, the Cultural Revolution is to the post-Mao reform regime what revisionism was to the Cultural Revolution.

But in both cases, trying to generate a political direction from a dialectic with a polar antithesis has proved imprecise: An aversive experience can provide motivation, but no clear direction. The Cultural Revolution legacy has been ambiguous, on the one hand, justifying a return to "top-down" legal formalization and institution building (and an overwrought horror of mass unrest) that has exacerbated elite-mass tensions, and, on the other hand, leading to a demythification and intellectual iconoclasm

---

53. See Anne Thurston, *Enemies of the People* (New York: Knopf, 1987).

the Party elite has grown uneasy with, invoking the Four Cardinal Principles to set bounds on ideological secularization. Criticizing the Cultural Revolution has created two different reform constituencies at loggerheads with each other: a political elite obsessed with stability, and an intellectual elite whose priority is liberty and civil rights.

If neither the founding era nor the Cultural Revolution provide clear guidelines for the future, what about the revisionist interregnum? It should be conceded at the outset that there are at least two important differences between revisionism and reform. The most significant of these is the complete disappearance from the Chinese political scene of the "proletarian revolutionary line." The cornerstone of that edifice was Mao Zedong himself, ably if controversially assisted by Kang Sheng, Chen Boda, Lin Biao, and, of course, the Gang of Four. With the deaths of the older radicals and the trial of the Gang, the Chinese leadership spectrum has for the first time in its history had its left wing amputated. The disappearance of this grouping has had a major emancipatory impact on the forces of reform. Upon overcoming the resistance of the "whateverists," who were inhibited by Mao's Thought (if unwilling to pursue its implications), the reformers have been able to venture much further than the revisionists of the 1960s. For example, before 1962 Liu and Deng had experimented with responsibility plots on a limited scale, but in 1979–1983 a series of agricultural reforms were introduced that amounted to de facto decollectivization. The reblooming of the Hundred Flowers beginning in the summer of 1985 went far beyond the original; whereas the revisionists were willing to accelerate trade in goods and even ideas (mostly, however, with other socialist countries), Deng's policy of opening to the outside world goes far beyond previous such ventures. Whereas Liu cloaked his support for material incentives in altruistic appeals, Deng has felt secure in making quite crude appeals to materialism.[54] In pushing the reforms beyond the intellectual premises set forth during the revisionist era, the reformers have had to resort to new sources of inspiration—such as the East Asian newly industrialized countries (NICs), the apparent origin of the Special Economic Zones (SEZs).

Of course, the fact that the political continuum has been chopped off at the left does not mean that there are no intraelite conflicts or purges, as the fall of Hu Yaobang and Zhao Ziyang illustrates. It does mean that there is simply no longer a politically viable ideological alternative to re-

---

54. In 1984 Deng said, "The superiority of the socialist system is demonstrated by faster and greater development of the productive forces than under the capitalist system.... Socialism means eliminating poverty. Pauperism is not socialism, still less communism." Deng, "Build Socialism with Chinese Characteristics," in *Deng Xiaoping*, pp. 95–98.

form. The post-Mao Left has become an essentially conservative grouping that opposes mass mobilization even more than the Right, and whose most effective opposition has coincided with economic retrenchment rather than new leaps forward. Indeed it is Deng Xiaoping who has become the most recent apostle of great economic leaps. Chen Yun, Deng Liqun, and other leftists stem from the same ideological pedigree (indeed Deng Liqun is a former secretary of Liu Shaoqi); although they continue to set more store in doctrinal orthodoxy than the radical reformers, they would never sanction another Cultural Revolution. The differences that roil the post-Mao elite are no longer differences of principle (what Mao called "antagonistic contradictions")—even when they result in purge.

A second difference is the international climate into which the reforms have been introduced. In the early 1960s China was still considered by the West to be a (maverick) member of the Communist bloc, which posed a continuing threat to Non-Communist regimes in the Third World. Hence containment policies and an economic blockade remained in effect even as the United States commenced wheat sales and Strategic Arms Limitations Talks with the Soviet Union. Among Mao Zedong's crowning foreign policy achievements was to break out of this encirclement by initiating rapprochement with the West, a policy that bore fruit in the normalization of Sino-American relations at the beginning of 1979. Thus the revisionist experiments of the 1960s were introduced in an international context in which China still felt obliged to defend the principles of socialism (indeed, the ideological dispute with the Soviet Union tended to enhance this need). However, the reforms of the late 1970s and 1980s were introduced in a very different international context: Chinese relations with the Soviet Union and the rest of the Communist bloc had deteriorated severely and relations with the United States and the rest of the free world had become not only quite friendly but essential to national security. Thus the "open door policy" of the 1980s, which has become a prime source of innovation in the reform effort, would have been completely impracticable in the international context of the early 1960s. In 1989 the whole Communist bloc of course disintegrated, making good relations with the West the only feasible alternative to international isolation.

With the exception of the two preceding qualifications, it may be said that the post-Mao reforms stand in direct line of descent from the revisionist experiments of the 1960s. Indeed, it should surprise no one that Deng Xiaoping, the "number two Party person in authority taking the capitalist road" (after the late Liu Shaoqi), whose first political priority upon gaining personal revindication (for the second time) in July 1977 was to rehabilitate about three million cadres and Party members who had been purged during the Cultural Revolution, should proceed to rebuild the system he had helped introduce in the early 1960s and again (in the face of much stiffer resistance) in 1974–1976—certainly it would not have surprised Mao Zedong, who anticipated as much in 1976. A certain amount of official sheepishness about this development remains, as indicated by the fact that since 1979 the epithet "revisionism" seems to have disappeared from the Chinese political vocabulary, even in referring to the Soviet Union. This seems to arise from the apprehension that despite the comprehensive repudiation of cultural radicalism, some of the Maoist criticisms of revisionism were perhaps valid after all. All this betrays a certain sensitivity to the fragility of the reform program: If revisionism resulted in the Cultural Revolution, was Tiananmen the result of reform?

Despite such indications of unease, the general tendency has been to revert to the revisionist pattern. Traces of revisionism in the politics of reform can be seen first and foremost in the priority given to institution building in general and to Party building in particular. Liu's rehabilitation coincided with the adoption (at the Fifth Plenum of the Eleventh CC) of "Guiding Principles for Inner-Party Political Life," designed to rectify Cultural Revolution–inspired factionalism and restore inner-Party democracy. The Party has begun to resuscitate its traditional organizational and disciplinary techniques, including small-group "criticism and self-criticism," the personnel management system (with nomenklatura features, such as secret dossier management with regularized evaluation procedures), and Party rectification campaigns.

Thus the Party rectification campaign launched at the Twelfth Party Congress in September 1982 eschewed all Cultural Revolution innovations, such as open-door rectification or any form of mass monitoring of cadres. It began with elaborate preparations, including rotational training classes held under work team jurisdiction among 580 selected branches at the center and in 29 provinces, with municipalities and autonomous regions responsible for training cadres to conduct the campaign. The campaign was then implemented "from top to bottom," both with regard to the hierarchy as a whole and within each unit, and in sequential shifts (*fen qi fen pi*, or stage by stage and group by group)—as in Liu's 1964 plan for the Four Cleans—rather than in nationwide "wavelike advances." In terms of ideological objectives, rectification involved a "struggle on two fronts," placing virtue in the middle of the road and targeting cadre corruption on the Right and the "three types of person"[55] on the Left. Unity would be achieved through the intensive study of

---

55. I.e., *san zhong ren* (three types of people)—remnant elements of the Lin Biao-Jiang Qing counterrevolutionary clique, those who gained power during the Cultural Revolution by "rebelling," and the "smash-and-grabbers."

thousands of pages of selected documents, accompanied by criticism and self-criticism sessions. Substantively, the campaign emphasized "revolutionary values that have no practical resemblance to the social values that the Party is trying to establish."[56] Nevertheless it did not engender "contradictions" between rectification and reform—as had the short-lived parallel campaign against spiritual pollution. This was partly because Party rectification proceeded relatively sedately ("gentle breeze and mild rain"), and partly because rectification was hermetically insulated from society, in accord with classical Leninist "closed-door" Party-building principles.

A second earmark of the revisionist approach manifests itself in the attitude toward the masses, who are generally treated like a pack of wild horses that might run amok, to be pacified with economic blandishments if possible but repressed if necessary. There have been cautious attempts to permit feedback from the masses, first in the Beijing Spring or Democracy Wall movement, which was initially encouraged (in the summer and fall of 1978) as a vehicle for Deng's comeback, and later in the (1980–1981) introduction of multiple-candidacy county-level elections. But these experiments (let alone the mass protests of 1985, 1986, and 1989) proved too effervescent and unpredictable for the tastes of shell-shocked Cultural Revolution survivors, and the general inclination has been to reduce mass participation in politics to a ceremonial role. Deng Xiaoping's Four Cardinal Principles were designed to protect and to consecrate Mao's Thought, socialism, the Dictatorship of the Proletariat, and Party leadership (the last of which is most important). The "socialist spiritual civilization," introduced by the reformers in 1985 as an antidote to radical heaven storming, shows the same deferential, ritualistic emptiness, with its Five Stresses (civilized behavior, decorum, hygiene, discipline, morals), Four Points of Beauty (the mind, language, behavior, the environment) and Three Deep Loves (the motherland, socialism, the Party).

In short, having repudiated the campaign style of elite-mass intermediation because it culminated in the Cultural Revolution, the reform leadership found in its timid experiments with more democratic arrangements no acceptable alternative, thereby gradually stripping the elite-mass relationship of any avenue for communication about national political issues. Even in Hong Kong, which is not scheduled to revert to Chinese sovereignty until 1997, when democratic elections were first introduced on an extremely modest scale in the summer of 1985, Xu Jiatun,

---

56. See Hong Yung Lee, "The Strategy of the Party Rectification," in Sang-Woo Rhee, *China's Reform Politics* (Seoul, Korea: Sogang University Press, 1986), pp. 67–94.

head of the Hong Kong New China News Agency (NCNA) branch and Beijing's highest local representative, expressed his displeasure and sought to bring the process to a halt; every democratic concession in the Crown colony has come grudgingly. It would appear that capitalism is less threatening to the reform leadership than democracy.

That would not be inconsistent with the underlying premises of revisionism. Recall the Liuist assumption that it was useful to maintain a functional division between politics and economics, in order to protect the elite moral subculture from social contamination while permitting the economy (and other functionally specialized realms) to operate according to its own "objective laws." The reform regime shares this assumption, seeking to separate enterprise management from the factory Party committee or even from its superior ministry[57] (for example) and generally to draw a clearer distinction between Party and state bureaucracies.[58] A rightist movement in the economic and cultural realms thus might easily coincide with a leftist movement in the Party, as occurred during the simultaneous Party rectification and anti–spiritual pollution movement launched after the Twelfth Party Congress. The idea of subsystem autonomy delighted artists, scientists, journalists, and other intellectuals, who proceeded to take advantage of their expanded professional freedom but could seldom resist expanding it into the political sphere. This type of ethical relativism had outraged Mao Zedong and the radicals, who insisted that politics and economics are indivisible, that any corrupting influence must be aborted *in utero* (*principiis obsta!*). Whereas the Maoist attempt to put politics "in command" and maintain social "monolithicity" (*yiyuanhua*) proved untenable over the long run, it nonetheless seems clear that Mao's insight into the flaws of Liu's attempt to create a

---

57. According to the urban reforms introduced in 1984, the enterprise is to become an independent legal entity endowed with specific rights and responsibilities, able to enter contracts and seek redress, entitled to a measure of protection against governmental encroachment, and so forth. Thomas P. Lyons and Wang Yan, *Planning and Finance in China's Economic Reforms* (Ithaca: East Asian Program, Cornell University, 1988), pp. 24–27.

58. The principle is that, though overlapping jurisdictions and joint appointments will not be altogether curtailed, no leading figure in one hierarchy will also be a leader in the other. Although this principle was first used to divest Hua Guofeng of his premiership, it has been quite systematically applied throughout the bureaucracy (in fact more effectively at the lower levels than at the top). By 1989, the holding of concurrent posts by individual leaders had been eliminated at most organizational levels. At the local levels the power of appointment of government staff has been shifted from the Party secretary to the Ministry of Personnel. Zhao Ziyang announced in his report to the Thirteenth Party Congress a plan to dismantle the Party groups in government, education, and military organs, to facilitate the separation of Party from government—a policy whose implementation has been deferred by Tiananmen. Sullivan, "Leadership and Authority," pp. 49–65.

political monastery for the cultivation of revolutionary virtue was quite prescient.

A general tendency in all industrializing systems, it seems, has been to obscure the distinction between politics and economics. Even in a free market system like that of the United States, in which classic economic liberalism qua Adam Smith's "invisible hand" likewise endorses a strict distinction between politics and economics, interpenetration has waxed vigorously since the Great Depression, in the form of governmental control of fiscal and monetary policies, wage-price controls and incomes policies, industrial and commercial regulation, and so forth; the private sector has in turn exerted its influence over relevant public policy through lobbyists, political action committees, and media campaigns. State Socialist systems have not been as troubled by this interpenetration as democratic political theorists, for according to Marxist thinkers it is to be assumed that politics is an expression (according to some, a mere reflection) of economic forces, and in any case the classic communist partystate had proprietary rights over the economy and managed it like a huge firm. The problem arises when an autonomous market mechanism and private or quasi-private ownership is introduced into a planned economy. Inevitably the question of ideological identity arises: What is capitalist, what is socialist, how far can the reforms go without trespassing the line of demarcation? This issue has in the course of reform been resolved with increasing latitude for market innovation (with certain well-known setbacks)—yet it also caused the NPC Standing Committee, a presumptive democratic organ, to stall passage of an industrial reform and bankruptcy package from 1986 to 1988.

Once the bird is released from the cage, the question is how to keep it from flying away: There are ministries for every industrial sector under the State Council, but for the regulation of markets there are few tools and limited knowledge. What is the proper relationship between the Party and this vigorous new sector? The revisionists have certainly been much more receptive to experiments mixing market and plan and less dogmatically rigid about the socialist economy than the Maoists—yet they, too, have difficulty here. The Liuist obsession with a firm "line of demarcation" against social penetration ("corruption") to preserve Party purity would result in an elite-mass communications breakdown and tension if it were a realistic prospect, but it is not; lacking formal channels, the Party is subject to penetration by myriads of informal inroads. The hope to limit the penetration of market forces and the market mentality to the economic realm seems as ill-fated as Zhang Zhidong's analogous attempt to maintain a distinction between Western utilitarian knowledge and a Chinese essence (*Zhongxue wei ti, xixue wei yong*). Market spillover takes the form of bribes and corruption (*bu zheng zhi feng*);[59] cultural spillover takes the form of the consumer revolution and Western popular culture at the mass level and academic social science at the elite level. Technology transfer is, of course, officially encouraged, under the naive assumption that it can be detached from its cultural base.

The underlying dilemma has to do with the function of the Party in an age of reform. As might be expected, the Party's legitimacy is based on the premise that it is the vanguard of the proletariat, needed to lead that class in overthrowing the old, rotten bourgeois class structure and mode of production and in establishing first a socialist, and then a communist, mode of production and political order. The implicit assumption of revisionism is that with the socialization of the means of production the unique historical role of the revisionist vanguard has basically been completed; its future task is to administer the planned economy efficiently and increase the capacity of the forces of production (e.g., science and technology).[60] This was the besetting crime of the revisionists, in the view of the radicals, who were convinced that the Party's function must include leading the march into the communist utopia; without sustained

---

59. According to my informants, corruption has increased since the advent of the reforms. Perhaps the best recent attempt by a Western social scientist to comprehend its distinctive qualities is that of Clemens Stubbe Ostergaard, "Political Corruption and Local Administrative Elites in the People's Republic of China" (Unpublished paper prepared for a workshop on comparative political corruption, ECPR Joint Sessions of Workshops, Freiburg im Breslau, March 20–25, 1983. See also excellent articles by Alan Liu, "The Politics of Corruption in the PRC," *American Political Science Review*, 77:3 (September 1983), pp. 602–623; and Wojtek Zafanolli, "A Brief Outline of China's Second Economy," *Asian Survey*, 25:7 (July 1985), pp. 715–737.

60. The problem of functional obsolescence is a poignant one for cadres. Ironically, in somewhat the same way Mao Zedong asked cadres to lead a revolution dedicated to their own criticism and purge, the reformers are asking cadres to preside over the quiet eclipse of their own power. In the countryside the dissolution of the communes and introduction of the responsibility system has already freed peasants from a good deal of cadre regulation and control, and industrial reforms promise to do the same for urban workers and especially for the professional middle classes. Middle-and lower-level cadres who wish to avoid such an eclipse have roughly three options: The first is not to implement the reforms, or to implement them half-heartedly. This risks incurring the wrath of the authorities, able to impose whatever sanctions they choose. The second is to join the new middle classes in the pursuit of wealth from their official positions. This option adheres to the old tradition of "bureaucratic capitalism" and utilizes the "connections" cultivated in official careers but is usually defined as "corrupt" (certainly it is inconsistent with Liu's ethos of austere self-cultivation) and runs the same risk as the first option. The third is to organize those who have for one reason or another failed to profit from the reforms and thus suffer the "red-eyed disease," mobilizing them in an attack upon those who have prospered most conspicuously. Such a throwback to the egalitarian rhetoric of the Cultural Revolution runs the risk of being labeled one of the "three types of people" and therewith purged. Chinese media abound with reports of all three of these deviant responses, but their relative frequencies have not been tabulated.

momentum in that direction not only would the Party lose its legitimacy, it would reverse course and take the "capitalist road."

The radical critique of revisionism turns out to be correct in the sense that in the absence of further progress toward distinctively socialist goals the Party loses its ideological legitimacy and with it its raison d'être. It becomes more and more like Western socialist or social democratic parties, with a vague commitment to social justice for the working classes but with no transcendent claim to legitimacy. It is interesting to note that whereas during the Cultural Revolution it was science that had to be legitimated in terms of Mao Zedong Thought, in the reform era it is the Party that claims to be "scientific"—the Party must borrow its legitimacy from institutions it once subvened. Its mass support is contingent simply on running the economy competently. This does not place the CCP in any immediate jeopardy, as the CCP's economic record has been quite good. Over the longer term its appeal is likely to fade, however, particularly to the young people and intellectuals for whom ideals tend to be important. The CCP will continue to attract adherents because it is the ruling party and has the power to advance cadre careers or interests. But even here its attractiveness is likely to fade, eclipsed by the relative vitality of the market sector (the state-owned sector's proportion of total GNP is facing gradual extinction).[61]

Conclusions

Like the Confucian intellectuals at the turn of the last century who absorbed so much of Joseph Levenson's attention, Deng Xiaoping and the reformers have sought to build their nation's future on a workable compromise between stability and innovation, between Chinese tradition and Western technology.[62] Just as Liu Shaoqi and the revisionists sought a balance between Confucian self-cultivation and Marxist-Leninist revolution, and between the relatively stable 1950s and the catastrophic attempt

---

61. In 1991, state enterprises were responsible for only 52.8 percent of the country's industrial output, compared to 54.5 percent in 1990 and well over 80 percent a decade ago. And the trend is clear. In 1992, the output of state industries grew only 8 percent, whereas collectives recorded output growth of 18 percent; private enterprises, 24 percent; and foreign-invested enterprises, 56 percent, according to Zhang Zhongji, director of the General Statistical Department of the National Economy of the State Statistical Bureau. The nonstate sector accounted for 95 percent of the nation's agricultural output and 46 percent of gross industrial output by 1990, according to an Asian Development Bank report released in April 1992. By the end of the century, China's nonstate sector could account for 75–80 percent of China's GNP.

62. Joseph Levenson, *Confucian China and Its Modern Fate*, 3 vols. (Berkeley: University of California Press, 1964).

at breakthrough in the Great Leap Forward, the reformers have sought to synthesize the revisionist innovations of the early 1960s with an awareness of some of the flaws in that program exposed in the trenchant Cultural Revolution critique. Probably to an extent far beyond their initial expectations, they have succeeded. Deng and his colleagues, now freed from the ideological constraint of Mao's Thought as Mao would have construed it, have taken revisionist pragmatism far beyond what Liu Shaoqi would have deemed feasible. It has, however, become evident that under the aegis of Mao's Thought revisionism was not only prevented from fully realizing its inherent potential, but also was protected from disintegrating into a melee of competing forces. Without that ideological grid, one of Liu's guiding assumptions—that political fixed principles and values can be isolated from economic and cultural vicissitudes—has already proved chimerical. Chen Yun is correct in pointing out that as long as modernization is allowed to proceed with doors open to the West, there will be continuing pressure for bourgeois liberalization.

The revisionist-reformist attempt to maintain a functional division of labor between politics and economics, between Party elite and social environment, will probably prove untenable in the long run. The Party has about the same chance of turning back the economic tide it has set in motion as Canute. Three alternative "lines" seem open at this juncture. The first would be to abandon the functional division of authority and reassert "politics in command," reaffirming the Party's special role and imposing its authority on the rest of society—via the central plan, the military and security apparatus, the propaganda network, and the Party-state apparatus. This line seemed to be the preference of the Party's ascendant left wing upon the suppression of the Tiananmen protests, but it soon proved to be indefensible in view of its negative economic repercussions.

The second, and most challenging, alternative would be to redefine the Party's mission and ideology to offer inspiring leadership to the rest of society while providing efficient and flexible economic management. This option might build on the Party's vanguard traditions and claims to political virtue, taking advantage of the once-promising nexus between intellectuals and Party cadres to foster a creative synthesis. There have been promising forays in this direction over the past several years, but they have typically been nipped in the bud by friction between prematurely outspoken intellectuals and ideologically touchy CCP elites.

The third, and perhaps the most likely, alternative is for the Party to attempt to neither resist nor actively steer the perplexing socioeconomic transformation now under way, but rather to cling to its present status and attempt to adapt to changes on a pragmatic, case-by-case basis, resorting to force as that seems necessary. This low-risk option would foresee the Party's gradual decline over the long term from its vanguard role to a more passive position vis-à-vis increasingly autonomous social forces, managing crises as they emerge rather than seeking to maintain a distinct elite subculture and lead society toward some foreordained Valhalla.

3

Political Leadership and Succession

Leadership has been one of the major strengths of the PRC political system since 1949, clearly distinguishing the regime both from its immediate predecessor (viz., the hapless KMT regime, forced to take refuge in Taiwan upon its defeat) and from nearly a century of humiliating national weakness and disunity. If we may draw an analytical distinction in the evaluation of political leadership between efficacy (in the purely technical sense of being able to implement policies) and the more value-laden issue of what we might term "wisdom" (whether the policies actually achieve what they were designed to achieve), the CCP has rather consistently (particularly since 1935) been endowed with a leadership of extraordinary efficacy. This fledgling regime succeeded, in its first ten years in power, not only in rescuing an imperiled fraternal socialist country (the Democratic People's Republic of Korea) from otherwise certain collapse by staving off the mightiest power in the world (despite the withdrawal of Soviet air support on the eve of intervention) but also in transforming the domestic economy from its "half-feudal, half-colonial" form to socialist ownership under a comprehensive communist party-state. These changes were wrought in the context of an economic revival that is perhaps somewhat exaggerated in contrast with the abnormal trough reached at the end of the Sino-Japanese and civil wars but is still impressive. It is true that toward the end of its first decade the leadership began to commit serious errors, such as the quickly aborted Hundred Flowers experiment (1957), or the more protracted Three Red Flags program (the People's Commune, Great Leap Forward, and General Line) (1958–1959), which contributed to a famine in which demographic statistics noted the loss of more than 18 million people from the normal projected birth rate.¹ Yet the fact that the leadership survived such debacles and was even able in its tenacious self-confidence to go on to commit analogous blunders in the Great Proletarian Cultural Revolution (1966–1976), gives backhanded testimony to its efficacy, if not to its wisdom.

How can we account for this level of leadership efficacy? The Chinese Communist Party classics display a curiously ambivalent attitude about the value of leadership. In place of the Leninist cult of the elite, we find in Chinese Marxism an assertive populism: "The people, and the people alone, are the motive force in the making of world history," in Mao's famous shibboleth.² Mao almost sounded at times as if the native intelligence of the masses made leadership superfluous: "Three shoemakers are equal to Zhugo Liang," as he put it in 1943. And, "the masses contain enormous forces for creativity. There are thousands of Zhugo Liangs among the Chinese people; there are some in every small market town."³ With the passage of time, he became, if anything, more outspoken in this conviction. "The masses have an immense force of enthusiasm for socialism," he said during land reform. They "are endowed with an unlimited creative power." In 1968: "Humble people are the most intelligent and prominent people the most idiotic." The implication was that the leadership was helpless without mass support: "However active the leading group may be, its activity will amount to fruitless effort by a handful of people unless combined with the activity of the masses."⁴ In possible retrospect, referring to the disastrous phase of "proletarian hegemony" when the CCP leadership arbitrarily imposed radical policies that were out of phase with mass interests, Mao emphasized that "unless they [viz., the masses] are conscious and willing, any kind of work that requires their participation will turn out to be a mere formality and will fail."⁵

Yet this faith in the masses' innate good sense was alloyed with an awareness that in practice the masses were all too gullible, all too willing to allow themselves to be hoodwinked by shadowy "backstage" backers. Particularly in his critiques, Mao backhandedly attributed great in-

---

1. There is now ample documentation of the severity of the politically induced famine in 1959–1961; see, for example, Thomas P. Bernstein, "Stalinism, Famine, and Chinese Peasants: Grain Procurements During the Great Leap Forward," *Theory and Society*, 13:3 (May 1984), pp. 339–377; Judith Bannister, "Population Policy and Trends in China, 1978–1983," *China Quarterly (CQ)*, no. 100 (December 1984), pp. 717–742; and Jurgen Domes, *The Government and Politics of the PRC* (Boulder: Westview Press, 1985), pp. 38, 274.

2. Mao Zedong, *Selected Works*, 4 vols. (Peking: Foreign Languages Press, 1965), vol. 3, p. 257 (hereinafter *SW*).

3. *SW*, vol. 3, p. 236.

4. *SW*, vol. 3, pp. 118–257.

5. See S. Bernard Thomas, *"Proletarian Hegemony" in the Chinese Revolution and the Canton Commune of 1927* (Ann Arbor: Center for Chinese Studies, University of Michigan, 1975).

fluence to leadership, especially intellectual leadership. Indeed the Cultural Revolution, which he himself always ranked among his foremost achievements (and which is usually deemed a form of populism run amok), was based on the notion that leading ideas, emanating from the "cultural superstructure," could play a decisive role in certain phases of historical development—and that this idea system was at least to some degree autonomous from developments in the economic "base" (i.e., the "forces of production"). Otherwise, the superstructure might have been expected in the normal course of things to adapt to the socialization of the means of production, which had been completed ten years previously.

Where do these leading ideas come from? Notwithstanding rhetorical claims that they percolate up from the "masses" or that they come exclusively from "practice," a superficial historical survey indicates that the CCP leadership has been the final arbiter of the pivotal ideas in Chinese politics. This emerges more clearly from cases of leadership failure than success (responsibility for which is widely diffused). Why did the Party falter (as it often did, by CCP admission)? Always, according to official histories, due to leadership errors. This follows logically: History advances with infallible inexorability; therefore all setbacks must be blamed on subjective miscalculations. Thus during the Cultural Revolution, apparently chaotic mass activities were conceived to follow two ideological lines clandestinely sponsored by opposing leadership factions: the "bourgeois reactionary line" and the "proletarian revolutionary line." The "cult of personality" is one logical consequence of this set of assumptions. Good leaders were superior human beings, able to work harder and longer, to suffer and sacrifice their personal well-being without losing their comprehensive vision of the common weal—the future salvation toward which all efforts must be funneled. Potential leaders were selected carefully for their conduct under fire or in a campaign, then "cultivated" for years before acquiring major responsibility. And once they had satisfactorily acquitted themselves, they were to be obeyed by those following in their footsteps, "without question."[6] As Mao pointed out in reprimanding radical Red Guard anarchist proclivities: "The Shanghai

---

6. Unquestioning obedience was associated with the discredited Liu Shaoqi, particularly as postulated in his famous book, *How to Be a Good Communist*, and was repudiated during the Cultural Revolution. But this was an authoritative tenet of Party doctrine before that time and seems to have been reinstated with the official rehabilitation of Liu at the Fifth Plenum of the Eleventh CC in March 1980. It is no coincidence that this rehabilitation coincided with promulgation of a document on the strengthening and improvement of Party leadership. See Siegfried Klaschka, *Die Rehabilitierung Liu Shaoqis in der chinesischen Presse* (Munich: Minerva, 1987), pp. 99–121.

People's Council office submitted a proposal to the Premier of the State Council in which he asked for the elimination of all chiefs. This is extreme anarchy; it is most reactionary. . . . Actually, there always have to be chiefs."[7]

The exact shape of this leadership has, to be sure, been a matter of persistent controversy, among CCP elites no less than among Western China-watchers. The contest between an emphasis on obedience to organizational superiors and a need to stimulate mass initiative, between adherence to formal procedure and the resort to more flexible informal expedients, and between collective leadership and a cult of personality has lasted for decades, and the leadership itself has changed its form from time to time depending on who prevailed. But one generalization remains fairly constant. As a general rule, CCP leadership has been *essentially monocratic*.[8] There has normally been a Paramount Leader (hereinafter the PL), though he has not necessarily held the highest formal positions, and the prerogatives and role expectations of the PL have differed perceptibly from those of his colleagues. These include the right to final say over major national decisions, including the nation's disposition to the rest of the world (alliance, war, or peace), whether and what kind of propaganda campaign to launch, which policy line to promote, and so forth; consequently, the PL has had ultimate command of the Party, the armed forces, and domestic security apparatus. There are occasional exceptions to this rule, as we shall see, but these exceptions tend to give rise to various political deformations and are viewed as pathological among Chinese participants.

The PL, as *primus inter pares*, is normatively expected to defer to his colleagues on the Politburo and to leading members (or recent veterans) of other central institutions (e.g., the State Council, the NPC Standing Committee, the CAC, the CMC). These senior colleagues have certain prerogatives as well—they do not owe their positions solely to his favor but usually have their own independent power bases (*zhengzhi jichu*).[9]

---

7. "Chairman Mao's Speech at His Third Meeting with Chang Ch'un-chiao and Yao Wen-yuan" (February 1967), as trans. in *Joint Publications Research Service*, 1:49826 (February 12, 1970), pp. 44–45.

8. Hence Schapiro and Lewis were correct in contending that the CCP has a "leadership principle" (*Führerprinzip*). See Leonard Schapiro and John Wilson Lewis, "The Roles of the Monolithic Party Under the Totalitarian Leader," in J. W. Lewis, ed., *Party Leadership and Revolutionary Power in China* (Cambridge: Cambridge University Press, 1970), pp. 114–148. Whereas in the Nazi party the führerist leadership pattern was uncontested, in China it was (according to Schapiro and Lewis) combined with the Bolshevik or Leninist principle of collective leadership, forming an uneasy compromise that lasted from the *Zhengfeng* movement in Yanan until the Cultural Revolution, at which point führerism predominated. Deng Xiaoping's ascendancy represents a reassertion of collective leadership with a strong informal undercurrent of personal leadership (as we shall see below).

9. See my article, "Bases of Power in Chinese Politics: A Theory and an Analysis of the Fall of the 'Gang of Four,'" *World Politics* 31:1 (October 1978), pp. 26–61.

Aside from controlling the usually important vertical hierarchies under their jurisdiction, they have the right to advise and consult in the high-level meetings they attend, to argue forcibly for their positions before a decision is made, and to "reserve their opinion" even should the majority decide otherwise. This is what is meant by "collective leadership." But it does not imply that there is equality between the PL and other Politburo members, even though formally all have but one vote. For one thing, whether a vote is even called is determined by the PL.

Although a Politburo member cannot be arbitrarily dismissed by the PL without cause (as can members of a U.S. president's cabinet), they may be excluded from meetings of committees of which they are formal members, cut off from the vital flow of "internal" information at the PL's behest, or even (in extreme cases) subjected to mass ridicule and trenchant media criticism. The PL is accorded the right to convene meetings of the elite when he wishes, set the agenda, specify the participants, and hence dominate the proceedings. The power balance is so lopsided that it has been exceedingly rare for a PL to be directly challenged by a member of the Politburo (and still more rare to be successfully challenged), whereas it has not been rare at all for a Politburo member to be purged based solely on the dictum of a PL.

Many organizational and systemic consequences flow from these generalizations about top-level Chinese leadership. Some consequences are structurally implied, and others result because popular emulation of "models" focuses on symbolic individuals defined by, and often personified by, top leaders. One corollary of the essentially monocratic nature of CCP leadership is that the PL's vital statistics become of great analytical utility, thereby justifying the type of biographical approach we undertake below. Structurally, the dominant position and prolonged tenure of the incumbent makes for a bureaucratic order in which the prevailing orientation is upward, and little personnel mobility occurs unless prompted from above. The leader is assumed to be infallible, whereas everyone else is deemed to be fallible. This assumption is in effect even when it is not explicitly defended (as it was in connection with the personality cult). This encourages an even greater reliance on seniority than is normally associated with bureaucracies, with consequent "gerontocratic" tendencies tacitly reinforced by the Chinese tradition of ancestor worship.[10] Under these circumstances certain historical "moments" become more pivotal than others: The overwhelming advantages of incumbency tend to inhibit change that transcends established paradigms within the life-

---

10. Compare Ada Elizabeth Sher, *Aging in Post-Mao China* (Boulder: Westview Press, 1984), pp. 7–85.

time of a given PL; only in the context of leadership transition is a fundamental departure from the status quo conceivable.[11]

Hence in this chapter we examine two leadership regimes—those of Mao Zedong and Deng Xiaoping (really, one and one-half, as Deng's regime is, at this writing, still extant). Although this is a very small case sample, the historical period is long enough to note certain clear trends. The dominant trend during this period, we assert (not without a certain bravado), has been a shift from mere leadership efficacy to leadership wisdom. Such a transformation has usually been discussed in the social science literature in terms of *charismatic routinization.* The concept of charisma has had an illustrious career since Max Weber first appropriated it from theology in the early twentieth century, and almost every social scientist to use the term since has added his or her own definitional twists, features, or subtypes.[12] Without prejudice to such refinements, I intend to focus here on what I take to be the term's central distinguishing characteristic—its iconoclastic, specifically revolutionary animus: "'It is written . . . but I say unto you.'"[13] Christ himself, the original charismatic leader, scourge of the Pharisaic religious establishment, frontally challenged not only the Fifth Commandment but ancient Hebrew norms of filial piety in his scornful retort to a would-be disciple whose father had died: "Let the dead bury their dead."[14] Charismatic leadership is marked by heroic, all-or-nothing ambition, a taste for conflict and paradox, a will-

---

11. For a similarly bimodal conception of change, see Thomas Kuhn's well-known *The Structure of Scientific Revolutions* (Chicago: University of Chicago Press, 1962). In the case of Chinese politics, we are proposing that the transition from "normal" change to paradigm-shattering change rests not in the cognitive properties of the ideas involved but in the physical mortality of their advocate. Of course, the status quo may be a dynamic one, as in the case of Mao's theory of "continuing the revolution under the dictatorship of the proletariat," but the point is that this dynamism evolves along lines implicit in certain first principles preconceived by their author.

12. See, for example, Arthur Schweitzer, *The Age of Charisma* (Chicago: Nelson-Hall, 1984); Ann Ruth Willner, *The Spellbinders: Charismatic Political Leadership* (New Haven: Yale University Press, 1984); Douglas Madsen and Peter G. Snow, *The Charismatic Bond: Political Behavior in Time of Crisis* (Cambridge: Harvard University Press, 1991); Ronald M. Glassman and William Swatos, Jr., eds., *Charisma, History, and Social Structure* (New York: Greenwood Press, 1986); and Joseph Nyomarkay, *Charisma and Factionalism in the Nazi Party* (Minneapolis: University of Minnesota Press, 1967).

13. Max Weber, "Charismatic Authority and Charismatic Community," in M. Weber, *Economy and Society,* ed. Guenther Roth and Claus Wittich, 2 vols. (Berkeley: University of California Press, 1978), vol. 1, p. 243.

14. Matthew 8:21–22, as quoted in Martin Hengel, *The Charismatic Leader and His Followers,* trans. James Greig (New York: Crossword, 1981), pp. 8, 19 et passim. The thrust of Christ's challenge was, of course, a demand that any would-be disciple should be ready to give up safety and possessions to follow him unreservedly.

ingness to spurn established rules and customs, a rabble-rousing appeal to the downtrodden and poor of spirit. As Weber indicated, its strong point is its efficacy in time of crisis; its weak point is its instability—its incompatibility with any form of routine.

Both Mao and Deng were very much aware of this besetting flaw of charismatic leadership—particularly at the time of approaching succession for each, when his own eminent demise made it necessary to consider how the nation's leadership could best be maintained, and if possible, improved. If, as some Existentialist thinkers contend, the true meaning of life is revealed only in death, the ultimate test of any leadership regime is succession. At this point both took hesitant steps to alleviate the leadership uncertainty they had been wont to capitalize on earlier to enhance their influence. Thanks partly to these efforts, and partly in response to the functional requirements of the system, the *routinization of charisma* achieved measurable progress during this period. Routinization may be subdivided into two processes: *institutionalization*, entailing a shift from the magical powers ascribed to an heroic decision-maker to the establishment of prescribed rules and procedures, and *depersonalization*, implying a shift from personally validated commands to organizationally prescribed roles within a formal division of labor. As we shall see, the former aspect of routinization has on the whole been relatively successful; the latter is not yet complete.

Mao Zedong

Since the May Fourth Movement (circa 1915–1924), the progressive forces and the reactionary forces in China have been symbolized by youth and age, respectively. Mao, as leader of the revolutionary forces that ultimately succeeded in uniting the country, brought the contrast between the two value systems into sharp relief. The most memorable slogan articulated at the inauguration of the PRC—China Has Stood Up—captured that occasion in the imagery of freshly matured youth, as did the youth, vigor, and seeming purity of the CCP leaders. We argue below that to Mao, charisma became crystallized in terms of a crusade to sustain revolutionary values; and these values came to be identified with the vigor, courage, and idealism of youth. As first leader of the new order, Mao was first to be challenged by the poignant riddle: How can a leader deal with the experience of personal aging and death within an institutional context that transcends personal mortality?

The following discussion consists of two parts. In the first, Mao's thinking about the political implications of age and youth is reviewed as it evolves over the course of his life. In the second, Mao's pattern of adaptation to his own aging and anticipated demise is examined.

Youth and Age in Mao's Thought

Harrison Salisbury, following John King Fairbank, attempted to place Mao Zedong in China's long dynastic tradition, as a successful peasant rebel who then proceeded to model himself after his imperial forbears.[15] It is true that Mao steeped himself in such dynastic classics as *The General Mirror for the Aid of Government* (*zi zhi tong jian*) and the *Records of the Historian* (*shi ji*), as an acquaintance with his internal conversations (as recorded in the *Wan sui* collection) bears out.[16] Certainly his ambition rivaled that of any emperor, as his poetry indicates; Kissinger testified that he met no one, "with the possible exception of Charles DeGaulle, who so distilled raw, concentrated will power."[17] But to rank him among China's emperors is neither fair nor accurate. Mao availed himself of the annals of China's proud imperial tradition, but he was first and foremost a rebel. Even assuming that his acquaintance with Marxist scholarship came late in life and was perhaps less than deep,[18] Mao made major contributions to the canonical tradition in both his actions and his writings.

Mao was the firstborn male child in a family of five, and according to Lucian Pye he displayed a certain jealousy toward his younger siblings, abandoning one to die in Jiangxi upon his departure on the Long March, for example.[19] But what comes through most clearly in his own description of his early family life is a classic Oedipus complex, played out in the form of rebellion against his father and devotion to his mother. "He was a severe taskmaster," Mao remarked with regard to his father. "He was a hot-tempered man and frequently beat both me and my brothers. He gave us no money whatever, and the most meager food." The results? "Reflecting on this, I think that in the end the strictness of my father

---

15. Harrison E. Salisbury, *The New Emperors: China in the Era of Mao and Deng* (Boston: Little, Brown, 1992); John King Fairbank, *The United States and China*, 3rd ed. (Cambridge: Harvard University Press, 1977).

16. According to Salisbury, Mao also relied heavily on two Chinese encyclopedic dictionaries, *Lexicon of Words* (*Ci hai*) and *Origins of Words* (*Ci yuan*). When he moved into Zhongnanhai after Liberation, a colleague reportedly dropped in to see his library and remarked about the plenitude of China's great literary and historical works and the contrasting dearth of Marxist classics—the omission was quickly corrected! Salisbury, *New Emperors*, pp. 8–9.

17. Henry Kissinger, *White House Years* (Boston: Little, Brown, 1979), p. 1058.

18. Mao's superficial acquaintance with Marxism was first noted by Wittfogel, more recently by Meissner—though the issue remains controversial, with vigorous counterarguments. See Werner Meissner, trans. Richard Mann, *Philosophy and Politics in China: The Controversy over Dialectical Materialism in the 1930s* (Stanford: Stanford University Press, 1990); for a contrasting view, see Brantly Womack, *The Foundations of Mao Zedong's Political Thought, 1917–1935* (Honolulu: University Press of Hawaii, 1982), and Stuart Schram, *The Thought of Mao Tse-tung* (New York: Cambridge University Press, 1989).

19. Lucian Pye, *Mao Tse-tung: The Man in the Leader* (New York: Basic Books, 1976), pp. 69–111.

defeated him. I learned to hate him." The basis for this hatred was not merely his father's age, but his selfishness, discipline, and calculating ambition, which Mao contrasted with his mother's kindness and generosity:

> My mother was a kind woman, generous and sympathetic, and ever ready to share what she had. She pitied the poor and often gave them rice when they came to ask for it during famines. But she could not do so when my father was present. He disapproved of charity. We had many quarrels in my home over this question.[20]

Though the conflict was already in a sense ideological, age entered into it as his father used his seniority to justify his prerogatives and demand his son's deference: "My father's favorite accusations against me were of unfilial conduct and laziness." Mao, however, demonstrated an early resourcefulness and pre-Marxist dialectical agility in using the classics to refute such accusations. "I quoted, in exchange, passages from the Classics saying that the elder must be kind and affectionate. Against his charge that I was lazy I used the rebuttal that older people should do more work than younger, that my father was over three times as old as myself, and therefore should do more work. And I declared that when I was his age I would be much more energetic."

Thus, although age was an incidental aspect of the confrontation, it does not seem unreasonable to infer that Mao acquired his first negative stereotype of age-based authority from this experience. And among the most firmly established generalizations of developmental psychology is the proposition that early traumatic experiences tend to endure, having a formative impact. Of course, this picture of Mao's family life must have been colored by the circumstances of the telling—as a rebel leader with a price on his head holed up in a Yanan cave he may have projected his current plight backward with a bit of tongue-in-cheek hyperbole. Yet we find a lifelong parallel between the characteristics Mao found in his father and those he attributed to subsequent antagonists, as well as in the "struggle" tactics he used to contend with such antagonists.

In coping with what he obviously considered an unjust paternal regime, Mao adopted the rather "un-Chinese" strategy of direct confrontation. "My mother advocated a policy of indirect attack," he recalled. "She criticized any overt display of emotion and attempts at open rebellion against the Ruling Power. She said it was not the Chinese way." Yet when Mao defied this maternal counsel and explicitly confronted his father, he was pleasantly surprised to discover that this proved far more

---

20. Edgar Snow, *Red Star over China*, (New York: Grove Press, 1977), pp. 131–132.

effective than adherence to a "Chinese way" of indirect attack. When he was ten years old he ran away from home for three days to protest the despotic ways of a local elementary school teacher, and upon his return he discovered that his father "was slightly more considerate and the teacher was more inclined to moderation. The result of my act of protest impressed me very much." Three years later, in a sudden dispute with his father in the presence of guests, Mao successfully faced him down and forced an acceptable compromise by threatening to throw himself into a pond.[21] Not only did Mao thus vindicate his choice of culturally outlandish tactics, he claimed to have successfully mobilized allies to his point of view, creating a "united front" coalition of the young (his two brothers and he), the female (his mother), and the proletariat (the hired hand) against the figure he called "the old man," allowing the Oedipal dimension of the confrontation to emerge quite clearly (it seems certain that Mao had heard of neither Oedipus nor Freud, either at the time of the incident or during its recounting).[22]

In Mao's subsequent revolutionary career, his attitude toward age-based leadership became less pertinent, for although the early membership and leadership of the Chinese Communist Party was decidedly youthful, its chief antagonists—the Nationalists (Kuomintang), and then the Japanese imperialists—were not clearly distinguishable from the Communists on the basis of age. Furthermore, as a Marxist, the categories through which he should seek to discover political coalitions were economic, and thus he shifted to class analysis. Mao did, however, occasionally express himself about Chinese youth as a category. Surprisingly, during the early and middle stages of his career his comments about youth were rather skeptical. In his 1939 essay commemorating the May Fourth Movement, for example, he noted that "in the youth movement of the last few decades, a section of young people have been unwilling to unite with the workers and peasants and have opposed their movements; this is a countercurrent in the youth movement." He continued:

> How should we judge whether a youth is a revolutionary? How can we tell? There can be only one criterion, namely, whether or not he is willing to integrate himself with the broad masses of workers and peasants and does so in practice. If he is willing to do so and actually does so, he is a

---

21. Snow, *Red Star*, pp. 131–132.
22. Thus the evidence of an Oedipal complex is quite explicit. Such a "family constellation" is, of course, extremely widespread—indeed, Freud considered it universal—but Mao's characterization of the conflict in revolutionary terms suggests that it was exceptionally violent, and his recurrent spontaneous return to the father-son theme throughout his life suggests it was unresolved.

revolutionary; otherwise he is a non-revolutionary or a counterrevolutionary. If today he integrates himself with the masses of workers and peasants, then today he is a revolutionary; if tomorrow he ceases to do so or turns round to oppress the common people, then he becomes a non-revolutionary or a counterrevolutionary.[23]

Why should Mao be so suspicious of that age cohort whose interests would most likely coincide with those of the CCP? Probably when Mao spoke of "youth" as a distinct category, he was also thinking of "students," or "intellectuals." Young workers or peasants would in contrast simply be included in the category of "workers" or "peasants," without undergoing the stage of studious incubation implied by the term "youth." This hypothesis is reinforced by another statement Mao made only a few months later, in which he spoke in similar terms about the "intellectuals":

The intellectuals often tend to be subjective and individualistic, impractical in their thinking and irresolute in action until they have thrown themselves heart and soul into mass revolutionary struggles, or made up their minds to serve the interests of the masses and become one with them. Hence although the mass of revolutionary intellectuals in China can play a vanguard role or serve as a link with the masses, not all of them will remain revolutionaries to the end. Some will drop out of the revolutionary ranks at critical moments and become passive, while a few may even become enemies of the revolution. The intellectuals can overcome their shortcomings only in mass struggles over a long period.[24]

In another passage written several years later, Mao identifies himself as having been a previous member of this cohort, at the same time suggesting some of the reasons for his mixed feelings about youth, students, and intellectuals:

I began as a student and acquired the habits of a student at school. I then used to feel it undignified to do even a little manual labor, such as carrying my own luggage in the presence of my fellow students, who were incapable of carrying anything, either on their shoulders or in their hands. At that time I felt that intellectuals were the only clean people in the world, while in comparison workers and peasants were dirty. But after I became a revolutionary and lived with workers and peasants and

---

23. "The Orientation of the Youth Movement" (May 4, 1939), in *SW*, vol. 2, p. 246.
24. "The Chinese Revolution and the Chinese Communist Party" (December 1939), in *Selected Works*, vol. 2, p. 322; as quoted in *Quotations from Chairman Mao Tse-tung* (Peking: Foreign Languages Press, 1966), chap. 30, "Youth," pp. 292–293.

with soldiers of the revolutionary army, I gradually came to know them well, and they gradually came to know me well too. It was then, and only then, that I fundamentally changed the bourgeois and petty-bourgeois feelings implanted in me in the bourgeois schools. I came to feel that compared with the workers and peasants, the unremolded intellectuals were not clean and that, even though their hands were soiled and their feet smeared with cow-dung, they were really cleaner than the bourgeois and petty-bourgeois intellectuals.[25]

Again, a more light-hearted Mao remarks: "I myself originally was an intellectual, had all kinds of thought. . . . We prayed to bodhisattvas; once I also made a pilgrimage to the Southern Peak, to fulfil my mother's promise; I believed in anarchism. Hey! That anarchism is great: also believed in the idealism of Kant. . . . Only later did Marxism really penetrate me, change my mind."[26]

It begins to become clear that what was most objectionable to Mao about youth is that they harbored, *in statu nascendi*, the same selfish, individualistic ambitions that drove Mao's father: the desire to transcend the working classes and become part of the elite, with clean hands (and feet!). To Mao, snared in an unresolved Oedipal complex, becoming like his father was the one thing that was absolutely forsworn. It is perhaps also worth noting that Mao's principal rivals for leadership in the Party at the time these comments were made were Wang Ming, Bo Gu, Luo Fu, and the "returned student" faction. Although this designation referred to the fact that they had returned to China from the University of Toilers of the East in Moscow, members of this faction were indeed "students" of Marxism-Leninism, and they based their sense of superiority over Mao on their mastery of the (Marxist) classics, putting his own previous attempts to transcend his class background through schooling in an unfavorable light.[27]

From the time of Liberation until the late 1950s Mao's statements about youth became somewhat more detached and neutral, as other matters (notably the socialization of the means of production) took pride of place on his agenda. Mao continued to emphasize the need for education, in order to enhance the political reliability and economic utility of young

---

25. *Selected Works*, vol. 3, p. 73.
26. "On the Correct Handling of Contradictions Among the People" (Speaking Notes), (February 27, 1957), trans. in Roderick MacFarquhar, Timothy Cheek, and Eugene Wu, eds., *The Secret Speeches of Chairman Mao* (Cambridge: Harvard University Press, 1989), p. 154.
27. Robert Scalapino has drawn attention to the importance of Mao's status as a "petty intellectual" in that he never acquired the proper credentials and was never accepted by the Beida graduates and other bona fide intellectuals. See Scalapino, "The Evolution of a Young Revolutionary: Mao Zedong in 1919–1921," *Journal of Asian Studies*, 42 (November 1982).

people, but the type of education he had in mind was relatively conventional, and his concern about the wayward propensities of youth did not seem exceptional. "We must strengthen ideological and political work for youth; we must teach them not to despise labor so that they will be able to construct our nation successfully!" he said in 1957.[28] In the same year, he noted that "bureaucratism is extremely grave; in some places, in quite a few schools the problems cannot be solved, because there has been no such training. The youth, particularly the youth in the schools, must be disciplined."[29] And in 1953 he said:

> Apart from continuing to act in coordination with the Party in its central task, the Youth League should do its own work to suit the special characteristics of youth. New China must care for her youth and show concern for the growth of the younger generation. Young people have to study and work, but they are at the age of physical growth. Therefore, full attention must be paid both to their work and study and to their recreation, sport and rest.[30]

These statements are by no means distinctive and in fact might have been made by any member of the CCP leadership. Mao no longer had any obvious reason to distrust youth particularly, nor did he necessarily place great hope in them.

Protracted Succession

Mao periodically toyed with the idea of retirement throughout his postrevolutionary incumbency, and each such flirtation precipitated a bitter power struggle. Mao seems to have had some inkling that he was essentially a revolutionary leader with little talent for economic administration (although he was very defensive if anyone else pointed this out); he also disliked ceremonial duties, such as receiving diplomatic credentials. At the same time, he began to have periodic health difficulties as early as 1946, and in 1953 he suffered from dizzy spells related to overwork and circulatory problems. Thus he first proposed the division of the leadership into "two fronts"—a "first front" responsible for ongoing routine work, and a "second front" where Mao himself and a small

---

28. "Talk at the National Propaganda Work Conference of the CCP" (March 12, 1957), as quoted in Peter Seybolt, ed., *Revolutionary Education in China* (White Plains, N.Y.: International Arts and Sciences Press, 1973), p. 26.

29. Helmut Martin, ed., *Mao Zedong Texte,* 4 vols. (Munich: Carl Hanser Verlag, 1979), vol. 2, p. 185 (my translation).

30. "Talk at the Reception for the Presidium of the Second National Congress of the Youth League" (June 30, 1953), as quoted in *Quotations from Chairman Mao,* p. 293.

personal staff could ponder larger problems—in Politburo sessions as early as August–October 1952. Whether he did so for the aforementioned health and division-of-labor reasons or as a mere tactical ploy is unclear, but Mao did in fact retire to a less active role in 1953, without, however, abdicating any of his formal posts.[31]

Two groups of colleagues soon emerged in contention for leadership of the first front. Their different handling of the issue seems to have affected Chairman Mao's favor and his consequent adjustment of the line of succession. One might have expected Mao's favor to go to Gao Gang, a supporter of Mao's leftist proclivities and a reputed favorite of the Chairman, to whom Mao is said to have confided his grievances concerning the more moderate Liu Shaoqi and Zhou Enlai. But when Mao suggested in December 1953 that he take charge of the first front, Liu modestly demurred, on grounds that the Chairman's leadership was still required, as new China had so recently been established; Liu agreed only to a temporary delegation of responsibility. Gao Gang, in contrast, seems to have taken Mao at his word, disagreeing with the proposed delegation and arguing that leadership should be exercised by rotation in Mao's absence. "When I retreat to the second front, he [Gao] wants to be the Party vice-chairman," Mao concluded to Luo Ruiqing in the fall of 1953. The upshot seems to have been to postpone the issue of the first front. Liu took charge of routine work for much of 1953 while Mao remained at his post, and other organizational expedients were undertaken to relieve him of his burdens (e.g., a chair of the NPC Standing Committee was created by the 1954 State Constitution to help assume ceremonial duties). Meanwhile, Gao Gang's frustrated ambition began to take clandestine channels. He began appealing to sympathizers such as Peng Dehuai, Zhu De, and Lin Biao, hoping to polarize Red Area forces against the White Area group ensconced in the line of succession (viz., Liu and Zhou). As soon as Mao came out against Gao, denouncing his networking as a "struggle between two headquarters," the conspiracy promptly collapsed, and Gao and Rao were disgraced.[32]

Mao's retirement and the functional division of labor between two fronts then became an apparent dead letter. Mao made a vigorous resurgence in the mid-1950s against "old women with bound feet" to accel-

---

31. This seems to have been the time when the prickly Mao became annoyed with his subordinates' presumptiveness. See "Liu Shao-chi and Yang Shang-kun Criticized for Breach of Discipline in Issuing Documents in the Name of the Central Committee Without Authorization" (May 4, 1953), in Mao, SW, vol. 5, pp. 92–93.

32. Frederick C. Teiwes, *Politics at Mao's Court: Gao Gang and Party Factionalism in the Early 1950s* (Armonk, N.Y.: M. E. Sharpe, 1990), pp. 24–42, 117, 142, 151 et passim.

erate agricultural collectivization; he then launched the first attempt at an economic leap forward in 1956 and presided over the 1956 Party Congress that celebrated completion of the transition to socialism (though references to Mao Zedong Thought were removed at that meeting, in tune with de-Stalinization efforts throughout the bloc). However, this early miscue set the stage for the succession struggle that began in earnest at the end of the 1950s. It was during these years that several problems were emerging for which there were no obvious answers, unlike the problems of socialist reconstruction when China explicitly patterned itself after the Stalinist model. Upward mobility had become frozen, as members of Mao's generation monopolized leadership positions and clung to them until they were either promoted or died in office—the notion of voluntary retirement, let alone limited office tenure, does not seem to have occurred to anyone.[33] The first spontaneous urban protests emerged in China at around the time of the uprisings in Poland and Hungary.[34] The initial revolutionary objectives of the new leadership had been successfully dispatched with the transformation of the extended family and the completion of socialization of the means of production, and it proved difficult either to arrive at a consensus on a new mission or to agree to let the revolution expire. Amid this uncertainty Mao began increasingly to seize the initiative, unilaterally launching new programs, the most significant of which were the Hundred Flowers experiment in 1957 and the Great Leap Forward the following year. Both failed ignominiously.

If one of the hallmarks of this stage in Mao's career was a thrashing around for new programs in an attempt to regain the conceptual initiative, another quite contrary impulse also made its reappearance—a movement in the direction of retirement. Mao reaffirmed his interest in a less active role in the leadership in February 1957 and put it in writing in early 1958. He then proceeded to resign from the largely ceremonial posi-

---

33. The obstruction of upward mobility has been demonstrated in numerous empirical studies. E.g., see Derek J. Waller, "The Evolution of the Chinese Communist Political Elite, 1931–1956," in Robert Scalapino, ed., *Elites in the People's Republic of China* (Seattle: University of Washington Press, 1972), pp. 67–149; Michel Oksenberg, "Local Leaders in Rural China, 1962–65: Individual Attitudes, Bureaucratic Positions, and Political Recruitment," pp. 155–216, and Ying-mao Kau, "The Urban Bureaucratic Elite in Communist China: A Case Study of Wuhan, 1949–65," in A. Doak Barnett, ed., *Chinese Communist Politics in Action* (Seattle: University of Washington Press, 1969), pp. 216–271.

34. See T. J. Hughes and D.E.T. Luard, *The Economic Development of Communist China, 1949–1958* (London: Oxford University Press, 1959), and Charles Hoffman, *The Chinese Worker* (Albany: State University of New York Press, 1974), pp. 146–147, for a discussion and statistics indicating the magnitude of the 1956–1957 strikes and protests.

tion of chief of state in April 1959, yielding that position to Liu Shaoqi, whom he later explicitly identified as his heir apparent.[35] He discussed this arrangement frankly and with what at the time seemed considerable foresight, in terms of his own preparations to "see Marx very soon" and the concomitant need to give his successors the opportunity to gain valuable preliminary experience at the helm—to be leadership interns, as it were.[36]

Three hypotheses have been proposed attempting to link Mao's movement toward retirement with his countervailing movement in the direction of revolutionary revivalism. The first is that Mao was *forced* to retire in the wake of the resounding failures of the Hundred Flowers and, especially, the Great Leap Forward, which precipitated a catastrophic famine that left from fifteen to twenty million people dead.[37] Although this hypothesis draws sustenance from Mao's own complaints in the summer of 1966 that his colleagues had been neglecting him, ignoring his directives, treating him like a dead father at his own funeral, and so forth, the timing of the decision belies his statements. Mao first indicated his intention to retire before the failure of the Leap had become apparent, before the Hundred Flowers had even bloomed, at a time when he still had every reason to be optimistic.

The second hypothesis links retirement and revivalism tactically, in a means-end relationship: Retirement was offered to possible opponents of

---

35. He hinted at a wish to step down in his contradictions speech and stated it explicitly in Article 60 of the "Sixty articles on work methods" (February 1958). Liu assumed the chief of state position at the first session of the Second National People's Congress, at which point Mao probably retired to the "second line." Roderick MacFarquhar, *The Origins of the Cultural Revolution: 1. Contradictions Among the People, 1956–1957* (New York: Columbia University Press, 1974), pp. 105–107, 152–156. The ambivalence is unveiled in the fact that when Mao proposed, "I should no longer be chief of state; I should retreat from the stage and let others take the position," he did not name anyone else to assume the responsibility. At last, Deng Xiaoping broke the ice: "If no one else makes a nomination, I nominate Liu Shaoqi for the position." Nobody disagreed and Mao did not oppose the nomination. All present applauded. Hei Yannan, ed., *Shi nian dong luan* (Ten years of chaos) (Hong Kong: Xing Chen, 1988), p. 50.

36. As Lin Biao put it in an October 24, 1966, speech to the Central Work Conference: "In his speech, Mao Zedong made it clear: my fault was to set up the first front and second front. Why did I do this? The first reason is that I did not feel well and the second is the Soviet lesson. I did it purposely. But I never dreamed that things would go to this extreme. Last September and October . . . I already felt that my opinions had no weight in Beijing." Hei Yannan, *Shi nian*, p. 132. See also Mao's January 9, 1965, interview with Edgar Snow in *The Long Revolution* (New York: Random House, 1972), pp. 195–222.

37. The famine is examined in Bernstein, "Stalinism, Famine, and Chinese Peasants," pp. 339–377; the measurable impact upon demographic statistics is examined in Bannister, "Population Policy and Trends in China," pp. 717–742.

the Leap as a quid pro quo in order to procure their support. This hypothesis fits more plausibly into the political context at the time. Mao's prestige had sunk considerably from its high point in mid-1955, when he was able to accelerate collectivization successfully, overcoming the resistance of "old women with bound feet" (viz., more cautious colleagues). After Khrushchev's 1956 critique of the cult of personality and the echoing Chinese attempt at the Eighth Party Congress to place greater emphasis on collective leadership (not to mention the disappointing outcome of the "mini-Leap" in 1956), Mao may have needed to make special concessions to generate a consensus in support of new radical initiatives. (Liu and Deng were certainly conspicuous in their early support of the Leap.) However, it should also be noted that the upshot of the Hundred Flowers was to strengthen the Left rather than the Right by discrediting the liberals, many of whom were purged in the subsequent antirightist movement. Thus Mao did not really need to make a self-damaging concession in order to have his way.

The third hypothesis, which is perhaps most defensible, is that Mao was genuinely ambivalent, with conflicting impulses to withdraw and prepare for his inevitable demise, on the one hand, and to rebel against it, on the other. It is perhaps no coincidence that "contradiction" and "struggle" (as in his innovative distinction between "antagonistic" and "nonantagonistic contradiction," or the "struggle between two lines") should emerge so prominently in his thoughts at a time when he was experiencing deep internal conflict. Mao seems to have been undergoing something of an identity crisis at about this time, a crisis Erikson calls "ego integrity versus despair."[38] In 1959 he visited his birthplace for the first time in thirty-two years in an inspection tour of the effects of the Leap (the natives assured him the economy was in great shape), survived bouts of debilitating illness, and occasionally ruminated with visitors about the future of socialism in China after his death.

The succession arrangement he set up reflected this ambivalence: Mao did not fully retire, but he did play a less active role in policymaking. The "two fronts" arrangement was revived, with the first being led by Liu Shaoqi as first CCP vice-chair (and chief of state) and Deng Xiaoping as Party secretary general and with the second led by Mao and a few personal confidants (apparently consisting of Kang Sheng, Chen Boda, and a politically reactivated Jiang Qing). Whereas the first front was preoccupied with resolving the budget crisis and recovery from the "three bad years" (1959–1962), the second was concerned with more long-term issues, such as the Sino-Soviet polemical dispute and the direc-

---

38. See Erik H. Erikson, *Childhood and Society* (New York: W. W. Norton, 1963), p. 268.

tion of the international Communist movement. But foremost among these issues in Mao's mind was succession:

> Why did we make this division into first and second lines? The first reason is that my health is not very good; the second was the lesson of the Soviet Union. Malenkov was not mature enough, and before Stalin died he had not wielded power. Every time he proposed a toast, he fawned and flattered. I wanted to establish their prestige before I died; I never imagined that things might move in the opposite direction.[39]

The political repercussions of this arrangement set off a succession crisis that was to roil the waters of Chinese politics for the next twenty years. Succession is both important and problematic for all Communist regimes.[40] It is important because power is highly "variable" and concentrated among a few incumbents at the top; it is problematic because no reliable means for the transfer of power has yet been devised in any Communist system. The two main types of succession arrangement are *premortem* succession, in which the departing incumbent attempts to stack the deck by installing an heir apparent and investing him with power before his own demise, and *postmortem* succession, in which the incumbent leaves a last will and testament—or not even that, letting the chips fall where they may. Premortem succession offers the best way of reducing the uncertainty of the transition, as it allows the successor to consolidate his power with the assistance of the retiring incumbent. The problem is that the incumbent may be ambivalent about the idea of arranging for his own succession, and this may prevent him from being altogether rational about it.[41] This brings up two other problems with premortem succession: that either the heir apparent may usurp power and kick out the incumbent, or that there may arise the problem of two

---

39. Mao, "Talk at the Report Meeting" (October 24, 1966), in Stuart Schram, ed., *Chairman Mao Talks to the People* (New York: Pantheon, 1974), p. 266.

40. See Myron Rush, *Political Succession in the USSR* (New York: Columbia University Press, 1965), and *How Communist States Change Their Rulers* (Ithaca, N.Y.: Cornell University Press, 1974); also see Valerie Bunce, *Do New Leaders Make a Difference? Executive Succession and Public Policy Under Capitalism and Socialism* (Princeton: Princeton University Press, 1981).

41. This seems to have been the case with Mao vis-à-vis first Liu Shaoqi and then Lin Biao. After Mao changed his mind about Lin Biao and decided that his erstwhile closest comrade-in-arms would no longer be an appropriate successor after all, Lin became so irate that he stopped referring to the Chairman as a "genius" and called him a paranoid monster, allegedly instigating a plot to blow up his train. See Michael Ying-mao Kau, ed., *The Lin Piao Affair: Power Politics and Military Coup* (White Plains, N.Y.: International Arts and Sciences Press, 1975).

rival centers of power.⁴² Thus most incumbent leaders prefer to arrange a postmortem succession. Yet here they are likely to fail even more egregiously, for once death claims the leader, the whole situation and balance of forces changes.⁴³

A succession crisis is (according to Myron Rush) a crisis not because the system necessarily threatens to fall apart but because for the time being no significant decisions can be made, for each such decision begs the question of who is to make it. Because this question cannot be answered until the succession crisis is resolved, and because many at the highest level fear that their own positions or even lives might be jeopardized by such a resolution, significant decisions can be arrived at only through circuitous and time-consuming consultation and compromise. This is known as "collective leadership" and may last for a period of several years. In the absence of authoritative (i.e., monocratic) leadership, tendencies toward rift, vacillation, and deadlock are prone to reduce the political efficacy of the regime. This crisis scenario has, however, been disputed by Valerie Bunce.⁴⁴ Whereas Rush argues that succession crises paralyze the regime's capacity for political innovation, Bunce argues that such crises stimulate political innovation, as potential successors strive to consolidate their hold on power with policies calculated to appeal to a politically significant consituency, making succession an opportunity for renewal analogous to electoral turnover in bourgeois democratic systems. Although the meaning of succession is thus conceived quite differently by Rush and Bunce, for both the immediate outcome is similar: For Rush, collective leadership is followed by eventual return to personal rule to end vacillation and rift; for Bunce, too, strong personal rule is

---

42. An example of the first type is Erich Honecker's succession to Walter Ulbricht, Nicolae Ceausescu's to Gheorghe Gheorghiu-Dej, or Leonid Brezhnev's succession to Nikita Khrushchev; an example of the second problem is Liu Shaoqi's growing power when he was named chief of state and Mao's heir apparent in 1959. Although there is no credible evidence that he used this power to plot against Mao, more and more people were turning to him as an alternative, partly because of a loss of faith in Mao's leadership after the Great Leap Forward, partly because he held the key to the future.

43. For example, Lenin wrote a famous last testament expressing grave misgivings about Stalin and left explicit instructions that it be read to the next Party Congress, but Stalin had successfully consolidated his power base as Party secretary and was able to ignore these instructions. Stalin's heir apparent, Georgi Malenkov, was ultimately outmaneuvered by Khrushchev. In late 1975–early 1976 in China, Zhou Enlai tried to arrange for Deng Xiaoping to succeed him, but these plans were undone when Mao managed to outlive Zhou Enlai. Andrei Kirilenko seems to have been Brezhnev's choice as his successor, but Yuri Andropov got the job; and Mikhail Gorbachev was probably Andropov's favorite, but Konstantin Chernenko was preferred by the rest of the Politburo.

44. See Bunce, *New Leaders*.

the ultimate outcome of successful political innovation. Yet again, the implications for postsuccession policy developments are different: For Rush, the new monocratic leadership can afford to innovate boldly; for Bunce, there is a danger of stagnation as the structural incentive for innovation is removed.

China is unique in having had such a protracted premortem succession crisis, lasting from Mao's first vesting of an heir apparent in 1959 until Deng's consolidation of power in 1979. This was even longer than the USSR's (Union of Soviet Socialist Republics) last series of successions (1981–1985), and arguably more disruptive—though of course not everything that happened in China during these years was directly related to succession, there were broad ramifications. Generally the Chinese crisis conforms to the Rush model, as characterized by fragmentation of leadership and an incapacity to make and sustain new programmatic initiatives. There were attempts at policy initiatives, as Bunce predicts, but the crisis atmosphere was inhospitable, inclining the leadership to vacillate (with accelerating tempo) between opposing alternatives. The crisis was initiated by Mao's illness and premortem succession arrangements; it was kept alive by the unwillingness or inability of Mao's various heirs apparent to seize power from him before he was willing to relinquish it and by Mao's own mixed feelings about retirement. The reasons for the inability of the putative successors to resolve this long crisis remain speculative but may be attributed in part to enduring Chinese traditions of deference to seniority and to the lack of any provision in Chinese culture or in Communist career arrangements for a "retirement" phase between the *vita activa* and death. The inability of the incumbent to decide the issue must be blamed on his own ambivalence, which manifested itself in an oscillation between periods of quiescent withdrawal and bouts of intense political activity.

Meanwhile, as Mao's thoughts became focused on death and succession, age took on increasingly negative connotations while youth assumed a correspondingly magnified value. If Mao (and his generation) must wither and die, China's youth must then live and wax vigorous, thereby reviving the nation's revolutionary vitality and assuring its future. As Mao put it in 1957, "In this world every new thing, every living thing, no matter what, everything develops through struggle with old objects, old things."[45] Or, later the same year, he stated, "The world is yours, as well as ours, but in the last analysis, it is yours. You young people, full of vigor and vitality, are in the bloom of life, like the sun at eight or nine in the morning. Our hope is placed in you. . . . The world

---

45. Mao, "On the Correct Handling" (Speaking Notes), p. 173.

belongs to you. China's future belongs to you."⁴⁶ And in a 1958 speech at the Eighth Party Congress, Mao delivered an extended disquisition on the virtues of youth and the decrepitude of age:

> Since ancient times, whenever the scholars or inventors created a new school of thought, they have always started young, possessed not much learning, and were scorned and oppressed. Not until later did they grow into adults and become learned. Are all the people like this? Is it a universal law? We cannot be completely sure, and it requires investigation and study. However, one can say that the majority are like that. Why did they become inventors, scholars, or heroes? They succeeded because their bearing was correct. Regardless of the amount of learning, if the bearing is wrong, it is of no use. "Man dreads fame and a hog dreads fat." The famous people are often the most backward, most fearful, and most lacking in creativity. Why? Because they have already attained fame. They have seniority and position, and are no longer oppressed. Being busy, they do not study any more. Of course, we cannot discredit all famous people. There are exceptions. Instances of young people knocking down the highly educated are numerous.⁴⁷

Mao then goes on to list and discuss with some erudition examples of people who allegedly achieved great merit in their youth, including Liu Bang, Xiang Yu, Confucius, Shakyamuni, poets Wang Bo and Li Ho (Tang dynasty), Li Shimin (first emperor of the Tang), Tang warriors Luo Shixin and Wang Bo, Song general Yue Fei, Marx, Lenin, Darwin, Hu Shi, and many more obscure figures. In this motley pantheon Mao perceived both brilliant originality and iconoclasm.

A review of Mao's poetry suggests possible reasons for his fascination with youth. He became obsessed with the fact that because time was short, one needed to make a deep and lasting impression on the world. As he put it in 1963:

> So many deeds cry out to be done,
> And always urgently;
> The world rolls on,
> Time presses.
> Ten thousand years are too long,
> Seize the day, seize the hour!⁴⁸

---

46. "Talk at a Meeting with Chinese Students and Trainees in Moscow" (November 17, 1957), in *Quotations from Chairman Mao*, p. 288.
47. "Miscellany of Mao Zedong Thought," in *Joint Publications Research Service*, 1:61269 (February 20, 1974), pp. 92–95.
48. "Reply to Comrade Kuo Mo-jo" (January 9, 1963), in Mao Tsetung, *Poems* (Peking: Foreign Languages Press, 1976), p. 46.

So far as the exact content of the deeds crying out to be done is concerned, his writings and statements convey a sense of urgency in the pursuit of radical initiatives ranging from health delivery to opera reform, but without detailed plans or clear priorities. In his poetry the logic of politics gives way to imagery, but that imagery may be a more accurate guide to Mao's feelings than his prose. Compare the following two passages, the first from a poem written in 1925 ("Changsha"), the second from one written in May 1965 ("Reascending Jinggangshan"):

> Young we were, schoolmates,
> At life's full flowering;
> Filled with enthusiasm
> Boldly we cast all restraints aside.
> Pointing to our mountains and rivers,
> Setting people afire with our words,
> We counted the mighty no more than muck.
>
> Thirty-eight years are fled
> With a mere snap of the fingers.
> We can clasp the moon in the Ninth Heaven
> And seize turtles deep down in the Five Seas:
> We'll return amid triumphant song and laughter.
> Nothing is hard in this world
> If you dare to scale the heights.[49]

Whereas such statements suggest unbounded (and perhaps unrealistic) faith in the potency of youth, the same ambivalence Mao exhibits toward his own death creeps into the attitudes he expresses toward the youth in whom he vests his hopes. They had not been through the revolution; they were untested, soft; they might easily succumb to the "silver bullets" of revisionism. Thus youth must undergo an ordeal, which he sometimes likened to "vaccination," or to "smelting iron in a blast furnace or making steel in an open-hearth furnace."[50] Conventional education no longer sufficed; children must learn in the school of hard knocks, growing up quickly to become heroes and martyrs. In his 1965 conversation with Edgar Snow, Mao saw "two possibilities" for the future: the first, the "continued development of the revolution toward Communism"; and the second, "that youth could negate the Revolution and give a poor performance: make peace with imperialism, bring the remnants of the

---

49. *Poems*, pp. 2, 49–50.
50. "Talks at a Conference of Secretaries of Provincial, Municipal and Autonomous Region Party Committees" (January 1957), and "Beat Back the Attacks of the Bourgeois Rightists" (July 9, 1957), both in Mao, *Selected Works*, vol. 5, pp. 369–370, and 459, respectively.

Chiang Kai-shek clique back to the Mainland and take a stand beside the small percentage of counterrevolutionaries still in the country."[51]

In launching the Cultural Revolution (and there is no question that without Mao's personal intercession it would have been squelched promptly), Mao was attempting, among other things (such as entrapping and purging his political opponents), no less than the revitalization of the entire system. By mounting the Tiananmen reviewing stand in August 1966, donning a Red Guard brassard, and conferring his blessing on millions of China's young people, he was passing the baton to a new generation. In personal terms this permitted him to deny his membership in the aging authority group, against whom he sensed resentment being directed, and reclaim his youth vicariously through identification with the young rebels: "To rebel is justified," he told them. In what he himself deemed his most visionary experiment, he would rejuvenate the revolution, rejuvenate aging cadres, rejuvenate the entire system by exposing it to a salubrious critical bath.

The Cultural Revolution thus became a massive revolt of the young against the old, in both a literal and a metaphorical sense. Literally, with the isolated exceptions of Mao himself and a few of his senior cronies, the struggle pitted the young and relatively junior (young students, young workers, junior officials) against the old and senior, led by that forbidding *eminence grise,* the tall and white-haired Liu Shaoqi (why not Deng Xiaoping, who was short with a black crew-cut?). Metaphorically, the values and symbolism of the "proletarian road" were those that Mao associated (in his poetry, for example) with his own youth: awesome power and unbounded potency (usually expressed in images of natural disaster, such as "with the fury of a hurricane," "with the force to topple mountains and upturn seas," "with the power of thunder and lightning from the heavens"), and incandescent brilliance (expressed in metaphors of fire, flames, or above all, the sun.) In similar fashion, he stressed martial courage (the "small generals" published "battle tabloids" and even manufactured rudimentary weapons, if they were unable to steal a supply from PLA armories), and pristine purity ("The turbulent stream of the revolutionary mass movement has been washing away the filth left by the old society," and "The roaring torrent of the great democratic movement under the command of the Thought of Mao Zedong is flowing on with surging waves under the bright sun, washing the whole of the old world"). This set of images was juxtaposed against the "bourgeois reactionary road," which embodied advanced age (e.g., the "four old") and decay: "devils," "freaks," "ghosts," and "monsters" from the darkness of

---

51. Snow, *Long Revolution,* pp. 195–222.

"Hell" (i.e., death), who represented "dirt," or "dog shit," but sought to withdraw, or hide underground, in "holes," and conceal themselves behind "masks" or "fig leaves" (i.e., to retire); who were weak and passive and sought to evade "struggle" (proposing abandonment of political Third World Wars of National Liberation, a "parliamentary road" to socialism, the "extinction of class struggle"), and who were in favor of patient "self-cultivation" under "absolute obedience" to established authority.[52]

The youth of China outdid themselves in trying to demonstrate that they could live up to Mao's ideals. The immediate (1966–1969) result of their enthusiastic but uncoordinated activities was to purge a large proportion of China's political and educational elite and thoroughly intimidate, and even traumatize, any survivors.[53] Although the number of those who claim to have been physically or mentally injured by the experience is vast indeed, the number of fatalities seems to have amounted to somewhat less than a million. This implies that most veterans and victims survived to discuss the experience. And surviving high-level victims were eventually likely to be politically rehabilitated as well; the first grouping after the fiery death of Lin Biao in September 1971 cleared the way. Although Mao had conducted the most sweeping purge of the Party and governmental bureaucracies since Liberation, it was not long before he began inviting the purge victims back into leadership positions, on the really quite implausible assumption that they had revolutionized their thinking. Having started out with an ambitious attempt to restructure the ruling apparatus in the form of Paris Communes or Revolutionary Committees, he soon dropped that idea and returned to classic Leninist organizational structures. Once rehabilitated to positions of leadership, former victims were only too apt, like Deng Xiaoping himself, to revert to their revisionist proclivities. The result was to doom the "newborn things" of the Cultural Revolution and restore the status quo ante. Mao's death and the third rise of Deng Xiaoping would, of course, fully unleash this tendency, resulting in a wave of revisionism far exceeding those experiments introduced in the early 1960s.

Why did Mao then permit the rehabilitation of the vast army of veteran cadres he had only recently consigned to political oblivion? The counterproductive outcome seems predictable enough in retrospect, and in view of the skepticism Mao expressed even during the height of the

---

52. See Lowell Dittmer, "Thought Reform and Cultural Revolution," *APSR* 71:1 (March 1977), pp. 67–85.
53. See, for example, Donald W. Klein and Lois B. Hager, "The Ninth Central Committee," *CQ*, no. 45 (January–March 1971), pp. 37–57, for an accounting of the impact upon the central leadership.

Cultural Revolution euphoria about what proportion of his cheering supporters had been truly converted, one might have expected him to anticipate this. The usual speculation concerning his course reversal is that management of the economy required the rehabilitation of cadres who essentially monopolized the requisite managerial and technical expertise needed to run it, particularly the planning apparatus and the modern industrial sector. This explanation would normally be plausible but gives insufficient credence to Mao's revolutionary commitments. Stalin had Mikhail Tukhachevsky executed for ideological reasons and decimated the Soviet officer corps (as well as the Bolshevik leadership, of course) with his purges on the eve of the Nazi invasion, and there seems to be no question that this gravely damaged the Soviet defense effort. But the Soviet Union nonetheless survived Hitler's onslaught, as it had survived a particularly sanguinary (and objectively unnecessary) collectivization of agriculture.[54] It is certainly true that the Cultural Revolution inflicted serious damage on the Chinese economy (though not as much as the Leap) and there is no doubt that Red Guard demobilization was functional from this perspective. After their banishment in August 1968, the economy made a fairly impressive recovery, however, along lines of local self-reliance and egalitarianism consistent with radical ideological priorities.[55] As Dwight Perkins has pointed out, Chinese economic performance remained reasonably good throughout the Cultural Revolution decade, although priorities were skewed to heavy industrial and strategic priorities and marginal productivity declined, demanding increasing capital investment.[56] This is not at all to argue that a radical road to development could be deemed economically desirable or even be sustainable in the long run; we can argue only that it was not so obviously disastrous by then prevailing historical standards for us to be able to account for Mao's course reversal on economic grounds alone. In view of Mao's lifelong radical commitments we are entitled to wonder why he

---

54. E.g., Sovietologist James Millar has called collectivization "an unmitigated disaster." Others, however, contend that "collectivization had very important positive aspects from a Soviet perspective," as discussed in Michael Ellman, *Collectivization, Convergence and Capitalism* (Orlando, Fla.: Academic Press, 1984).

55. A comparative analysis indicates that relative to population, some twenty times more Russians died from political violence under Stalin than Chinese under Mao. From 1934 to 1939, for example, more than 70 percent of the Soviet Central Committee members were shot, many after torture. In China, a similar proportion of Central Committee members were denounced and purged during the Cultural Revolution, but fewer than 5 percent of these perished. See Philip Short, *The Dragon and the Bear: Inside China and Russia Today* (London: Hodder and Stoughton, 1982), p. 172.

56. See Dwight Perkins, *China: Asia's Next Economic Giant?* (Seattle: University of Washington Press, 1986).

did not pursue that line more consequentially when the way seemed clear to do so.

The answer seems to be that Mao changed course because he became personally disheartened with the Cultural Revolution. He had plunged into the melee with great élan, at one point declaring that he wished to be remembered for only two things: having driven Chiang Kaishek from the mainland, and having launched the Cultural Revolution. Yet after two years of free-lance rebellion that tended to disintegrate into factional feuds, anarchy, and mindless vandalism, Mao became disillusioned. In the fall of 1968, Zhou Enlai induced him to make a tour of the countryside and he was apparently appalled by what he saw. He could not understand why different Red Guard factions should fight one another when there was no conflict of interest between them.[57] In one meeting (July 28, 1968) with Kuai Dafu and four other rebel faction leaders he made an emotional confession: "You have let me down," he said, with tears in his eyes. "And what is more, you have disappointed the workers, peasants, and soldiers of China."[58] As Deng Xiaoping (not the most reliable witness on this issue) later put it: "In the two years before his death Chairman Mao said that the CR [Cultural Revolution] was wrong in two respects: for one thing people wanted to 'overthrow everything,' for the other it came to a 'comprehensive civil war.'"[59]

Yet Mao's disappointment was quite apparent in the political resolution of the spontaneous mobilization phase of the Cultural Revolution, when the distribution of the spoils of the "power seizures" was decided. True, a handful of Red Guards, or "representatives of the revolutionary masses," as they were now called, successfully "seized power," but none attained line offices, most gaining only (what proved to be temporary) plenary seats on the Revolutionary Committees, or other showcase positions. The overwhelming majority achieved not upward but downward mobility, a total of some seventeen million being sent down to the villages or up to the mountains to feed pigs and plant crops for the rest of their lives. This was deemed a heroic and revolutionary mission, but there is little question that it was perceived by the young people involved as harsh punishment. The leadership cannot have been unaware of their

---

57. Mao, "Instruction Given During Inspection Tour," as cited in *Renmin ribao* (*RR*) editorial, "Promote Revolutionary Great Alliance Through Revolutionary Mass Criticism and Repudiation," September 14, 1967.

58. Quoted in *Far Eastern Economic Review*, 61:35 (August 29, 1968), pp. 377–378; see also William Hinton, *Hundred Day War: The Cultural Revolution at Tsinghua University* (New York: Monthly Review Press, 1972), p. 213.

59. Deng Xiaoping, "Interview with Oriana Fallaci" (August 21 and 23, 1980), as trans. in Helmut Martin, ed., *Die Reform der Revolution: Eine Milliarde Menschen auf dem Weg* (Berlin: Siedler Verlag, 1988), p. 65.

misery and thus must have intended it—certainly the peasants were not grateful to see these unskilled and unmotivated workers dumped in their midst.

Mao was returning to the role of his father, the "severe taskmaster" who always accused Mao of "laziness" and saw no use for learning except in an immediately utilizable capacity—for Mao to help his father keep books or defend him (by quoting the classics) in the lawsuits his sharp business practice provoked. Such severity in Mao's administration had consequences. For the last twenty years of his reign the average wage remained essentially frozen, while capital accumulation averaged an incredible 20–30 percent. Under the "open-door" system the schools became indistinguishable from labor reform camps, and cadres and intellectuals as well as students were sent out to do manual labor, on either a rotational or a more protracted basis. This was no necessary corollary of radicalism; although admissions to higher education were indeed democratized, the service being redistributed was thereby devalued, fostering considerable cynicism.

Regardless of the merits of either the emancipatory or the punitive phases of Maoist radicalism, a pattern begins to emerge that would recur with increasing frequency throughout Mao's waning years—a pattern of oscillation between incompatible alternatives. Seeing his time running out, he began to alternate between spurts of hyperactivity in which he wanted diverse Herculean tasks to be achieved instantly and periods of brooding, study, illness, and reclusion. It no longer seems plausible to attribute this oscillation to a deadlocked "struggle between two lines," for, after all, the "bourgeois reactionary line" had been thoroughly vanquished in the Cultural Revolution. Rather, it seems that Mao himself proved unable to push either policy line "through to the end," or, as his oft-cited rhetoric had urged, to "beat the dog in the water until it is dead." Much has been made of the surviving rivalry between the Gang of Four, who continued to mobilize a series of criticism campaigns, and the "moderates," who managed the economy, but, without denying that such a rivalry existed, the fact remains that both of these factions were dependent on Mao's favor—he had created the radicals *ex nihilo*, and the moderates survived (or were rehabilitated) only by his grace. Ultimately Mao's own ambivalence played a much larger role in this policy vacillation than has generally been recognized.

Not all policy arenas were equally affected. There was, for example, an overall consistency in agricultural policy throughout the radical decade, despite occasional attempts to raise the unit of accounting from the team to the brigade or to reduce private plots. There was no major change in China's foreign or defense policy posture after the limited opening to the West in 1971. Most visibly affected were the arena of mass participation and the issue of Mao's personal succession—the former because here, above all, the conflict between authority and spontaneity could play itself out; the latter because Mao's ego was directly involved.

With regard to mass participation, Mao no longer found the Party's standard "from the top down" approach adequate, and, in unexpectedly rebuking Liu and Deng and ordering the work teams withdrawn, he authorized a momentous departure from previous traditions of Party-mass linkage. However, having ventured this innovation, he found it impossible either to allow the rebels to consummate their victory or to permit the entire experiment in spontaneous "from the bottom up" mobilization to be negated. Instead, from 1968 through 1976 he vacillated, sometimes permitting repression of the "revolutionary masses," sometimes permitting the masses to kick over the traces and rise in relatively untrammeled anarchy (up to a point); as a result, mass mobilization became devalued either as a mechanism for elite implementation of policy or for the purpose of popular monitoring of deviant elites. Only during the brief Lin Biao period (1968–1971) was mobilization so tightly harnessed that it did not interfere with production, and this created friction between the military and the civilian radicals. The immediate post–Lin Biao period (1971–1972) was marked by moderate demobilization, but in the summer of 1973 the radicals (with, we now know, Mao's personal blessing) regained the initiative in their Campaign to Criticize Lin Biao and Confucius (*pi-Lin pi-Kong*), which escalated in the spring of 1974 until it reached pandemic proportions in May–June (spontaneous big-character posters appeared criticizing cadres, workers began traveling throughout the country to foment protest activities, factional violence arose), resulting in a drop in industrial production and a discouraging agricultural outlook, whereupon the campaign was demobilized.[60] The same pattern was pursued in 1975, with radical mobilization under the campaign to study the dictatorship of the proletariat and to criticize "bourgeois rights," followed by a moderate countermobilization of officials for the implementation of the Four Modernizations. The spring and summer of 1976 were something of a free-for-all because of the deaths of first Zhou Enlai and then Mao Zedong, witnessing first a radical mobilization against Deng Xiaoping, followed by "spontaneous" moderate countermobilization (in the Tiananmen Incident of April 5) in support of Zhou Enlai, then by radical countermobilization against the moderate countermobilization, and so on. Mobilization throughout assumed a self-

---

60. See Wang En, "Yi-jiu-qi-si nian zhonggong zhengju yanbian tedian" (Characteristics of Chinese Communist political developments in 1974), *Zhanwang* (Outlook) (Hong Kong), no. 311 (January 16, 1975), pp. 9–11; *New York Times*, September 22, 1974, p. 31, and August 1, 1974, p. 58.

frustrating yo-yo-like pattern, reaching only a certain threshold before economic damage was incurred justifying demobilization qua suppression.

Mao's behavior concerning his own succession assumed a Don Juan pattern, where he would first embrace an heir apparent enthusiastically and with exaggerated expectations, only to later grow disillusioned, finally casting off the object of his previous ardor. This love-hate metamorphosis is clearest with respect to Lin Biao. During the 1966–1969 period, Mao seems to have been quite taken with Lin, publicly embracing this "closest comrade-in-arms" as he had never embraced another. He joked and laughed with Lin during their joint appearances at mass rallies, glancing benevolently over his shoulder at the text as Lin struggled through a speech. The two seemed inseparable. Indeed, Lin made it a point never to appear in public except in Mao's company (about forty times altogether between the first mass rally in August 1966 and the Ninth Party Congress in April 1969), and he was always photographed with Mao. The two went on private retreats together for two months or more on half a dozen occasions during this period.

Then, sometime after demobilization of the Red Guards in August 1968, something seemed to trigger Mao's suspicions. As was the case with Gao Gang and Liu Shaoqi, that trigger seems to have been the successor's attempt to consolidate the heir apparency, allowing Mao to perceive that their participation in the mutual admiration society had ulterior motives. At the Ninth Party Congress Mao made Lin his official successor, even having this written into the constitution, though he allowed Zhou Enlai to redraft Lin's report before publication (suggesting a certain rivalry between the two men). When Lin attempted to fill the post of chief of state vacated by Liu Shaoqi—nominally with Mao, but actually (Mao suspected) with himself—Mao took umbrage and proceeded to sponsor a media criticism campaign against Lin's supporter Chen Boda; then Mao toured the country marshaling forces against Lin himself. According to the only document by the Lin "conspirators" that has come to light, Lin reacted bitterly:

> Today he uses this force to attack that force; tomorrow he uses that force to attack this force. Today he uses sweet words and honeyed talk to those whom he entices, and tomorrow he puts them to death for some fabricated crimes.... Looking back at the history of the past few decades, [do you see] anyone whom he had supported initially who has not finally been handed a political death sentence? ... He is a paranoid and a sadist.[61]

---

61. Quoted in Ying-mao Kau, ed., *The Lin Piao Affair* (White Plains, N.Y.: International Arts and Sciences Press, 1975).

The inside story of the climactic confrontation between the two remains shrouded in mystery to this day, but, whatever the details, it culminated in Lin's violent death. Mao went through a phase of postpartum withdrawal, retiring from active politics amid (reasonably credible) reports of serious illness. Between his August–September 1971 tour (to muster support for his anticipated confrontation with Lin) and the Tenth Party Congress in September 1973, he made no public speeches and appeared only once before the Chinese people. He apparently made no public statement explicitly condemning Lin, which is puzzling in view of the heinousness of the crimes the latter is said to have committed.

Mao then reportedly became briefly infatuated with Wang Hongwen, who had been a young and low-ranking Shanghai enterprise cadre before the Cultural Revolution, vaulted to municipal leadership in the 1966–1969 period, and then was suddenly lofted to the vice-chairmanship of the Party at the Tenth Congress by Mao himself. Handsome and idealistic, he is said to have reminded Mao of himself when he was in his prime, and the aging Chairman took him into his private residence to live (replacing the banished Jiang Qing). Then Mao, reverting once again to the role of his father, seems to have grown exasperated with Wang's political naiveté. Particularly irked by his handling of a protracted strike in Hangzhou in the spring of 1974 (Mao had a summer home in Hangzhou), Mao dropped him from favor.[62] Although he did not lose his vice-chairmanship, Wang returned to Shanghai in May 1975 and played no apparent role in the final succession drama. Whether Mao intended his wife, Jiang Qing, to figure in the succession is unclear, but she presumed that he had. It is interesting that this pattern of infatuation and betrayal unveiled itself only with regard to radicals; both Liu Shaoqi and Zhou Enlai stood first in the line of succession at specific times, but Mao always kept his distance from both men, and certainly his relationship with Deng Xiaoping never seems to have been other than utilitarian.

Why this pattern of terminal vacillation? In psychological terms I would suggest that it derived from Mao's own ambivalence about the meaning of his life in the face of its imminent end. Throughout his early career he had played the archetypal rebel against authority, and he came to identify all the more intensely with the ideals of his youth—bold self-sacrifice and revolutionary vitality—even as he grew older. As illness

---

62. In 1974 Mao reportedly sent both Deng and Wang to Hangzhou and asked each upon their return: "After I die, what will happen in China?" "The whole country will certainly follow Chairman Mao's revolutionary line and unite firmly to carry the revolution to the end," said Wang. "Civil war will break out and there will be confusion throughout the country," said Deng. Mao preferred Deng's answer. *Qishi niandai* (The Seventies), (Hong Kong), March 1977.

and his first taste of serious defeat in the late 1950s caused him to see death approaching, he found himself thrust also into the role of his father, as perhaps all men do as death approaches—he visited his father's grave for the first time, ruminated over his own unfulfilling experience with fatherhood (one son dead, one insane). Unable to resolve the deep conflicts between the values of youthful idealist and shrewd, cynical, power-maximizing father figure, he oscillated continually from one to the other, lashing out at its inverted doppelganger. Fundamentally, he remained a rebel, yet he could not permit the rebels to triumph. Death's approach thus not only gave rise to a tendency to identify with the revolution and seek immortality by fusing his ego with this collective abstraction,[63] but even raised questions about whether the revolution should succeed after all—feelings that may ultimately be traced back to an unresolved identity conflict.

In the last months of his life he looked upon China's youth with despair. "Young people are soft. They have to be reminded of the need for struggle," he told Julie Nixon Eisenhower on December 31, 1975. "The Chairman told us, there will be struggle in the Party, there will be struggle between classes, nothing is certain except struggle."[64] In the end he characterized himself as "an isolated poor *old man* standing alone."[65]

One is tempted to infer that the inconclusive outcome of the Cultural Revolution demonstrates the inherent inadequacies of charismatic politics. However disruptive, Mao's approach to politics effected incredibly sweeping changes—yet the transformations he wrought seem at this point to have left surprisingly little trace, aside from Mao's own still-lingering reputation. Mao's inability to give them greater permanence was not entirely because they were culturally alien (not all aspects of Maoism were incompatible with Chinese culture) but was also due to an underlying ambivalence that induced the Chairman to criticize and disrupt any order, even one he himself had established. The result was very damaging to the crowning project he had wished to leave as his legacy, as the Cultural Revolution lost its symbolic purity in a bewildering succession of tactical zigs and zags, and the question of an appropriate successor to carry the revolutionary torch could not be resolved at all but had to left to be sorted out postmortem. Mao's ultimate successor would be a man he had purged twice in the last decade, indicating his reservations clearly enough. The aversion might seem to have been mutual, as

---

63. See Robert Jay Lifton, *Revolutionary Immortality: Mao Tse-tung and the Chinese Cultural Revolution* (New York: Random House, 1968).
64. Ms. Eisenhower's interview is recorded in *Ladies' Home Journal*, January 1976.
65. Quoted in *China Aktuell* (Hamburg), November 1976, p. 581 (emphasis supplied).

Deng lost no time dismantling the Cultural Revolution and everything it stood for. Yet that perception would be an oversimplification, as we will see.

Deng Xiaoping

Deng Xiaoping preferred to be called the "chief architect" (*zong shejishi*) of Chinese reform (while Mao was the continuing revolution's "great helmsman," or *weidade duoshou*), and he cuts a much less romantic figure. Less than five feet tall and partly deaf (Mao used to complain that he sat with his deaf side to him), he struck one interlocutor as a "cold fish,"[66] and Kissinger, albeit greatly impressed with Mao and Zhou Enlai, put him down (in 1974) as "a nasty little man."[67] Yet Mao at least at one point deemed this world-class bridge player "highly intelligent,"[68] and Helmut Schmidt, who (in 1984) found Deng "mentally quick, with a sense of humor, alert and competent in every phase of the conversation," said he surpassed "all other statesmen in the world in the 1980s."[69] Tough and candid to the point of bluntness, Deng lacks charisma either in the popular sense of conspicuous magnetism or in the more specific sense used here of iconoclastic originality: To the contrary, Deng seems to apotheosize the conventional wisdom and common sense of his generation of Chinese Communists.

Despite his forthright demeanor, Deng is a more complex character than generally assumed. After spending much of his life in the shrewd and aggressive pursuit of personal power, he steadfastly declined the highest offices of the party and state when they were within his grasp, preferring to pull strings from behind the scenes. An ardent advocate of law and order, Deng did not shrink from contorting China's embryonic legal system in political show trials or from upsetting painstakingly arranged succession arrangements in whimsical reshufflings. Ever eager to disprove Mao's 1976 verdict that he had "never been a Marxist"[70] by repressing ideological dissent, he was, in fact, never much of a theoretical innovator ("I am quite unimportant" in the development of Mao Zedong

---

66. Based on a talk by Lucian Pye at the Forty-fifth Annual Meeting of the Association for Asian Studies, March 25–28, 1993, Los Angeles, Calif.
67. See Fox Butterfield's article in *New York Times Magazine*, August 1, 1976.
68. During his 1957 visit to Moscow, Mao pointed to a member of his delegation: "See that little man there? He's highly intelligent and has a great future ahead of him." Strobe Talbott, ed., *Khrushchev Remembers: The Last Testament* (Boston: Little, Brown, 1974), p. 288.
69. Helmut Schmidt, "Einleitung," in Deng, Martin, ed., *Die Reform.*
70. *RR*, March 10, 1976.

Thought, he once conceded).[71] Yet his pragmatic admixture of Marxist and market principles seemed to many theorists to have far-reaching theoretical implications[72]—implications he refused to admit, cracking down hard on any attempt to extend theory beyond the rather simplistic taboos of the Four Cardinal Principles. Although he prided himself on rebuilding the institutions of the Party-state after the Cultural Revolution, he also unleashed a set of economic reforms whose ramifications tend to undermine it. Yet despite such inconsistencies, his place in history seems assured as the leader who opened China to the outside world as never before and who, by launching a reform movement that he perhaps did not entirely understand or even fully concur with, unleashed a socioeconomic revolution no less profound than Mao's political revolution.

Like the previous sketch, this one will be divided into two sections. The first will summarize Deng's career; the second will analyze his attempt to come to terms with the fallout of charismatic leadership and his succession arrangements in particular.

Career Vicissitudes

Deng was born August 22, 1904 (Gregorian calendar), in Paifangcun Village, Sichuan province, a region as isolated as Mao's native village of Shaoshan, in Hunan province, of well-to-do Hakka landowners. Unlike Mao's family, which was nouveau riche, the Dengs had some inherited wealth and cherished a tradition of scholarship, public service, and local leadership; they had been pillars of the community for generations. Deng's father, Wenming, the richest landlord in the county, was on a first-name basis with the governor; in addition to farming some eighty mu (thirteen acres) of land (a goodly farm by local reckoning), he was in effect high sheriff (chief of the local militia for eight counties) and had a good education. Like Mao an oldest son, Deng Xixian (Xiaoping was a later alias) was the second child of his father's first concubine (his wife remained heirless) and was held in high esteem by a family that rested its hopes in him.

From what little we know of his childhood, Deng's relationship to his father was (in contrast to Mao's early rebelliousness) correct and

---

71. Deng, "Interview with Oriana Fallaci," in Martin, ed., *Die Reform*, p. 75. Deng took pains at Tiananmen to disprove Mao's contention that he had never been a Marxist, but he was notoriously ill-read in the theoretical classics. During his well-publicized trip to Shenzhen in the spring of 1992, he admitted, for example, that he had never even read *Das Kapital*. Personal communication from Professor Joseph Fewsmith.

72. See Bill Brugger and David Kelly, *Chinese Marxism in the Post-Mao Era* (Stanford: Stanford University Press, 1990), especially Chap. 6.

respectful: He recalls one incident in which he submitted without a word of protest to his father's technically justified caning before explaining to him that the money he had taken was to help a friend in a family emergency. Although his resolution of the conflict cannot fairly be likened to the "counter-Oedipal" Confucian pattern of abject submission[73]—Deng had, after all, stolen his father's money—he played by the prevailing rules. The authority, he characteristically presumed, deserved to "save face" even if one disagreed with him.

After middle school, Deng took a preparatory course for candidates to be selected for study in France as worker-students, then embarked in the fall of 1920 (having just turned seventeen) for study at the University of Lyon. Thus he entered the elite fraternity of young Chinese whose backgrounds allowed them to see themselves as future leaders and whose experience in the outside world had a broadening, politicizing effect. Though he remained in France for five years (acquiring a lifelong taste for croissants—he lived on a croissant and glass of milk a day), he did not study much because he had to work to survive: He was employed at the Schneider-Creusot Iron and Steel works, the "Chaussures" (rubber galoshes) division of Hutchinson, and the Renault automobile plant, and worked as a locomotive fireman. Most of his free time was dedicated to revolutionary activities; he led a highly peripatetic life, living at the margins of society. In 1922 he joined the Chinese Socialist Youth League (a branch had been established in France by Wang Ruofei) and the French branch of the CCP upon its founding in 1924.

Deng's energy, intelligence, and ambition quickly propelled him to positions near, but not at, the pinnacle of both the Youth League and the CCP—a political vantage point he seemed to prefer for the rest of his career. In 1923 he was elected to the leadership organ of the Youth League and in 1924 to the "Central Organization of the CCP in Europe." These responsibilities brought him into his first contact with Zhou Enlai, secretary of the Youth League and then of the French branch of the CCP—and Deng's first patron. When the Party and the League jointly launched *Chiguang* (Red light), Zhou was the chief editorial contributor and Deng was his right-hand man, the "doctor of duplication" who hand-stenciled and mimeographed the pages. Without ever displaying any apparent theoretical originality or rhetorical flare, the "small cannon" built a reputation on his willingness to make himself useful in whatever capacity the occasion demanded.

Upon Zhou's return to China in the summer of 1925 Deng inherited some of his power and might conceivably have moved into the leader-

---

73. See, for example, the story of Xue as cited by Richard Solomon, *Mao's Revolution and Chinese Political Culture* (Berkeley: University of California Press, 1971), pp. 35–36.

ship slot, but instead he soon departed for Moscow, where he studied at the Sun Yatsen University from January to August 1926 (with Yang Shangkun). He then took advantage of a state visit by then Communist sympathizer Feng Yuxiang to attach himself (along with ninety-eight Comintern advisers) to Feng's entourage. Upon the delegation's return to Xian, Deng's first post was that of instructor at the Political Department of the Sun Yatsen Military Academy that Feng proceeded to found there; he also helped reorganize Feng's army along Soviet lines, becoming political commissar of the Seventh Corps. The triumph of Chiang Kaishek's "northern expedition" (*beifa*) in 1926–1927 (and the anticipated spoils of that victory) soon disabused Feng of any revolutionary sympathies, however, and Deng was thrown out along with all his Comintern confederates when Feng joined the increasingly anti-Communist KMT.

On August 1, 1927, along with an illustrious list of later notables including Zhu De, Zhou Enlai, Chen Yi, Lin Biao, Ho Long, Liu Bocheng, and Nie Rongzhen, Deng helped launch the Nanchang uprising; though the putsch was promptly crushed, this event would officially mark the birthday of the Red Army. For the next two tempestuous years Deng worked in the CCP Central Organization in Shanghai; then, in his first independent Party assignment, Deng was sent to Guangxi province to organize Soviets (*suweiai*), as part of an effort to mobilize the peasantry (whose revolutionary potential had been ignored during the first united front, according to contemporary postmortems). Largely for reasons beyond his control, this effort turned out disastrously, as the Soviet was dissolved and much of the Seventh Red Army he had been sent to help organize (as its political commissar) was decimated by Nationalist forces. Abandoning his forces on the point of a withering attack, Deng adjured them to fight their way through to join Mao's forces at Jinggangshan while he made his way to Shanghai to report to the Central Committee, then headquartered there. By August 1931 he was in Ruijin, the capital of the Central Soviet of Jiangxi, then commanded by Mao Zedong and Zhu De. As Party secretary of Ruijin County, he quickly terminated the so-called A-B conspiracy prosecution, an internecine factional fight that was decimating the organization.

This was the first nadir of Deng's personal career, as well as a generally desperate time for the CCP. When the returned student leadership vacated Shanghai to seek refuge in Ruijin in the early 1930s, its members naturally sought to assert their authority there; Deng was demoted along with Mao for promoting a "rich peasant line" and for committing errors in repulsing Chiang Kaishek's fourth "encirclement" campaign. Deng was sent to the General Political Department of the Red Army in Ruijin to be "struggled." He wrote a number of self-criticisms, but refused to go far enough to satisfy his critics and seemed to have been relegated to political obscurity. In the attendant furor, his beautiful second wife, Jin Weiying, divorced him to marry his leading critic, one Lo Man (an offspring of this remarriage, a future education commission head named Li Tieying, is rumored to be Deng's belated progeny). It is interesting to compare Deng's behavior in this affair of the heart with Mao's roughly contemporaneous experience: Whereas Mao insisted on marrying the demimondaine, Jiang Qing, in the face of the contrary advice of the majority of the Politburo (and was hence obliged to keep her out of the public eye for the next several decades), when Deng's wife was pursued by a Party superior he readily gave her up.

Not until the famous Zunyi conference in January 1935 (which Deng attended, as reporter qua editor of the army newspaper, *Red Star*) was he to make his comeback. Deng had thrown his lot in with Mao at Ruijin and taken his lumps; his political career now began to ascend on the coattails of his new patron. Although so severely stricken with typhoid that he barely survived, Deng participated in the Long March, briefly serving as director of the CC Secretariat and then the Propaganda Department. But his most historically significant assignment was that of political commissar of what was then the 129th Division (later to become the Second Field Army) with Commander Liu Bocheng. The "Liu-Deng Army" held together for the next thirteen years, established the Jin-Ji-Lu-Yu military region (consisting of contiguous base areas in Shanxi, Hebei, Shandong, and Henan provinces), inflicted (together with Peng Dehuai's troops) a costly loss on Japanese forces in the "Battle of the Hundred Regiments" (August–October 1940), and waged the culminating Battle of Huaihai against Nationalist Armored Forces in January 1949. Deng returned to Yanan only three times, and briefly, from the Long March to the end of the anti-Japanese war.[74]

Upon Liberation, Deng came into his own. He was appointed a member of the Central People's Government Council and the Revolutionary Military Council in 1950 (both provisional central organs, set up until more permanent organs could be established by the adoption of a state constitution in September 1954) and also assumed effective control of the Southwest (which included his home province): He was first Party secretary of the Southwest Office of the CC (Liu Bocheng, second secretary; third secretary, He Long), and deputy director of the Southwest China Military and Administrative Council (under Director Liu Bocheng). He seems to have been a crack regional implementer of central policies, which concentrated at the time on "socialization of the means of produc-

---

74. Yang Guoyu, Chen Feijin, and Wang Quanhong, eds., *Ershiba nian qian: cong shizhengwei dao congshuji* (Twenty-eight years ago: From division political commissar to secretary general) (Shanghai: Shanghai wenyi chubanshe, 1989), p. 19.

tion" (particularly the land revolution), a policy he zealously supported. But he was already more than a regional satrap. Mao realized that one of the possible consequences of his decision to intervene in the Korean War would be an American attack on the homeland, and in preparation for this eventuality he began a massive relocation of Chinese industry in the early 1950s—if Chiang Kaishek could shift his headquarters to Sichuan in response to the Japanese invasion, Mao would pursue the same strategy on a far more ambitious scale. Deng Xiaoping, as Party leader in the host site, was put in charge. In this connection Deng helped set up factories in hidden mountain valleys and caves and created a rail network linking Chongqing with Chengdu. This policy of industrial relocation, pursued more consequentially as the "third line" in the early 1960s when the Sino-Soviet dispute revived the specter of invasion or nuclear attack, was to continue through the end of Mao's tenure at enormous cost, consuming 40 percent of the nation's capital budget in 1963–1965, 53 percent in 1965–1970, 45 percent in 1970–1975.[75] Although in retrospect the program might be deemed economically disastrous and even of questionable strategic value in a nuclear age, Deng implemented it efficiently and without question.

Beginning in 1952 Deng was promoted to vice-minister and in 1953 became minister of finance and chairman of the Economic Affairs Committee of the Central Administrative Council (antecedent of the State Council), once again working under Zhou Enlai. By the mid-1950s Deng had shifted his base of operations almost entirely to the central level. When Mao began to complain of his onerous administrative burdens, Liu Shaoqi suggested (and Mao readily agreed) to appoint Deng secretary of the CCP Central Committee (in May 1954). In this capacity Deng assumed responsibility for the investigation and disposition of the case against Gao Gang and Rao Shushi, whose purge at the National Party Conference of March 1955 earned the gratitude of Zhou Enlai and Liu Shaoqi (whose careers had been at stake). Deng then assumed Rao's vacancy as director of the Organization Department of the CCP. At the Fifth Plenum of the Seventh Central Committee (April 1955), Deng (along with Lin Biao) was elected to the seventeen-man Politburo. As Party secretary, Deng made organizational preparations for the watershed Eighth Party Congress, where his office was expanded (to CCP General Secretary), and he was elected junior member of the newly established six-man Standing Committee of the Politburo (ranking just below Mao Zedong, Liu Shaoqi, Zhou Enlai, Zhu De, and Chen Yun).

Upon his arrival in the highest leadership circles, Deng quickly gravitated into a coalition with Liu Shaoqi, whose views and general approach

---

75. Salisbury, *New Emperors*, p. 128.

he shared. As a member of a CCP delegation led by Zhu De that attended the Twentieth Party Congress of the Soviet Union in Moscow, he was among those to be surprised by Khrushchev's secret speech denouncing Stalin. When the domestic implications of this volte-face split the CCP leadership, Deng aligned with Liu Shaoqi and Peng Dehuai in support of "the profound significance of adhering to the principle of collective leadership and combating the cult of personality"; in his report to the CCP's Eighth Congress on amendment of the Party Constitution (September 1956), Deng endorsed the deletion of the articles pledging allegiance to Mao Zedong and his Thought and the extinction of class struggle after socialization of the means of production—somewhat softening the blow with a long and faithful recitation of Mao's "mass line."[76] Again, when Mao launched his bold experiment with liberalism in the 1956 Hundred Flowers initiative, Deng helped erect bureaucratic hurdles that delayed implementation until the spring of 1957, joined the leadership majority in favor of aborting the campaign once "blooming" started to generate unexpectedly trenchant criticisms, and led the subsequent antirightist movement against dissidents that would result in the classification of some 800,000 people (mostly intellectuals) as "rightists" between 1957 and 1958. (Deng has subsequently admitted that the movement's scale was too broad, but continues to insist that the struggle "was not wrong in and of itself.") Though both Deng and Liu joined a united front in support of the Great Leap Forward in 1958 (and reluctantly endorsed the 1959 purge of Peng Dehuai at Lushan when he prematurely objected to the Leap), Liu and Deng again cooperated in rescinding various radical initiatives in the wake of the devastating economic depression the Leap precipitated. Deng's Secretariat thus put forth the "60 articles on agriculture" in the spring of 1961, which included permission to allocate production quotas to individual peasant households; a few months later the Secretariat announced "70 articles on industrial labor," which provided for implementation of piecework wages, "chopping down" unproductive industries, and a shift of investment priorities to light industry.[77]

This new Liu-Deng alignment soon evolved into a self-sufficient alternative policymaking center, thanks to a functional division within the leadership whereby Mao withdrew to the "second front," leaving Liu to convene important Party conferences while Deng used his authority to convoke "central work conferences" in lieu of CC Plenums. Mao seemed

---

76. Deng, "Report on the Revision of the Constitution of the CPC" (September 16, 1956), in *Deng Xiaoping: Speeches and Writings*, 2nd expanded ed. (New York: Pergamon Press, 1987), pp. 1–40, hereinafter *Deng Xiaoping*.

77. Uli Franz, *Deng Xiaoping* (Boston: Harcourt Brace Jovanovich, 1988); Ching Hua Lee, *Deng Xiaoping* (Princeton: Princeton University Press, 1985).

at first to accede to this arrangement, making a self-criticism for the mistakes of the Great Leap at a meeting of 7,000 cadres in January 1962 and agreeing four months later to a five-year consolidation phase after Liu and Deng conducted an audit revealing a 2 billion *yuan* budget deficit. But beginning with a work conference at Beidaiho (an elite lakeside summer vacation resort) in August 1962 and during the Tenth Plenum of the Eighth CC a month later, Mao reversed course, calling for a revival of "class struggle." Mao complained of a rift (which Deng later admitted), accusing Deng of setting up an "independent kingdom" in the Secretariat, noting his failure to brief him often and his tendency to distance himself physically at meetings. As he put it in 1966:

> Deng Xiaoping never came to consult me: from 1949 to the present he has never consulted me over anything at all. In 1962 suddenly the four vice-premiers, Li Fuqun, Tan Zhenlin, Li Xiannian and Bo Yibo came to look me up in Nanjing, and afterwards went to Tianjin. I immediately gave my approval, and the four went back again, but Deng Xiaoping never came.[78]

Mao's wife, Jiang Qing, reentered politics after the Lushan confrontation with Mao's apparent blessing; Deng seems to have had a long-standing animus against the woman; he never bothered to conceal his contempt for the "revolution" she sought to launch in culture. Policymaking became more complicated in this increasingly factionalized context, as each factional grouping sought to thwart or modify the other's initiatives while protecting its own.[79]

Finally, with the help of his wife and the "kitchen cabinet" of radical intellectuals she had assembled, Mao launched the Great Proletarian Cultural Revolution, building momentum at the mass level beyond Liu's and Deng's reach to "topple" the Party-state apparatus they controlled, while prohibiting them on penalty of purge from cracking down on the "revolutionary masses." Deng Xiaoping confessed publicly that he had been "guilty of arrogance, complacency and a belief in my own infallibility ... I sought the advice of neither my comrades nor the masses and neglected to report to the chairman"[80]—but his self-criticisms were

---

78. Mao, "Talk at the Report Meeting" (October 24, 1966), in Schram, *Chairman Mao*, p. 266.

79. See, for example, the conflicting policy lurches in the course of implementation of the Socialist Education Movement (Four Cleans) of 1962–1965, as detailed in Richard Baum and Frederick Teiwes, *Ssu-ch'ing: The Socialist Education Movement of 1962–66* (Berkeley: Center for Chinese Studies, 1968); also see Richard Baum, *Prelude to Revolution: Mao, the Party, and the Peasant Question, 1962–66* (New York: Columbia University Press, 1975).

80. Deng, "Self-Criticism" (October 23, 1966), as trans. in Martin, ed., *Die Reform*, p. 84.

rejected as "insincere." After more than two years of chaotic factionalism, with the government barely held together by media-coordinated mass criticism of "China's Khrushchev" and "the other top Party person in authority taking the capitalist road," Liu and Deng (and most of their known disciples) were purged from all leadership positions and "sent down" to do manual work in penance for their ideological errors.

Deng's punishment was slightly less severe than Liu's (i.e., he was never evicted from the Party or criticized by name in the official press), probably because he was not perceived to pose a threat to Mao's leadership position. Liu died in captivity in 1969, but Deng survived his banishment (and the crippling of one of his children) to rise again. Working in a tractor repair factory in Fuzhou, Deng got wind of Lin Biao's death in the "September 13 [1972] Incident" and promptly wrote a letter to Mao, abjectly apologizing for his mistakes and offering his services in the criticism campaign. Zhou induced an ailing Mao to accept the offer (after circulating Deng's self-criticism and Mao's response to the Politburo), and the "small cannon" was reintroduced by none other than Jiang Qing at a reception in April 1973.[81] Deng quickly proved himself invaluable, helping Mao regain control of the PLA in the wake of the purge of Lin Biao's supporters and assuming control of the State Council when Zhou became terminally ill. In 1973 he was referred to as vice-premier; by 1974 he became a member of the Politburo and (in April) delivered an important address to the United Nations (propounding Mao's Theory of Three Worlds).

By the Tenth Party Congress in January 1975, Deng had become acting premier as well as first vice-premier and vice-chairman of the Standing Committee of the Politburo, in position to succeed Zhou Enlai. Although Mao made a fairly transparent bid for Deng's loyalty upon his return with lavish public praise, the latter quickly gravitated back to his original political base and revisionist policy line (though he did serve Mao's purposes in restoring order in Hangzhou and other strife-torn cities). Evidently hoping to structure the succession scenario to his advantage while Zhou (who had terminal cancer) was still alive to front for him, Deng used the power he had regained to launch the ambitious Four Modernizations program in 1975, designed to revitalize his bureaucratic base by way of restoring order to the economy. As nominal first vice-premier, but functioning in effect as acting premier because of Zhou's hospitalization, Deng made his plans clear with characteristic vitriol:

---

81. Lin Qingshan, *Fengyun shinian yu Deng Xiaoping* (A decade of turmoil and Deng Xiaoping) (Beijing: Jiefangjun chubanshe, 1989), p. 267.

How can an individual be allowed casually to absent himself from work whenever he feels like it? If a man doesn't come to work, cross his name off the payroll. If he refuses to work, tell him to leave![82]

Owing to the sabotage by Lin Biao and his like, there are quite a few problems besetting our army . . . : bloating, laxity, extravagance and inertia.[83]

The key here is to set up a responsibility system. In many places we often find that there is no one who takes responsibility for the work. . . . We must be bold and not be afraid of making mistakes or of being criticized.[84]

Deng's priorities flew squarely in the face of the radical Gang of Four, for whom he expressed undisguised contempt, adding insult to injury by spreading rumors about the incompetent management of their own cultural sector and even launching his own competing propaganda organ. The Four, however, took advantage of their access to Mao to strike back, staging a confrontation at a November 5, 1975, Politburo meeting in which Deng refused to back down. In late November Mao thus authorized public criticism of the "reversal of just verdicts" (i.e., Deng's rehabilitation of purged cadres) and within weeks of Zhou Enlai's funeral in January 1975 (at which Deng, at Zhou's behest, gave the memorial address) Deng was once again forced to "stand aside." He had taken an accurate measure of the public's disenchantment with radical rhetoric, however, as indicated by a cascade of wreaths and other tokens of sympathy for Zhou Enlai at the Qingming festival (roughly equivalent to Memorial Day) on April 5, 1976. Mao and the Four held Deng responsible for this display (the evidence for which is unclear but plausible), resulting in Deng's second purge from all leadership positions (but still not from Party membership).

Deng bode his time for the next six months under ostensible house arrest in South China, clandestinely engaging with Ye Jianying and other veteran cadres in the conspiracy that eventually resulted in the purge and arrest of the Gang of Four and in Hua Guofeng's attendant power seizure.[85] As in the aftermath of the Lin Biao affair, Deng availed himself of the resulting power vacuum to proffer his services (again amid abject

---

82. Deng, "Some Problems Outstanding in the Iron and Steel Industry" (May 29, 1975), in *Selected Works of Deng Xiaoping (1975–1982)*, p. 21, hereinafter, *Selected*.

83. Deng, "The Task of Consolidating the Army" (July 14, 1975), speech to the CMC, in *Selected*, p. 27.

84. Deng, "Some Comments on Industrial Development" (August 18, 1975), in *Selected*, p. 45.

85. Lin Qingshan, *Fengyun*, p. 440.

expressions of admiration and loyalty). By July 1977, Deng had regained all previous positions. The price Hua extracted in return was yet another self-criticism (circulated throughout the Party), in which Deng inter alia assured Hua he would never seek to displace him (which turned out to be correct, but only technically).

Suspicion persisted between Deng and the younger man, and not without reason. Deng's first priority was the criticism of the remnants of the Gang of Four; he skillfully manipulated the situation to purge surviving Maoists and rehabilitate moderate cadres ousted during the Cultural Revolution, at the same time ending class struggle and removing the "class enemy" label from "landlords, rich peasants, counterrevolutionaries and bad elements." In the spring and summer of 1978 Deng staged a media debate on the "criteria of truth," in which he undermined the legitimacy of Hua's succession by criticizing dogmatic adherence to Mao's Thought as a manifestation of the personality cult. And when Democracy Wall protesters came to his support in the fall of 1978 with posters and tabloid publications embarrassing to Hua, Deng for the first and last time in his career defended their right to freedom of speech. Although Deng's big political breakthrough was achieved at the Third Plenum of the Eleventh CC in December 1978, he continued to use Hua as a foil for his reform movement for the next several years.[86] When the (rather poorly conceived) Great Leap Westward (*yang yao jin*), launched in February 1978 (which involved signing contracts with foreign joint venture partners worth several hundred million dollars), resulted in a budget deficit and an overheated economy (inflation rose from 2 percent in 1979 to 6 percent in 1980), Deng held Hua Guofeng responsible and joined forces with Chen Yun to impose economic retrenchment: About a thousand joint venture contracts (including the notorious Baoshan iron and steel complex) were rescinded, and state enterprise capital investment was actually cut in 1981. Meanwhile, the public trial of the Gang of Ten (the Gang of Four plus survivors of the Lin Biao plot) completed the demolition of Hua's ideological base. Using various face-saving "reforms" as a pretext, Deng removed Hua in successive stages from his premiership and then from his chairmanship of the Party (at the Twelfth Party Congress).[87] Yet he was never publicly humiliated and was even allowed to retain a seat on the CC.

---

86. See Shanbi Han, *Deng Xiaoping: Biography*, 2 vols. (Hong Kong, 1986–1987); Ching Hua Lee, *Deng*; Lin Qingshan, *Fengyun*.

87. Hua was induced to step down from his premiership as part of the separation of Party from government (i.e., eliminating "many hats"); he was divested of the CC chairmanship by eliminating the positions of chairman and vice-chairman and allowing the general secretary (then Hu Yaobang) to assume those functions.

Upon the elimination of residual Maoist opposition, Deng's reform program surged forward in the early 1980s, with the generally excellent economic results noted in Chapter 1. However Deng, like Mao, has managed to jeopardize the staying power of his legacy by some ill-considered actions during the terminal years of his reign.

Deng's Leadership Legacy

If we can say that Mao Zedong managed to synthesize the influence of traditional imperial statecraft with that of Marxist revolution, we can explore a similar synthesis in Deng's leadership: The two figures who shaped his views more than any other were the antipodal Liu Shaoqi and Mao Zedong. From Liu Shaoqi he seems to have derived his basic theoretical premises and policy preferences, known during Mao's heyday as "revisionist" and more recently rechristened "reform" ("revisionism" vanished from the Chinese political vocabulary in 1978). The roots of this theoretical and policy heritage were laid bare during the campaign to laud Deng Xiaoping Thought (*Deng Xiaoping sixiang*) that began in the late 1980s, accelerating in preparation for the Fourteenth Party Congress in October 1992. Here we learn that "the heart of Marxism" is to "develop productive forces" and raise living standards:

> We advocate communism. But what does that mean? It means the principle of from each according to his ability and to each according to his needs, which calls for highly developed productive forces and overwhelming material wealth. Therefore, the fundamental task for the socialist stage is to develop the productive forces. The superiority of the socialist system is demonstrated by faster and greater development of the productive forces than under the capitalist system. . . . Socialism means eliminating poverty. Pauperism is not socialism, still less communism.[88]

The impact of Mao Zedong is more difficult to encompass, because it is less obvious: In most respects Deng Xiaoping is Mao's antithesis. If Mao fits the textbook stereotype of a charismatic leader, launching vastly ambitious projects and deeming political vision or "standpoint" sine qua non, Deng's indifference to ideology has been immortalized in the

---

88. Deng, "Build Socialism with Chinese Characteristics" (June 30, 1984 talk with a Japanese delegation), in *Deng Xiaoping*, pp. 95–98; for a sampling of the Deng Thought campaign, see Jiang Zemin, "Accelerating Reform and Opening Up" (Political Report to the Fourteenth National Congress of the CPC), in *Beijing Review*, 35:43 (October 26–November 1, 1992), pp. 10–33; Liao Xuan, "Correctly Understand the Essence of Socialism: Understanding Gained by Studying Comrade Deng Xiaoping's Important Talks," *Qiushi* (Seeking Truth), no. 20 (October 16, 1992), pp. 6–9; and others.

Chinese saying, "White cat black cat (if it) catches rats, good cat"—and the resulting ideological secularization has facilitated a shift from totalitarian to authoritarian rule. Although Deng's commitment to the revolution cannot be questioned, he did not personify rebellion the way Mao (however ambivalently) did. To the contrary, Deng's experience as a target of "struggle" during the Cultural Revolution seems to have made him averse to any form of spontaneous mass participation. Taking to heart the charismatic injunction to forsake one's family in pursuit of the cause, Mao led a thoroughly Bohemian lifestyle (with sundry bedfellows) right to the end,[89] whereas Deng's family life, with wife, children, and numerous grandchildren on constant display, epitomizes Confucian *xiao*, or filialism. Whereas Mao hated bureaucracy and often flouted its rules, for example, by circumventing the Central Committee if its support was in question (after 1959 he did not even attend regular Politburo meetings),[90] by convening the Supreme State Conference or an ad hoc meeting of provincial Party chairmen or some other "expanded" session, or by turning directly to the masses (as in the Cultural Revolution), Deng inherited Liu's belief in bureaucratic institutionalization and the rule of law, and he has been highly skilled in advancing his program through bureaucratic channels.

Only during the later stages of Deng's career have certain points of tangency between Deng and Mao become evident, either due to unconscious personal identification or simply because Deng now occupies the position of PL. The two on which we shall focus are (1) the issue of succession, where Deng's concerns about the fragility of monocratic leadership stand in direct line of descent from those of his predecessor, and (2) the concrete implementation of arrangements for his *own* succession, where Deng has ensnared himself in the same sort of ambivalence that frustrated Chairman Mao.

Deng was alerted to the issue of succession during the Cultural Revolution, when Mao's precipitous attempt to promote a generation of young "rebels" to positions of influence forced him to face the prospect of a protracted insurrectionary future—as in 1975 when he overheard Wang Hongwen reconcile himself to exile with the thought that the radicals could afford to wait another decade before reckoning accounts.[91]

---

89. See Salisbury, *New Emperors*; see also Roger Faligot and Remi Kauffer, *The Chinese Secret Service*, trans. Christine Donougher (London: Headline, 1989), p. 216 et passim.

90. David Shambaugh, in a speech to the Center for Chinese Studies, University of California, Berkeley, on April 2, 1993.

91. Deng, "Senior Cadres Should Take the Lead in Maintaining and Enriching the Party's Fine Traditions" (November 2, 1979), in *Selected*, p. 218.

Political Leadership and Succession

Like Mao, Deng's solution to the likelihood of a succession crisis was premortem succession, but he proceeded to institutionalize such arrangements much more systematically. Particularly noteworthy in this regard have been his endeavors

1. To stimulate the circulation of elites. The Fifth Plenum of the Eleventh CC abolished the practice of guaranteed lifelong tenure for Party cadres, and two different retirement packages (*lixiu* for cadres, and *tuixiu* for others) were introduced. With the help of Chen Yun and Hu Yaobang, Deng has vigorously encouraged veterans to retire.[92] Most leading officials are now limited to two five-year terms, and there is a "normal" retirement age for officials.[93]
2. To disperse power. By dividing power into different spheres of competence (separating Party from government, and supplementing the CC with the CDIC and the CAC), and by spreading executive power among individual offices (the troika of premier, Party secretary, and chair of the CMC), Deng undertook to disperse power so that the whole system would not hinge on one man's mortality. Party rules now stipulate that decisions be taken by majority vote,

---

92. The effort to retire aging veterans began as soon as they had served their purpose in the inner-Party struggle against the "small gang of four" and other Maoists. At the Twelfth Party Congress (September 1–12, 1982), 172 veteran officials stepped down from the Politburo, the CC, and other front-line positions of leadership and took seats in the newly established CAC. The CCP's National Conference of Party Delegates held in September 1985 seems to have been particularly successful in its efforts at rejuvenation, retiring 131 senior veteran top-level leaders; half a dozen members of the Politburo (including Ye Jianying, Deng Yingchao, and Wang Zhen) had resigned a week earlier. These resignations created an opportunity for the conference to elect 179 younger leaders during the week-long session, including 56 Central Committee seats and 34 alternates. Fifty-six older officials were elected to the CAC and 33 to the Central Commission for Discipline. The conference was presided over by Hu Yaobang, signaling his special interest in this reform. A subsequent CC Plenum on September 24 elected 6 new full members to the Politburo (10 having retired), bringing the total to 22, and 5 to the Secretariat (which lost three of its old members), bringing the total to 10. See Richard Baum, "China in 1985: The Greening of the Revolution," *Asian Survey*, 26:1 (January 1986), pp. 30–54; also see Hong Yung Lee, "China's New Bureaucracy?" in Arthur L. Rosenbaum, ed., *State and Society in China: The Consequences of Reform* (Boulder: Westview Press, 1992), pp. 55–77. Although the purge of Hu Yaobang brought a temporary quietus to the rejuvenation campaign, at the Thirteenth Party Congress more than 90 CC members, including such senior leaders as Chen Yun, Li Xiannian, and Peng Zhen were induced to join Deng in leaving both Politburo and CC.
93. The plan adopted by the Standing Committee of the NPC called for requiring officials of ministerial rank to retire at 65, and vice-ministers and department directors at 60. The plan also called for creation of state councilors, to be equal in rank with vice-premiers, as counterparts to the CAC in the Party.

and intra-Party elections permit candidate lists to exceed the number of posts being filled.[94] The 1992–1993 appointment of Jiang Zemin as concurrent Party general secretary and chief of state is one of several indications that this effort has not been consistent at the top, but the holding of concurrent posts by individual leaders has been eliminated at all organizational levels below the center.
3. To coax veteran leaders into a less active role as "councillors" (in the Government) or "advisors" (in the Party). In 1982 Deng established a Central Advisory Commission (along with provincial counterparts) as a way of facilitating graceful and decorous career termination. This represents formalization and institutionalization of Mao's informal division of the leadership into two fronts—the first for routine business, the second a sort of advisory board concerned with more general issues. This aspect of the reform proved to be the most problematic, but may have been preferable to doing nothing at all; in any case, the CAC was abolished (as promised) at the Fourteenth Party Congress.
4. To try to deal with the question in generational rather than individual terms. Thus the "first echelon" (including Mao, Zhou Enlai, Kang Sheng, among others) referred to the revolutionary veterans; the "second echelon" (including Deng, Chen Yun, Peng Zhen, and others) referred to those who had risen to leadership since 1949; and the "third echelon" (e.g., Jiang Zemin, Li Peng, Qiao Shi) would carry the nation into the twenty-first century. This represents a bureaucratic systematization of Mao's search for "revolutionary successors"—while orienting the search to a quite different type of candidate. Though this policy is sometimes resented by other cadres as a vehicle for accelerated promotion of children of high cadres (the "princes' party," or *taizi dang*), it has resulted in a sweeping rejuvenation.

Yet in regard to arranging his own personal succession Deng has repeated an all-too-familiar pattern. First, he has failed to retire from politics, vacillating between withdrawal and spirited comebacks designed to ensure the viability of his reform legacy. Second (and relatedly), he has failed to make an irrevocable decision in favor of an heir apparent, falling rather into Mao's love-them-and-leave-them pattern. As in Mao's case,

---

94. This provision, first adopted at the Thirteenth Congress in October–November 1987, made it possible to oust Deng Liqun, who had reportedly hoped for promotion to Party secretary general. Gu Zhibin, *China Beyond Deng: Reform in the People's Republic of China* (London: McFarland, 1991), p. 98.

the result has been a classic succession crisis in which policy innovation is either paralyzed or gives way to policy zigzags. The recurrence of this pattern has reinforced gerontocratic tendencies in the short run and cast a shadow on the attempt to institutionalize the uncertainties of succession over the longer term.

First, let us consider Deng's handling of his own retirement. Like Mao, Deng dangled the prospect of succession before his cohorts long before making any concrete arrangements, speaking as early as 1979 of his sincere desire to step down soon: "As for me, I'd like to retire right now if the Party would let me. I really mean it. That's the truth. But in the interest of our cause as a whole I can't retire yet, nor do I think you would agree to my doing so."[95] And in 1980 he not only reiterated this wish but began what would prove to be his long march toward retirement by resigning from his post as vice-premier (part of a package deal that included Hua's "retirement" from the premiership).[96] He tied his retirement to the broader problem of generational succession, which served at once to promote more systemic reform of the tenure system and to delay his own case. Thus in 1982 he retired to the second front (at this point the reconstituted Party Secretariat under Hu Yaobang was to function as the first front), while retaining chairmanship of the CMC, the CAC, and a Politburo seat. At the Thirteenth Party Congress in 1987 he ceded chairmanship of the CAC to Chen Yun and resigned from the Politburo, while retaining chairmanship of the CMC and the right to pass on all Politburo decisions.[97] After using this power base to eliminate Zhao Ziyang at the Fourth Plenum and install Jiang Zemin as the next "leadership core,"[98] he finally relinquished his chairmanship of the CMC (also to Jiang) at the Fifth Plenum (November 1989). Finally, he seemed to have reached the end of the line; as he put it on June 16:

> When I talked with Comrades Li Peng and Yao Yilin, I stessed that after the new leadership establishes its working order, I will refrain from bothering about, or interfering in their work. . . . Of course, if you want to discuss something with me, I will not refuse you. But I will not do as I did in the past. . . . Now it is obvious that if I play too great a role, this will be harmful to our country and party. . . . The US policy for China is

---

95. Deng, "Senior Cadres Should Take the Lead," in *Selected*, p. 220.
96. Deng, "Interview with Oriana Fallaci," in Martin, ed., *Die Reform*, p. 72.
97. The constitution had to be amended to allow Deng to retain his chairmanship of the CMC without being a member of the Politburo. *RR*, November 19, 1987, p. 4.
98. "Deng Xiaoping's speech to members of the new Politburo Standing Committee" (June 16, 1989), in Michel Oksenberg, et al., eds., *Beijing Spring, 1989: Confrontation and Conflict* (Armonk, N.Y.: M. E. Sharpe, 1990), p. 383.

based on whether I fall ill, or die. Many countries in the world also base their China policy on my life. I realized this problem several years ago. It is unhealthy and dangerous to base the fate of a country on the prestige of one or two persons.[99]

Yet on September 4, the same day he submitted his resignation from the CMC to the Politburo Standing Committee, Deng made a *neibu* speech in which he hinted that Jiang Zemin was not yet qualified to assume supreme power and lacked military experience: "If I retire now and live on, I can still play a role, because I am known to many people in the world and they take me into account in their relations with China." This time, however, his colleagues seemed to ignore him, as Chen Yun (with considerable accuracy) blamed the Tiananmen crackdown and China's consequent international ostracism on him and proceeded to use this to strengthen his own pro-planning and slow growth wing of the leadership. On as many as four different occasions over the next two years Deng attempted to reinsert himself into the policy process on behalf of more rapid growth.[100] But it was not until making his "trip south" (*nanxun*) in the summer of 1992, interspersed by several speaking engagements that he finally induced the national press to publicize, that he was able to reassert his leadership and reemerge as the dominant figure at the October 1992 Fourteenth Party Congress. The pattern of retirement followed by resentment of being pushed aside and a resurgent comeback is reminiscent of Mao's last days.

The striking feature of Deng's retirement pattern was not his ambivalence but his seeming success at having his cake and eating it too, retiring from formal positions as an example to other senior colleagues, at the same time clinging to informal power. Yet by playing this sort of shell game, Deng has thoroughly obscured the relationship between informal and formal power—a relationship blurred from the outset by the fact that Deng never claimed the highest formal positions, because of his oppo-

---

99. Ibid.
100. In a talk with Jiang Zemin, Yao Yilin, and Gu Mu in the summer of 1990, Deng complained of obstruction by "some old comrades"; on October 7 he met with Jiang, Li Peng, Yang Shangkun, Wan Li, Wang Zhen, Bo Yibo, Song Renqiong, and Xi Zhongxun and again called for an acceleration of reform in the context of preparations for the Eighth Five-Year Plan (1991–1995) and Ten-Year Plan (1991–1999). In February 1991 he met and joined forces with Shanghai's Zhu Rongji during his trip south for the spring festival; Zhu had several articles published in *Jiefang ribao* (Liberation Daily) (*JFRB*) under the pseudonym "Huangfu Ping," calling for a faster tempo. At the end of September–October 1991, Deng started a new push to promote reform in the preparations for the Eighth Plenum of the Thirteenth CC. In April 1992, there was a clash between Deng and Chen Yun (which ended inconclusively) at an informal summit meeting in Beijing. See *Zheng ming* (Contending) (June 1992), p. 11.

sition to the "cult." Thus he backed into power like a crab, refusing the Party chairmanship when it was his to take in June 1981, instead abolishing the position outright. This has tended to undercut the point of retirement, tacitly signaling to other senior cadres that they, too, might step down from their posts without actually giving up anything. Thus the diffusion of power at the top has been purchased at the cost of considerable uncertainty over the division of labor in general and, more specifically, over which position a potential successor should try to succeed to.

The second noteworthy feature of Deng's personal retirement scenario concerns his use (and abuse) of his heirs apparent. As in the case of Mao, Deng exploited succession as a tactic to motivate his junior colleagues during the twilight of his reign, abruptly shifting course if an heir apparent sought to seize power before he was ready to yield it. Whereas Mao tended to use "favorites" (such as Jiang Qing) to push pet projects he could not trust to formal members of the bureaucracy,[101] Deng has been prone to use his heir apparent in this manner, emitting broad hints of his policy preferences and expecting him to carry the ball. Moreover, Mao tried to protect his favorites, whereas Deng has been quite willing to use his heir apparent as an expendable scapegoat if the gambit fails. This was the fate of both Hu Yaobang and Zhao Ziyang.

Hu Yaobang, the former long-time head of the China Youth League and a man with a carefully cultivated retinue of younger followers, hearkened to Deng's comments about the need for rejuvenation and quickly became his point man on this issue. It was Hu who chaired the CCP's National Conference of Delegates, September 18–23, 1985, that retired a rather large proportion of the Central Committee, and he signaled his intent to continue rejuvenation apace in the upcoming Thirteenth Party Congress.[102] This reportedly antagonized many of the senior cadres at whom the policy was aimed. Compounding this misstep was Hu's

---

101. See my article, "Bases of Power in Chinese Politics," pp. 26–61.
102. Two million of the nation's 22 million Party officials would have stepped down by the end of 1986, he said, and 15 percent of the 210 CC members would be replaced by new appointees under the age of sixty. This was part of a coordinated campaign that included retirements from the State Council and NPC as well. Kwan Ha Yim, ed., *China Under Deng* (New York: Facts on File, 1991), pp. 206–207. "[We] must make up our mind to solve the problem of younger cadres in the 13th Party Congress next year," he proposed in 1986. "One third of the members and alternate members of the CC should be retired, coupled with 110 to 120 new comrades. Among these 110 to 120 new comrades, 80–90 percent should be around 50 years old." He reaffirmed his position in a talk with a delegation of journalists from the *Wall Street Journal* in October 1986. Yang Zhongmei, *Hu Yaobang Pingzhuan* (The biography of Hu Yaobang) (Hong Kong: Benma Chubanshe, 1989), pp. 222, 224, as cited in Peter N. S. Lee, "Informal Politics and Leadership in Post-Mao China" (Paper presented at the Forty-fourth Annual Meeting of the Association of Asian Studies, April 2–5, 1992, Washington, D.C.).

earlier suggestion that Deng Xiaoping himself should retire—a proposal he then leaked to the media.[103]

In the summer of 1986, succession politics became a political football in the popular reaction to economic retrenchment at a time when an anticipated new stage of reform failed to materialize (for a more detailed analysis, see Chapter 4). It is unclear who launched the drive for "political reform," but Deng climbed on the bandwagon in a June 1986 speech to the Politburo Standing Committee.[104] This high-profile opening unleashed a freshet of suggestions from the country's intellectuals on the conceivable dimensions and modalities of political reform, stoking expectations for a new breakthrough at the Sixth Plenum of the Twelfth CC. Instead, the plenum (which met for only one day—September 28, 1986—following sharp conflicts during the five weeks of preparatory meetings at Beidaiho and five days of formal preparation in Beijing) consigned the issue to a committee for "study" while approving a call for ideological revival entitled "Resolution of the CCP CC on the Guiding Principles for Building a Socialist Society with an Advanced Culture and Ideology." The reform wing of the Party was particularly incensed by this document's denunciation of bourgeois liberalization and sought to have it deleted, but it was retained at the insistence of none other than Deng Xiaoping. This untoward turn of events incited student protests, beginning December 5 and 9 on college campuses in Hefei and Wuhan and spreading to the capital by the end of the month. These demonstrations culminated in reported instances of traffic disruption and vandalism and were suppressed in early January.

We have noted that Deng was at least as guilty as Hu in initiating the

---

103. In early 1986, Hu went to Deng and asked him to give up his power once and for all: "Be an example. I cannot work efficiently while you are still in power." Not too long afterward, a reporter from the *Washington Post* interviewed Hu. "Who is going to replace Deng as chair of the Central Military Commission?" he was asked. "We will solve this problem once and for all at the Party's 13th Party Congress," Hu was quoted saying. "No one can be in a post forever." Pang Pang, *The Death of Hu Yaobang*, trans. Si Ren (Honolulu: University of Hawaii Press, Center for Chinese Studies, 1989), p. 42.

104. In his June 28 speech, Deng called for withdrawal of the Party from excessive interference in administration of the economy (complaining that "we advocate decentralized power but they take it back" by forming production "companies") and called for "reform of the political structure," asserting that "if we only carry out economic reform and not political reform we will not be able to carry the reform of economic structure through to its end." Beyond criticizing "unwieldy and overstaffed organizations and dilatory workstyle," Deng did not elaborate further on what he had in mind by reform of the political structure; but by making economic reform contingent upon political reform the latter acquired a prominence it had never been afforded before. See my article, "China in 1986: Domestic Politics," in John S. Major and Anthony J. Kane, *China Briefing, 1987* (Boulder: Westview Press, 1987), pp. 1–27.

movement that led to this turn of events. Whether Hu Yaobang defended the demonstrators in camera or simply became the scapegoat because of his zeal in pursuing the retirement of his seniors (including Deng) may never be known,[105] but in any case his fate was reportedly decided at an enlarged meeting of the CMC on December 11–25, 1986, and at an "expanded" Politburo meeting on January 16 he was forced to resign, along with the leadership of the CC Propaganda Department; several of Hu's intellectual protégés were also censured and purged from the Party—at Deng's personal behest.[106] Like the group that had met at Beidaiho to launch the campaign against spiritual pollution in the fall of 1984, or to draft the resolution on spiritual pollution in the summer of 1986, the group that decided on Hu Yaobang's resignation was dominated by senior cadres without formal Politburo positions: 17 members of the CAC and 2 members of the CDC nearly outnumbered the 18 Politburo members and 2 alternates present; the summary of complaints was read by another nonmember, Bo Yibo, vice-chair of the CAC.[107] Contrary to the constitution, the decision was announced without CC ratification (there was no mention of a CC meeting during the first nine months of 1987).

By the time of the Thirteenth Party Congress in November 1987, the reformers appeared to have recouped from the setback of early 1987, realigning the succession by shifting Zhao Ziyang from the premiership to Party general secretary and muting the campaign against bourgeois liberalization. The conservative Li Peng was selected to replace Zhao, reportedly at the sponsorship of Deng Yingchao (his foster mother), but with the full support of Zhao Ziyang (who mistakenly calculated that Li could be more easily manipulated than the more senior reformer Wan Li). Deng formally retired from the CC and the Politburo, though he still retained chairmanship of the CMC and continued to operate as the power behind the scenes—Zhao made this arrangement public when he met with

---

105. According to a former secretary, Hu himself suspected the scapegoat hypothesis. After Deng criticized him for mishandling the issue and told him he was no longer suitable to be the goalkeeper of the Party, Hu went back to his office. When a friend dropped by to elicit his reaction to Deng's criticism, he exploded: "Isn't it simply because I have frequented those old comrades' homes less than others?" he asked. "Rectifying me, getting rid of me; this is an outrageous practice from the Cultural Revolution." Peng Pang, *Death*, pp. 35, 43.

106. "I read the speech of Fang Lizhi," Deng stated on January 20; "no Party member speaks that way! Why should we keep that type of person in the Party? . . . he must be pushed out!" Deng, "Central Document No. 1: Put an End to Student Unrest" (Based on Talk in Central meeting on December 30, 1986), as trans. in Martin, ed., *Die Reform*, p. 148.

107. See Yang Zhongmei, *Hu Yaobang: A Chinese Biography*, trans. William A. Wycoff (Armonk, N.Y.: M. E. Sharpe, 1988), pp. 155–160.

Gorbachev shortly before his own purge.[108] Zhao moved to enlist Hu's intellectual and bureaucratic constituency at this point, for as a provincial official he lacked a national network.

But like Hu, Zhao was undone by Deng's erratic and irresponsible initiatives. In the spring of 1988, Deng surprised everyone by suddenly directing the government to forge ahead with price reform, announcing that it was better to have great pain for a short time than to protract the ordeal. Zhao seemed taken aback and did not express his support until five days after Deng's public endorsement.[109] Having embarked on this policy, Zhao perhaps overcommitted himself, bringing with him to Beidaiho a bold plan called the "New Order for the Socialist Commodity Economy," which foresaw ending all state price controls within four to five years while devaluing currency to encourage exports. But price reform stimulated a run on the banks and a consumption binge that drove prices up at an unprecedented rate. At this point Deng shifted his support from Zhao to Li Peng: "I will protect no one. Anyone who isn't doing a good job should be dismissed."[110] Zhao's proposal was rejected by a majority, and Chen Yun moved to dismiss him from his position. The motion was not put to a vote, however, and the meeting adjourned till mid-August. Upon reconvention, a compromise was arranged: Zhao could stay, but must relinquish his portfolio. Zhao would be obliged to make a self-criticism, and his role in economic policy would be curtailed—Yao Yilin and Li Peng would henceforth share responsibility for economics, Qiao Shi would supervise Party affairs, and Hu Qili would handle culture, propaganda, and ideology. Deng agreed, and the Third Plenum of the Thirteenth CC (September 29–October 1 in Beijing) formalized the arrangement and put the brakes on further economic reform under the slogan Deepen the Reforms, Improve the Economic Environment, and Restore Economic Order.

---

108. Although that was the first time it was made public in such explicit form, it had been revealed previously in interviews and could not be considered a state secret. In a July 1984 interview, Zhao stated that both the Party Secretariat and the State Council looked ultimately to Deng, who belonged to neither of those bodies. Before Deng decided to retire from the Politburo at the Thirteenth Congress, Zhao said again: "The role of Xiaoping does not lie in whether he stays in the Politburo. He is the policy-maker and the actual helmsman." A. Doak Barnett, *The Making of Foreign Policy in China: Structure and Process* (Boulder: Westview Press, 1985), p. 9; *Zheng ming* (Hong Kong), no. 122 (December 1987), p. 9.

109. Deng launched the idea in a talk with the Democratic People's Republic of Korea leader, O Chin-u, on May 18, 1988; the Politburo then held a meeting on May 30–June 1 to confirm its support of Deng's policy of moving ahead quickly in price reform. Xinhua, May 19, 1988, as trans. in *FBIS-China*, May 19, 1988.

110. See Dittmer, "China in 1988: The Crisis of Incomplete Reform," *Asian Survey*, 30:1 (January 1990), pp. 25–42.

Zhao, having lost control of the economic portfolio (which was in any case now under control of conservatives sponsoring a policy of retrenchment for which Zhao had little enthusiasm), launched a counterattack in the cultural sphere. He mobilized Hu's old intellectual constituency by permitting or perhaps even encouraging various theoretical meetings and symposia, the most prominent of which was a December 1988 discussion of the theoretical implications of the reforms initiated by the Third Plenum of the Eleventh CC.[111] Meanwhile, Zhao's conservative opponents tried to finish him off, holding him responsible for the still-spiraling inflation (which conservative retrenchment failed to bring under control). As in 1986, the protests of the intellectuals proved to be a dwindling political asset: Their public petitions only infuriated the senior veterans, now determined to have Zhao's head. Deng insisted that the issue be postponed until after Gorbachev's scheduled May summit visit, to keep up appearances. But (again, as in 1986) intellectual ferment (in addition to the fortuitous death of Hu Yaobang) precipitated sympathetic student protest, this time vaguely focused around the demand for greater democracy. The coincidence of protest with economic discontent from high inflation and the rampant corruption it stimulated lent these protests overwhelming popular support, and they spread like a prairie fire through China's major cities.

The leadership split again over how to react to these demonstrations. The decisionmaking council that emerged from the shadows during this crisis made a complete mockery of Deng's attempt to institutionalize succession arrangements by letting the first generation fade away. To muster sufficient power for the purge of Hu Yaobang in January 1987 Deng had been obliged to call senior veterans back out of retirement, and they continued to participate in the policy process. By dint of their seats on the CAC they could sit in on extended Politburo or Central Work Conferences, where they could throw their considerable weight into the fray and, according to some evidence, cast votes;[112] even if they lacked any formal position at all they might attend by invitation and in any case

---

111. Susan Shirk, *The Political Logic of Economic Reform in China* (Unpublished ms., San Diego, University of California, Political Science Department, March 1991).

112. I base this inference on the fact that authoritative decisions issue from such "expanded" meetings, at which nonmembers are reported to play an influential role. Thus an expanded Politburo meeting was held May 22–24 at which Deng Xiaoping, Chen Yun, Li Xiannian, Peng Zhen, Yang Shangkun, and Wang Zhen—all "older veterans with great prestige" (but only one of whom is a Politburo member)—decided to reaffirm the hard-line April 26 editorial and to denounce the May 4 speech. *Far Eastern Economic Review*, June 15, 1989, p. 13; *Ming Bao*, May 30, 1989.

could always buttonhole former colleagues informally.[113] Their status, without high formal posts but with great prestige and informal influence, allowed them to wield power without responsibility. Though not necessarily career military officials, all were Long March veterans with much more extensive experience in the use of violence than their younger colleagues. No doubt their views on reform varied, but all were inclined to be skeptical of new policy departures and to place a high priority on professions of due respect for the status hierarchy of which they formed the apex.

It is important to point out that their power was by no means the inevitable by-product of some deeply rooted cultural reverence for age: As in previous succession struggles—Deng Xiaoping versus Hu Yaobang, Mao Zedong versus Lin Biao or Liu Shaoqi—there have been those in the younger generation quite prepared to put the old people on the shelf and leave them there. Two political factors were decisive in this case. First, as the price of their retirement, the senior veterans had extracted the right to name their successors, who were expected to remain loyal to them.[114] Second, and more specifically, a secret agreement was made at the Thirteenth Party Congress that despite Deng's retirement from the Politburo, all major decisions must receive his approval. These two factors implied that the Thirteenth Congress was not quite the watershed it had seemed to outside observers at the time. The blanket assumption that younger Politburocrats were more sympathetic to reform was not reliable—one had to take patron-client ties into account.

At first it seemed that Zhao would be able to turn the demonstrations to his advantage; however, although the demonstrators supported Zhao's proreform stance, they not only declined his entreaties to vacate the square but took advantage of his soft line to metastasize their protest. Having by now exhausted his patience with Zhao's soft line, Deng ordered a harsh crackdown, once again (as in June 1988) reasoning that it would be best if it were done quickly.[115] Thus, once again, Zhao's own

---

113. In estimated rank order of prestige, this "sitting committee" consisted of Chen Yun (born in 1905), chairman of the CAC; Yang Shangkun (born 1907), chief of state and executive vice-chair of the CMC; Li Xiannian (born 1909), chair of the CPPCC; Wang Zhen (born 1908), vice–chief of state and CMC vice-chair; Bo Yibo (born 1908), executive vice-chair of the CAC; Song Renqiong (born 1909), vice-chair of the CAC; Peng Zhen (born 1902), retired former chair of the NPC Standing Committee; and Deng Yingchao (born 1904), widow of Zhou Enlai, former Politburo member and former chair of the CPPCC National Committee.

114. Thus Zhao Ziyang was beholden to Deng, Yao Yilin was beholden to Chen Yun, Li Peng was beholden to Deng Yingchao (and Chen Yun), Qiao Shi was beholden to Peng Zhen; Hu Qili, a veteran of Hu Yaobang's China Youth League group, was "adopted" by Zhao.

115. About Deng's personal responsibility for the decision there can be little doubt. When George Bush called after the massacre, Deng responded enthusiastically: "It appears that we have created new methods to deal with domestic insurrections and student demonstrations.

sympathizers succeeded in discrediting a sitting Party secretary for excessive liberalism and eliminating him from the succession scenario. Although Zhao was informally obliged to step aside after the declaration of martial law on May 20 (which he refused to support), his purge was not formalized until an enlarged Politburo meeting was held June 19–21, followed by the Fourth Plenum of the Thirteenth CC two days later. The latter was also an "expanded" session, attended by a full complement of the CAC and the CDIC, along with other "leading comrades from relevant departments" (a total of 557 participants in all), permitting no doubt about the outcome. The leading reformers to fall in Zhao's wake were Hu Qili (dismissed from the Politburo Standing Committee and the Secretariat), Rui Xingwen, and Yan Mingfu (both dismissed from the Secretariat).

After reemerging briefly to congratulate the storm troops and preside over the Fourth Plenum, Deng lapsed into a less salient position for much of the next two years. Having reneged on two heirs apparent, he tried for the third time to groom a successor in the person of Jiang Zemin. Jiang, however, feeling understandably insecure, became a political chameleon, trying to please every grouping within the leadership; by 1992 Deng had become so exasperated with him that he reportedly invited Liu Huaqing to take over his seat as chair of the CMC (Liu wisely declined). Meanwhile, Li Peng consolidated his hold on the economic portfolio, while chairing the Party's Leading Group on Foreign Affairs.

As of November 1993, Deng's position seems secure. Many who had previously distanced themselves from him have come back to his support as the strongest surviving advocate of reform—partly because he himself had eliminated all other conceivable contenders. Yet the enigma of his succession remains unresolved. Jiang Zemin's successorship seems assured, as he has been so careful not to offend anyone that his profile offers no target, but over the longer term this is unlikely to prove sufficient. Yang Shangkun, who with his half brother, Yang Baibing, had intended to move into Deng's position of informal strongman, was suddenly dumped in the fall of 1992, reportedly because he schemed to shed the blame for Tiananmen on Deng, once he passed away. For the next six months the military was subjected to its most sweeping purge since the fall of Lin Biao, in an apparent effort to eradicate the Yang family faction. Reformers' hopes have begun migrating to Zhu Rongji, a relatively recent arriviste among top CCP elites, who has a high reputation for competence. Li Ruihuan, the ex-carpenter and mayor of Tianjin, assigned since

---

It is of world significance and many countries will learn from us. It's better to have brief rather than prolonged suffering. What Hu Yaobang couldn't solve in several years, we settled in a few days." Pang Pang (pseud.), *The Death of Hu Yaobang*.

Tiananmen with the unenviable propaganda portfolio, seems to have been sidetracked, though Qiao Shi remains a contender. Meanwhile, the Party committee assigned to study the case of Zhao Ziyang returned a surprisingly lenient verdict (an outcome conceivable only with Deng's approval), suggesting that the "small cannon" wishes to keep that option alive.[116]

It seems likely that for the rest of Deng's life the Chinese leadership will be stalled in a Janus-like stance, eager to move forward yet guarding its rear. Deng's responsibility for the crackdown freezes the regime in an embarrassing international position, despite a generally adroit foreign policy; his paranoia about mass participation has poisoned China's Hong Kong policy and made Chinese public opinion a blank slate. The outlook is even more complex than it was during the late Maoist period, for it is not only a question of Deng personally but of the whole "sitting committee" of gerontocrats, who may follow Deng's lead and intercede at will (particularly after Deng passes from the scene) to correct any perceived deviations and rectify the succession lineup. Whereas our last glimpse of the Great Helmsman was of a "poor old man standing alone," we bid tentative adieu to Deng as a tough old man in a hurry, still eager to spur the prodigious growth rates on which his posthumous reputation will rest, while resisting to the end their political corollary.

Conclusions

We would conclude that the Chinese political system has consistently produced leadership of a very high level of efficacy and that it has been moving toward greater wisdom. Mao Zedong left his country stronger; Deng Xiaoping will leave it richer. Mao was able to transform profoundly the ownership system, the kinship structure, the class structure, and the political culture during his tenure. Deng's impact has been no less profound in a quite different direction, involving an opening to the outside world, a redistribution of usufruct and management rights, the proliferation of markets and entrepreneurial enterprises of diverse size and variety, and continued devolution of power from the center to regional authorities. Finally, both leaders have held the country together in the face of divisive pressures that might otherwise have turned it into a "sheet of loose sand." Yet any balance sheet must also record that monocratic leadership has been at times extraordinarily oppressive, harsh, and even totalitarian, resulting in massive suffering and death. The elimination of opposition that made the CCP so efficacious has also made it pos-

---

116. See Willy Wo-Lap Lam's article in *South China Morning Post*, April 29, 1992.

sible for the leadership to drive the nation to extremes before an error is recognized, with the result that the system has moved forward by lurching from one extreme to the other.

The fact that Mao and Deng came to represent opposing ideological and policy lines during their lifetimes has obscured certain underlying similarities between them, particularly in handling paramount leadership. Both men deem themselves Marxists and have been willing to sacrifice a great many lives without qualm on behalf of that value system, but neither has hesitated to modify Marxist ideology in major (albeit quite different) ways to suit his view of the national interest. Without having pursued Mao's esoteric historical research into the careers of his imperial forbears, Deng seemed to define his position much as Mao did, declining to form his own faction but assuming a position above the fray, playing rival "mountaintops" off against each other and interceding to arbitrate the issue.[117] Like Mao, who often used the guerrilla tactic of "luring them in deep," that is, allowing the foe to become fully extended before striking (e.g., his absences during the Gao-Rao controversy, his semi-retirement after the Great Leap), Deng has skillfully alternated periods of active advocacy with long periods of withdrawal from the political process (e.g., his disappearance during the 1959 Lushan confrontation, or the Party purge preparatory to the Twelfth Party Congress; his semiabdication in the post-Tiananmen period). Despite a period in the late 1970s and early 1980s in which he sought to undermine Mao via a critique of dogmatism and the cult of personality, since the purge of Hua Guofeng and the Gang trial Deng has sought increasingly to identify himself publicly with Mao, thereby preempting possible opposition under that flag.[118] Finally, notwithstanding his commitment to institutionalization, Deng has, like Mao, been willing to set that aside and resort to informal means if the stakes seemed high enough. These means included not only factional intrigue, as in the 1976 conspiracy against the Gang of Four, but reliance on close relatives (in Mao's case, his wife, Jiang Qing, and

---

117. This seems to have been Mao's strategy in the Gao-Rao incident, as well as during the struggle between the Gang of Four and the moderates that followed the death of Lin Biao. Throughout much of the 1980s, Deng likewise balanced radical reformers such as Hu Yaobang and Zhao Ziyang against the more conservative wing led by Chen Yun.

118. In Shanghai, a poster was printed in which Deng towers over crowds of soldiers and technicians just as Mao did in the posters of the Cultural Revolution. In 1983 the country's newspapers carried a photo of Deng swimming in the ocean—obviously patterned after the shot of Mao swimming across the Yangtze River that inaugurated the Cultural Revolution. Deng wrote the commemorative plaque for Mao's birthplace in his own calligraphy. Deng is also credited with the "enrichment and development" of Mao's Thought in "the new era," in which modernization is the main contradiction to be addressed. See Tiziano Terzani, *Behind the Forbidden Door: Travels in China* (London: Allen and Unwin, 1986), pp. 239–242.

nephew, Mao Yuanzi; in Deng's case, his daughters, Deng Nan and Deng Rong, who frequently accompany him and reportedly write some of his speeches).

Chen Yun once said that Mao's reputation would have stood much higher had he died earlier, and if Deng had truly retired at the age of 80 as he promised, his own reputation would be more secure. Having risen on a critique of Mao's personality cult, Deng has suspended all criticism of the Chairman (poor precedent for his own posthumous handling) and launched his own cult.[119] Having brought Hua Guofeng down for his "feudal" succession ("With you in charge, I am at ease"), Deng has not relinquished the Caesarean prerogative to select his own successor—nor to change his mind! Once a cautious and deliberate bureaucratic broker,[120] Deng as PL became more like Mao in his willingness to throw caution to the winds, as in his handling of price reform in 1988, or in his inclination to push rapid growth (in 1992 even calling for a "great leap") contra Chen Yun.

Yet that should not obscure his very real achievement. Through secularization he has relieved China of ideological totalitarianism, allowing a real distinction to arise between a public that is more public and a private that is more private (see Chapter 4). He salvaged the elite from chaos and

---

119. The *Selected Works of Deng Xiaoping (1975–1982)* appeared in Chinese in 1983 (and in English translation in 1984), in the same format in which the works of Mao and other major Chinese leaders (Liu, Zhou) had been published, and in 1992 a 2-volume *Treasury of Deng Xiaoping's Thought* appeared. The growing importance of Deng Thought was demonstrated by the effusive homage to Deng's theory of "building socialism with Chinese characteristics" at the Fourteenth CCP Congress in October 1992. In his political report, Jiang Zemin called Deng's theories a "magic weapon" for keeping the CCP on the correct path, hailing his "theoretical courage in opening up new perspectives for Marxism" and his "historical contribution" to the continued development of Chinese socialist thought and practice." Jiang Zemin, "Accelerating Reform and Opening Up," Political Report to the 14th National Congress of the CPC, in *Beijing Review,* 35:43 (October 26–November 1, 1992), pp. 10–33. The phrase "Deng Xiaoping Thought" has now become commonplace in the official political vocabulary of the PRC, and a flood of articles and books extolling and expounding on Deng's thoughts on a wide range of topics appeared in the late 1980s. Publishing houses have launched series devoted to research on Deng's life and thought, such as the 20 volumes announced by the Liaoning People's Publishing House in 1991. Xinhua (NCNA) (1991), "Beijing Holds Forum on Publishing Deng Xiaoping Life, Thoughts Series," June 15, 1991, in *FBIS-China,* June 16, 1991, 91–120, p. 18. A national "academic seminar" on Deng's economic theories was held in Chengdu in July 1991. Shu Zhu and Xiao Qi, "Roundup of Academic Seminar on Deng Xiaoping's Economic Thinking," *Guangming ribao,* July 5, 1991, in *FBIS-China,* July 6, 1991, 91–140, pp. 45–46. See also Li Junru, "Deng Xiaoping's 'Theory of Socialism with Chinese Characteristics,'" *JFRB,* June 5, 1991, in *FBIS-China,* June 6, 1991, 91–113, pp. 24–28.

120. Certainly he has been among the sharpest critics of Mao's recklessness. "Our experience has shown that one cannot push forward too fast or too hastily," he told the Liberian chief of state in May 1982. "We went too fast before and thus made a series of mistakes—left mistakes, as we say." In Martin, ed., *Die Reform,* p. 36.

humiliation and restored its prestige, and he freed the population to actualize more fully its keen business acumen. China has been opened to the outside world as never before, with perhaps the most profound repercussions of all.

Although Deng Xiaoping was not a bold theoretical or organizational innovator, his mission was (like Confucius!) to restore. Routinization—the establishment of rational patterns of leadership via constitutional engineering—was Deng's answer to the problem of impulsive and erratic charismatic leadership. If we distinguish here between institutionalization and depersonalization, the former has been his strong suit. The leadership organs have been put back on regular meeting schedules, their agendas and personnel arrangements placed on a businesslike footing, and some notion of division of labor and accountability among them has been introduced. Meetings of the State Council and the NPC Standing Committee have become more frequent and regular. The Thirteenth Congress in 1987 even announced a system of regular meetings of the Politburo, its Standing Committee, and the Central Secretariat, and a system whereby the Politburo Standing Committee would report regularly to the Politburo, and the Politburo report to the Central Committee.[121] Institutionalization has entailed some depersonalization as well, visible, for example, in the introduction of fixed terms of office, "normal" retirement ages, and the appearance of dissenting votes at acclamatory hearings (e.g., Li Peng's nomination as premier at the Eighth NPC in 1993 drew an unprecedented 10 percent negative vote).

But on the whole depersonalization is likely to remain a challenge for the next generation of leadership. Again, succession has been the major stumbling block. The price paid to incumbents to step aside has been a "personalization of the succession process," in which succession becomes a private transaction between incumbent leaders and their personal favorites.[122] This has permitted an informally based hierarchy to arise that is no less authoritarian for having divested itself of official responsibility for its acts. Without complete routinization, leadership transitions will continue to assume the "succession crisis" pattern—albeit alleviated by greater civility. In view of the cultural importance of leadership example in China, Deng Xiaoping's obvious reluctance to "go quietly into that good night" must bear a large share of the onus.

Deng Xiaoping's case demonstrates that formal reforms of tenure

---

121. Chen Yizhi, et al., eds., *Zhengzhi tizhi gaige jianghua* (Talks on political restructuring) (Beijing: People's Publishing, 1987), pp. 44–45. Thus between the time of the Party Congress (October 1987) and June 1988, the Politburo held nine publicly announced plenary meetings.

122. Hsi-sheng Ch'i, *Politics of Disillusionment: The Chinese Communist Party Under Deng Xiaoping, 1978–1989* (Armonk, N.Y.: M. E. Sharpe, 1991).

arrangements may not go far enough: If the PL remains PL despite some facile reshuffling of formal roles, the problem remains—now immune from legal solutions. Our brief review of Deng's efforts at constitutional engineering arrived at a very mixed picture. Democratization, or other sweeping structural reforms, would constitute a sufficient but not necessary condition for stabilizing the CCP's leadership arrangements. A few relatively limited rule changes could have considerable impact. One useful reform would involve endowing the second-tier leadership (viz., the CC) with the authority to vote out a sitting PL and elect a replacement. Whereas the Soviet Union made a major step forward in this direction decades ago with the electoral deposal of Khrushchev, nothing of this sort has happened in the CCP since at least 1935 (Hua Guofeng, we would argue, was never a PL). An even more modest but probably helpful procedural reform would be the elimination of "expanded" sessions or at least a requirement that an "executive" session (formal members only) be convened for important decisions. The current situation is a highly irregular one in which important decisions are reached *only* in expanded sessions.

4

Emergence of a Public Sphere?

The demonstrations centered at Tiananmen Square in April–May 1989, the largest such spontaneously assembled gatherings since the founding of the People's Republic, were (thanks to the demonstrators' excellent access to international media) relevant not only to China but to the world—and particularly to the Communist world. Although the popular upsurge that swept through Eastern Europe later the same year also had its indigenous causes, its leaders were aware of and inspired by the Chinese precedent. Yet while the Eastern European masses (and, later, the Soviet masses) went on to prevail over their regimes, the first and by far the largest such spontaneous movement in Beijing came to a bloody and tragic end. Why was China such an exception? One of the reasons most frequently advanced is the absence of "civil society" in China. Poland had its Solidarity, East Germany had its Civic Forum, Hungary had its Petofi Club, but the Chinese demonstrators were unable to form a cohesive organization able to maintain discipline within its ranks and negotiate responsibly with the CCP.

Yet the victims of the crackdown did not die in vain, for Tiananmen also represents considerable progress toward civil organization. China has little historical precedent for a civil society as defined in the West, but then this notion has evolved over historical time even here, not reaching its present form until the onset of modernity. Chinese thinkers have long related to the "public," however, cherishing the concept even more single-mindedly than in the West. We thus begin below by contrasting Chinese and Western concepts of the public (it should be noted in this context that our chief interest is in the contemporary mainland, or "Chinese Communist," concept of the public, though in trying to explain that we occasionally venture more sweeping generalizations). We then show how politics interacts with the public-private dimension in the PRC.

Finally, we turn to the impact of reform on the Chinese Communist concept of the public, culminating in a discussion of the origins of Tiananmen.

Conceptual Background

The concept of "publicity" (*gongkai*) in contemporary China is derived from the age-old concept of the "public" (*gong*).[1] In the Confucian classics a prominent polarity exists between the terms "self" (*zi*) and "public" (*gong*), which is linked to an opposition between selfishness (*ziside; zixin*) and selflessness (*wu zi; wuzixindi*). This is part of the Chinese antithesis between *yang* and *yin*, outer and inner, male and female, bright and dark, sun and moon, heaven and earth, and so forth—sets of polarities that actually antedate Confucius, going back at least as far as the *Book of Changes* and most likely to the very roots of Chinese civilization. The juxtaposition corresponds to the Western "public-private" distinction, though it is more invidious. Selflessness is lauded for having the interests of all the people in mind, as selfishness is condemned for a cognitive or even a moral failure to perceive the self in terms of a more comprehensive social organism to which the person's fate is inextricably connected—such that "the universe and all things form one body."[2] Depending on the context and thinker, this larger entity is described as encompassing a network of social relationships, the physical matter that composes all things, and the natural patterns to which all things are subject.[3] The one-sided depiction

---

1. See Chang Hao, *Liang Ch'i-ch'ao and Intellectual Transition in China* (Cambridge: Harvard University Press, 1971); I-fan Cheng, "'Kung' as an Ethos in Late Nineteenth Century China: The Case of Wang Hsien-ch'ien (1842–1918)," in Paul A. Cohen and John Schrecker, eds., *Reform in Nineteenth-Century China* (Cambridge: East Asian Research Center, Harvard University, 1976); Prasenjit Duara, *Culture, Power, and the State: North China Villages, 1900–1942* (Stanford: Stanford University Press, 1988); Keith Schoppa, *Chinese Elites and Political Change: Zhejiang Province in the Early Twentieth Century* (Cambridge: Harvard University Press, 1982); Mary Backus Rankin, "'Public Opinion' and Political Power: *Qingyi* in Late Nineteenth Century China," *Journal of Asian Studies*, 41:3 (May 1982), pp. 453–484; William T. Rowe, *Hankow: Conflict and Community in a Chinese City, 1796–1895* (Stanford: Stanford University Press, 1989), and "The Public Sphere in Modern China," *Modern China*, 16:3 (July 1990), pp. 309–329, among others.

2. Although in principle the public-private juxtaposition is stark, in practice it is less so. Given the relatively modest bureaucratic resources available, it was practically impossible to compel compliance. Individuals had substantial autonomy within their nuclear or extended family, guild, *Landsmannschaft*, religious sect, secret society, literary club, and so on. Much social activity took place with little active regard for how it conformed to official orthodoxy, leading Whyte to infer the existence of a "de facto civil society" in late imperial China. Martin K. Whyte, "Urban China: A Civil Society in the Making?" in Arthur Rosenbaum, ed., *State and Society in China: The Consequences of Reform* (Boulder: Westview Press, 1992), pp. 77–103.

3. Donald J. Munro, "The Concept of 'Interest' in Chinese Thought" (Unpublished paper prepared for the Workshop on the Pursuit of Political Interest in the People's Republic of China, Ann Arbor, Mich., August 10–17, 1977).

of the two realms is perhaps at least partly due to the fact that the public realm happens to coincide politically with the formal institutional structure (i.e., the meritocratic Confucian bureaucracy, which wrote the official histories), the private with the inner court (eunuchs, consorts, palace guard, servants) and their informal organization (factional maneuver, conspiracies for favor or succession).

The Western concept of the "private" is less pejoratively defined than the Chinese, with a strong strain going back at least to Adam Smith construing the private sector as making an almost necessarily positive contribution to public welfare. Private interests per se are sanctioned by the free market model in economic thought, by social contract theory in politics, and by the adversary tradition in jurisprudence. Analogies may be (and are) drawn from any of these realms to promote the free play of private interests throughout society (as in Mill's *On Liberty*, which first likens public discourse to a marketplace). The public is, to be sure, also positively evaluated in the West (e.g., "public interest," "public weal"), but even though it is favorably evaluated it has subtly different connotations from the Chinese concept, as indicated below.

If the Chinese Communist revolution endeavored to override and reverse certain elements of traditional Chinese political culture,[4] with regard to the public-private distinction and its implications the impact seems to have been rather to reinforce the momentum of the past. Despite the fact that Marx himself (in his critique of Hegel) denied the existence of a public interest, conceding sociological authenticity only to classes, CCP leaders for the most part fit rather comfortably into Chinese philosophical tradition on this issue. Actually, CCP discussions of public opinion use two terms: *yulun*, which refers to leadership views, as reflected in the official media, which the masses are expected to share; and *renmin qunzhong de yijian* (opinions of the masses), referring to the more or less spontaneous opinions of a range of people, as reflected in letters to the editor, big-character posters, and so forth.[5] These two terms suggest not only an active impulse to build a consensus from above, but also an acknowledgment of a certain ambit for feedback from the masses below. In "On the Correct Handling of Contradictions Among the People," Mao Zedong attempted to sort these out:

> Our People's Government is one that genuinely represents the people's interests, it is a government that serves the people. Nevertheless, there are still certain contradictions between the government and the people.

---

4. As most cogently argued (outside the CCP canon itself) in Richard Solomon, *Mao's Revolution and the Chinese Political Culture* (Berkeley: University of California Press, 1971).

5. On big-character posters, see Goeran Leijonhufvud, *Going Against the Tide*, Scandinavian Institute of Asian Studies Monograph no. 58 (London: Curzon Press, 1990).

These include contradictions among the interests of the state, the interests of the collective, and the interests of the individual.[6]

Mao then goes on to draw his famous distinction between "contradictions among the people" and "contradictions between the people and the enemies of the people," in which the latter are to be resolved through "struggle" and the former through patient persuasion. Although Mao herewith seemed to be granting a measure of political autonomy to certain types of public contradictions, that autonomy is consistently lost in the act of realization. Resolution of either type of contradiction turns out to involve adaptation on the part of what might be called the private sector (viz., the "masses") to the Party-state, which hence emerges as the sole proper repository of the public interest. The only difference is that the resolution to "nonantagonistic" contradictions is voluntary and pacific, whereas "antagonistic" contradictions involve violence and coercion. Moreover, Marx's denigration of "bourgeois privacy" reinforces the traditional Chinese scorn for "self-interest" (*liyi*), resulting in the Chinese Communist tendency to associate private interests with the selfish "profit-maximizing" (*lijizhuyi*) characteristics of capitalist economies—in contrast to their own alleged concern with the "great public" (*da gong*). The legitimacy of material interests must be accepted, in view of their centrality to Marx's theoretical schema, yet there is an underlying tendency to give them a negative connotation and to attribute correspondingly idealistic motives to public concerns. There is also a tendency, particularly in the more radical version of Maoist ideology that emerged during the Cultural Revolution, to give paradigmatic status to those instances where public and private interests conflict and to demand that the former prevail absolutely: "Great public, nothing private" (*da gong, wu si*).[7]

What emerges, then, from the synthesis of traditional Chinese political culture and Marxist-Leninist ideology is a conception of the public that is recognizably parallel to that used in the West yet is marked by subtle but significant differences. First, the Western concept of the public includes a connotation of *objectivity*—ultimately deriving, perhaps, from the methodology of scientific verification (according to which hypotheses, experiments, and theories had to be publicly exposed to possible refutation) that achieved such prestige during the European Enlighten-

---

6. Mao, "On the Correct Handling of Contradictions Among the People," in Mao Tse-tung, *Four Essays in Philosophy* (Peking: Foreign Languages Press, 1966), p. 81, as cited in Munro, "Concept," p. 14, n. 27.

7. Ding Danian, *Gongchanzhuyi renshengguan* (Communist life view) (Shanghai: Huadong renmin chubanshe, 1953), p. 22, as cited in Munro, "Concept," p. 17.

ment. This Western notion has been exacerbated in the course of centuries of religious secularization and economic commercialism, during which the public sector, initially imbued with the bourgeois values of liberty, fraternity, and equality from the French Revolution, has progressively become eviscerated of any substantive content, aside from an essentially neutral set of rules of the game to govern the free play of private interests.[8] This nuance seems to be altogether lacking from the Chinese concept; to the Chinese, the concept of the public retains a distinct substantive content.

Precisely what is that content? Let us try to sum up some of the immediately salient characteristics. The PRC concept still has an unambiguously positive moral value, deriving from both Confucian and Marxist-Leninist philosophical traditions; in the West the public has become a neutral arena. Moreover, as CCP authorities deny the legitimacy of private interests, any public demand or grievance must be expressed in terms of universal validity. Obviously self-interested appeals are ruled out of court from the beginning; the rhetoric tends to be self-righteous, with a tendency to escalate. It is perhaps partly because of this moral coloration that Chinese Communist "news" tends to be euphemistic, whereas Western news is as likely to be pejorative as celebratory, seeking out sensationalism, scandal, the bizarre (man bites dog). It is not just the lure of the limelight that afflicts actors on the Chinese political stage but the even more powerful urge to strike a noble pose.

First, this pose involves a public emotional display of *care* for the people, again reinforced by both Confucian and Marxist-Leninist ideas. This display is traditionally referred to as "human feeling" (*renqing wei*).[9] In its absence, a public performance is apt to be rejected as "insincere." Thus during the Cultural Revolution, Marshal Chen Yi was able to convince his Red Guard interrogators of his sincerity in a spirited and frankly combative defense, while the more emotionally withdrawn Liu Shaoqi and Deng Xiaoping were not.[10] In the West, in contrast, the public

---

8. See Juergen Habermas, *Strukturwandel der Oeffentlichkeit* (Darmstad: Hermann Luchterhand, 1962), translated (by Thomas Burger) as *The Structural Transformation of the Public Sphere* (Cambridge: MIT Press, 1989); see also John Keane, *Public Life and Late Capitalism: Toward a Socialist Theory of Democracy* (Cambridge: Cambridge University Press, 1984). Independent reinforcement for this general argument may be found in Robert N. Bellah, et al., *Habits of the Heart: Individualism and Commitment in American Life* (Berkeley: University of California Press, 1985).

9. See the interesting article by Chung-fang Yang, "Conformity and Defiance on Tiananmen Square: A Social Psychological Perspective," in Peter Li, Steven Mark, and Marjorie H. Li, eds., *Culture and Politics in China: An Anatomy of Tiananmen Square* (New Brunswick, N.J.: Transaction, 1991), pp. 46–56.

10. True, other factors may have played a role—Zhou Enlai came to Chen's defense; Mao may have had it in for Liu and Deng. But the different public performances of these "human targets" also affected the outcomes.

sphere implicitly differentiates between politics and sports, on the one hand, where rule-bound rationality reigns supreme and the public display of emotion is proscribed,[11] and theater and the performing arts, on the other, where a full range of emotional display is appreciated.

Second, the Western concept of the public presumes diversity and internal contradiction, particularly in the American "melting pot," but also in all systems with low entry barriers to their economic and political markets. By contrast, to Chinese Communists, the public should represent unity and consensus (*yu lun yi zhi*); information that might mar this consensus should best remain private (one "should not wash dirty linen in public"). The Chinese Communist public realm is morally pure, hence it is relatively information-poor. Particularly during the Maoist period, when detailed street maps or telephone directories were labeled "classified," government offices could be detected only by their outsize street number plates, and libraries were tightly restricted (news of important PRC political events was often broken by foreign media).[12] The West's relative tolerance for public diversity is, to be sure, tenuous and hard-won,[13] coming only after centuries of fierce religious and ideological strife, during which diverse creeds learned to tolerate each other because they could not destroy each other. CCP politics, in contrast, has been characterized by a series of "winner-take-all" conflicts, in which disagreement is ruthlessly extirpated.[14]

Third, the public sphere in mainland China is politically inclusive; in the West, it is more circumscribed. That means, first of all, that it is pro-

---

11. See, for example, the case of Senator Edmund Muskie, whose emotional response to a newspaper attack proved politically suicidal to his 1975 presidential candidacy. In the world of sports, tennis player John MacEnroe's notoriously emotional public outbursts incurred severe financial penalties.

12. News of the fall of the Gang of Four was first announced by a British News Agency dispatch. The Voice of America broke the story of the 1986 student demonstrations. Liu Binyan, *China's Crisis, China's Hope*, trans. Howard Goldblatt (Cambridge: Harvard University Press, 1990), p. 95.

13. Indeed, there is also a *tendance* in the West, perhaps more dominant in continental (e.g., Rousseau, Hegel, Croce) than in Anglo-American philosophical traditions, to define public opinion as "pressure toward conformity." According to this way of thinking, the "public" media are not neutral instruments of enlightenment, but rather tools whereby elites manipulate and enforce mass conformity. See Elisabeth Noelle-Neumann, *The Spiral of Silence: Public Opinion—Our Social Skin* (Chicago: University of Chicago Press, 1980); Alvin Gouldner, *The Dialectic of Ideology and Technology* (New York: Oxford University Press, 1978), especially chap. 4; and Frederick Pollock, "Empirical Research into Public Opinion," in Paul Connerton, ed., *Critical Sociology* (New York: Penguin, 1976), pp. 225–236.

14. Tang Tsou, "Twentieth Century Chinese Politics: The Game to Win All—A Theoretical Perspective and a Research Design" (Unpublished paper, University of Chicago, December 1991).

portionately larger and more socially pervasive, partly because the socialization of the means of production carried out by the CCP in the 1950s included socialization of the means of communication—meaning not only mass media but also public squares, statues, main streets, and the calendar of public rituals (holidays, festivals, anniversaries, and other ceremonies). Even ostensibly private ceremonies, such as weddings or funerals, were co-opted by the state, incorporating heavy ideological symbolism. Courtship, family planning, food consumption, child rearing, travel, belief systems, and all aspects of life became matters of legitimate public concern. Thus, on the one hand, people feel quite free to ask in casual conversation what in the West would be deemed impertinent questions without any sense of intruding into "private" life. On the other hand, there is relatively little sense of responsibility for the public sector, due to the fact that it has been monopolized by the "dictatorship of the proletariat" (now termed "people's democratic dictatorship") throughout the post-Liberation era.

Fourth, the state (in this case, the Party-state) has a much stronger claim to define the public sector than in the West. In the West, too, the state is a dominant actor, but it must share the public realm with various nonstate actors contending to represent the public interest (political parties, public interest lobbies, religious denominations, entertainment media, the market), whose autonomy is not recognized in the PRC. Indeed, in the most recent period, there has been an increasing (albeit not yet unanimous) tendency in the West to view the public as *nothing but* a function of the intercourse among private interests. In contrast to the Western tendency to view the public as the playground of private interests, the Chinese inclination is to view it as the exclusive or even proprietary preserve of the state. It is certainly possible to entertain a distinction (as when the emperor is found to have violated the "mandate of heaven," or when a "clean official" [*qing guan*] confronts and upbraids a corrupt superior), but this is usually discernible only posthumously.[15]

For the most part, these contrasts in the Chinese concept of the public held true under the empire and were reinforced rather than alleviated by the triumphant CCP's creation of a strong centralized state. The implication of these cumulative differences is that the whole context of meaning differs correspondingly. "Publicity" is not a morally neutral grilling in an openly competitive public arena whereby the objective truth will be sifted out but is rather a bright spotlight of virtue that gives prominence to superior individuals or achievements, which others should observe and

---

15. For an articulate defense of the dissident tradition, see Franklin W. Houn, "Rejection of Blind Obedience as a Traditional Chinese and Maoist Concept," *Asian Thought and Society*, 7:19 (March 1982), pp. 18–31; 7:21 (May 1982), pp. 264–279.

follow. "Publication" via the various media is in most cases just a final confirmation of authoritative judgments; it is not really necessary for different publication outlets to compete in the discovery of "news" or in the articulation of different editorial opinions—indeed, it does not normally make much sense for them to do so. That might confuse people unnecessarily, giving rise to "chaos" (*luan*). Once the authorities (viz., those authorized to define the public interest) arrive at a consensus on a "correct" political agenda, the various media can be expected to relay this information more or less in unison. This typically gives rise to a bandwagon-like process that contrasts with the more dialectical dynamic of the media in the West.

Having outlined some of the broad cultural differences in the way mainland Chinese understand their public sector, we will now show how the distinction between public and private plays itself out in the political arena. We shall then review how the concept of the public has changed in the course of the last ten years of economic reform and political stalemate. Finally, we will review the structure and history of the unofficial mass movements that have arisen to fill a void experienced in the post-revolutionary public arena, culminating in the confrontation and crackdown at Tiananmen. The latter represents a climactic synthesis of many of the tendencies unleashed during the foregoing reform of the Chinese public sphere; Tiananmen brings that reform to a crossroads.

The Structure of Political Publication

How does the public-private dichotomy relate to political power? Although both realms are repositories of power, that power takes quite different forms: The former manifests itself in public, in the light of day, to widespread applause; the latter is hatched in furtive plots, lurking in ambush, to emerge from hiding in surprise coups. Sun Tzu appreciated the potential of the private realm in his discussion of strategy (and Mao in turn appreciated Sun Tzu): "All warfare is based on deception. Therefore, when capable, feign incapacity; when active, inactivity. When near, make it appear that you are far away; when far away, that you are near. Offer the enemy a bait to lure him; feign disorder and then strike him."[16] In the trade-off between public and private, the private sector relinquishes legitimacy for offsetting gains in power, whereas the public realm displays civil virtue without any real power (in the sense of polit-

---

16. Sun Tzu, *The Art of War*, trans. Samuel B. Griffith (New York: Oxford University Press, 1971), p. 66. See also Douglas Stuart and William Tow, "The Role of Deception in Chinese Strategic Calculus," in Donald Daniel and Katherine L. Herbig, eds., *Military Deception* (New York: Pergamon, 1982), pp. 292–316.

ically significant choices). The reason for this bifurcation is that public performance implies conformity with the norms of selflessness, precluding the appearance of the particular interests that motivate political demands in China as in every other political system, not to mention the dirty tricks required for successful political war fighting, deal making, and power mongering. Power can be effectively pursued only in private, advertised in the form of policy only after cleansing all trace of its self-aggrandizing, "unprincipled," and conflictual origins. In the early stages of the policy process "privatization" is indispensable, however unseemly.

In answer to our question, we thus have two continuums, one between public and private, the other between power and legitimacy. Power corresponds to the private realm, policy to the public. In the passage from power to policy, a given decision must proceed through a series of forums, progressing from highly private ones to ever more public ones. Private forums are characterized by greater confidentiality, permitting *Realpolitik* to be conducted in businesslike, sometimes brutal fashion; they are also more informal in procedure, permitting the meeting's chair or convener to override various technicalities to cobble together an effective majority and crush any opposition. Public forums meet on a more regularly scheduled basis, are more apt to be governed by rules of procedure (e.g., minutes, a set roster of participants, announced agenda), and even provide avenues for public disclosure (e.g., sessions open to media coverage, a concluding communique).

As is consistent with the cultural assumption that publicity equals virtue, the CCP has historically opposed the privatization of meetings in principle.[17] Indeed, at the extreme end of the spectrum in terms of both privatization and unalloyed power mongering is the faction, which is prohibited. Factions must hence meet clandestinely, in a private venue. Those excluded or anticipating exclusion from formally sanctioned forums, due either to the nature of their affiliation or to the subject of their meeting, may form such a privatized cabal as a last-ditch expedient, but if they do so their activities will remain murky, win or lose, due to their illicit status. They of course honor no public disclosure requirement, and subsequent exposure of their activities is subject to polemical distortion. It is still not clear, for example, what Peng Dehuai and his "military club" did besides meet occasionally to complain of Mao's high-handedness, and the nature of Lin Biao's conspiratorial activities after the Sec-

---

17. Mao, for example, complained bitterly about Peng Zhen's privatization of the Beijing municipal Party committee when he was mayor in the early 1960s, referring to it as an "independent kingdom" so tightly controlled that one could not stick a pin in. Mao himself was not, however, immune from similar tendencies, having first his secretary and then his wife promoted to the Party Politburo itself.

ond Plenum of the Ninth Party Congress that put him on the defensive remains unclear in many areas. Deng Xiaoping seems to have formed a similar grouping with Ye Jianying, Xu Xiangqian, and others in South China after falling from favor in Beijing in the spring of 1976, but precisely how this group pursued its struggle has never been officially disclosed.[18]

Next along the continuum of power and publicity is the formally sanctioned small group meeting in an "expanded session," usually consisting of the Politburo Standing Committee and any number of other high-level participants based on the discretion of the convener. These sessions may have varying degrees of formality, ranging from expanded Politburo meetings (marked only by a report that a meeting was held, with no information about its substance), to Politburo Standing Committee meetings (with not even that), to "work" or "report" conferences known only by the place and time they are held. The major difference between a formally sanctioned small group meeting and a faction (aside from the question of legality) is that in the former all members are permitted to attend and express their views, whereas a faction includes only loyal coconspirators. In many other respects the two are really quite similar. Both tend to be procedurally open-ended, allowing the convener to set the agenda, designate speakers, shift the venue (e.g., before Tiananmen, Deng convened high-level meetings at his home), and stack the deck by inviting selected nonmembers. The convener can call a vote, but formal votes are usually not called, allowing the convener greater leeway to construe the consensus.[19]

A policy emerging from a formally sanctioned small group meeting must then be heard and approved by one or another large public forum—the Party Congress, the National People's Congress, the Chinese People's Consultative Congress, or all three—before it is deemed legitimate. The formally "correct" path of approval is for these meetings to meet seriatim, beginning with the Central Committee, then the Party Congress, the NPC, and the CPPCC; but during Mao's later years this sequence was frequently abridged, to the effect that many CCP policies were implemented without technically becoming laws. These assemblies' role has hitherto been essentially acclamatory, with a slight tendency to

---

18. See, however, Lin Qingshan, *Fengyun shinian yu Deng Xiaoping* (Beijing: Jiefangjun chubanshe, 1989), pp. 216, 219, 220, 223, 230–231.

19. A former high-level adviser of Zhao Ziyang has written: "In the past, apart from elections within the Party, we have rarely made decisions on important issues by voting. This has tended to result in discussions not reaching decisions or delayed decisions, and even allowing one or a few persons to make the decisions." Chen Yizhi, et al., eds., *Zhengzhi tizhi gaige jianghua* (Beijing: People's Publishing, 1987), p. 46.

assume a more influential role in the course of reform (thus, for example, when an NPC session approved the controversial Yangtze Gorges dam project in 1992, nearly half abstained).[20]

Following "congressional" approval the policy is announced to the public. Publication may flow through two channels, which may be termed official and unofficial.[21] The official channel in turn consists of a "dual communication network": On the one hand, we have the mass media; on the other, the internal (*neibu*) communication system within the bureaucracy.[22]

The mass media are among the least informative avenues of publication, purveying general and euphemistic reports often discounted or reconstrued by their readership. At least until the late 1980s the media prided themselves on their lack of prepublication censorship,[23] but the threat of postpublication sanctions (official or mass criticism, dismissal of editorial staff) has always been more or less present, resulting in fairly vigilant self-censorship.[24] The mass media are part of the propaganda "system" (*xitong*), which includes the Ministry of Culture; the Ministry of Broadcasting, Television, and Movies; the Bureau of Information and Publication; the Academy of Social Sciences; the Xinhua News Agency; the official central newspaper (*People's Daily*); and the official journal

---

20. See Kevin J. O'Brien, *Reform Without Liberalization: China's National People's Congress and the Politics of Institutional Change* (New York: Cambridge University Press, 1990).

21. Tsan-kuo Chang, "Reporting US-China Policy, 1950–1984: Presumptions of Legitimacy and Hierarchy," in Chin-chuan Lee, ed., *Voices of China: The Interplay of Politics and Journalism* (New York: Guilford Press, 1990), pp. 180–202; I have taken the liberty of modifying Chang's terminology somewhat.

22. Michel Oksenberg, "Methods of Communication Within the Chinese Bureaucracy," *China Quarterly* (*CQ*), no. 57 (January–March 1974), pp. 1–39.

23. This tradition seems to have been broken by the establishment of a State Media and Publications Office (*Xinwen chuban shu*) on January 27, 1987 (during the high tide of the antibourgeois liberalization campaign), under the direction of Du Daozheng, former editor of *Guangming ribao*. Although its precise functions are unclear, this agency seems to have been modeled on the censorship bureaus of Eastern Europe. See *China Directory, 1988* (Tokyo: Radio Press, 1987), p. 111.

24. Party organ newspaper editors are appointed by the Organization Department after discussion and decision by the standing committee of the Party committee at that level, and normally the managing editor and editor-in-chief are members of that Party committee. When necessary, they may attend standing committee meetings of the same level Party committee as nonvoting delegates to make sure they understand the intentions of the Party committee on sensitive issues. Party newspaper workers join the Party committee's unit and are "national cadres"paid by the central government. All newspapers on the national level have members from the Politburo or Secretariat who are assigned supervisory responsibilities as well as ideological supervision. Any member of the CC is permitted to criticize articles in the national papers, and the latter are usually obliged to recant. See Liu Binyan, *China's Crisis*, p. 84.

(*Qiu shi*). This system is under the jurisdiction of the Central Propaganda Department of the CCP (currently chaired by Ding Guangen, with gerontocrats Deng Liqun and Hu Qiaomu receding to an "advisory" role), which also controls the education system, the propaganda department in the military, scientific research, the Party school system, the "bourgeois democratic parties," and mass organizations. But a Politburo member normally outranks and may overrule the propaganda department: Mao himself wrote a number of key editorials,[25] as did Zhou Enlai in his prime; later Hu Yaobang took strong proprietary interest in *People's Daily*.[26]

More detailed reports are parceled out to the various bureaucratic "systems" on a need-to-know basis. The CCP divides the Chinese political structure into six systems: military; political and legal; administrative; propaganda; united front; and mass organization.[27] These systems, vertically integrated hierarchies between which lateral contact is minimized, then relay the information and directives downward through a wide variety of meetings: work conferences, symposia, transmission meetings, report-back meetings, mobilization meetings, and so forth.[28] This vertical communication system distributes by "dosage": Knowledge is power, so those highest in the hierarchy get most fully briefed, while the stream trickles out in the lower strata.

Although originally an exclusively oral network, the bureaucratic communications system has been supplemented over time by a wide variety of "internal" (*neibu*) printed media. The largest of these, a collection of wire-service translations known as "Reference News" (*Cankao xiaoxi*), has over time acquired a circulation of some nine million (larger than that of *People's Daily*, indeed perhaps the largest in the

---

25. A number of NCNA and *Renmin ribao* (*RR*) editorials were penned by Mao, the most famous being "Press Du Yuming to Surrender," "Carry the Revolution Through to the End," and "Five Criticisms White Paper."

26. Zhou Enlai once interrupted a meeting with foreign visitors to proofread the next day's front page of the paper. During the 1981 public criticism of Bai Hua, although *Jiefang ribao* published one criticism after another, *Renmin ribao* remained on the sidelines, not publishing a single criticism of Bai Hua. A former *RR* reporter says everyone knew this, and knew that it was politically possible for the paper to opt out because the campaign was not led by Deng. But as Hu's influence declined, the degree of freedom decreased. Liu Binyan, *China's Crisis*, pp. 88–89.

27. Yan Huai, *Understanding the Political System of Contemporary China* (Princeton: Center for Modern China, 1991), p. 30; as cited in Su Shaozhi, "Public Opinion and Ideological Control in China" (Paper presented at Voices of China Conference, University of Minnesota, October 4–6, 1991).

28. Oksenberg, "Methods," pp. 1–3 et passim.

Emergence of a Public Sphere?

world).[29] "Reference Information" (*Cankao ziliao*) also publishes translated articles and editorial commentary from abroad but is more comprehensive and restricted in circulation, delivered (initially twice daily, but since 1988 only once) not through the mails but by Xinhua personnel. Even more restricted is a three- to ten-page daily report called "Internal Reference" (*Neibu cankao*), which is distributed at the ministerial (*bu*) level and contains sensitive reports written by domestic and international Xinhua reporters. At the highest level of secrecy and restriction are Xinhua reports known as "red head reference" (*hong tou cankao*), Hand Copied Documents, and other materials, printed in large type so the "immortals" can read them, issued on an occasional basis to as few as a dozen people.[30] Members of the political elite also have their own restricted television channels and special access to foreign movies.

At the base of these systems is a honeycomb-like matrix of "basic units" (*jiben danwei*). Even the mass organizations are subdivided into units. The basic unit, defined functionally as well as by geographical proximity, exercises relatively comprehensive control over its membership, less, however, through disciplinary sanctions than through the calculated distribution of rewards. The unit distributes salaries, housing, bonuses, rations, school attendance, military service; during campaigns, the unit organizes the killing of flies and rats or the designation and criticism of class enemies. The unit keeps track of its membership in a complete set of personnel files (*dangan*); unit approval is needed to marry, to have children, to divorce, to form or dissolve a contractual relationship.

Unofficial communication, by comparison, consists of leaks, rumors, and (top-down) campaigns.

1. As defined here, the difference between leaks and rumors has to do with the amount of elite initiative: Leaks have an elite source, whereas rumors may not. Leaks disseminated on a not-for-attribution basis by public officials are not just informal but are illegal, according to the "Provisional Regulations on Safeguarding National Secrets," reinstated in

---

29. *Cankao xiaoxi* was introduced in the late 1950s amid some controversy—Mao Zedong once called it "the Communist Party running a newspaper for the bourgeoisie"—because it contained international news as well as fragments of Hong Kong and Taiwan news that could not be published in newspapers for sale to the general public. At first, a regulation limited access to cadres at or above the agency level. Later, because the CCP decreed that "the working class is the leadership class," access was expanded to include factory workers. When, after the rise of Deng Xiaoping, the CCP decided that "intellectuals are part of the working class," even secondary school teachers could read it. It is now simultaneously printed in twenty-five Chinese cities, and each copy is read by several readers.

30. See Jennifer Grant, "Internal Reporting by Investigative Journalists in China and Its Influence on Government Policy," *Gazette*, 41:1 (1988).

1979 after long suspension.³¹ Enforcement has been strict but uneven, however, due to the troubled history of the rule of law and to the skill of leaders at evading restrictions. The most flagrant violations took place during the Cultural Revolution, when leaks to the unofficial tabloid newspapers were widely used to smear factional opponents. Enterprising Red Guard reporters sometimes created their own leaks, breaking into the files and disseminating secrets to the public, smashing the distinction between public and private and creating "chaos."

During leadership disputes, leaders have their greatest incentive to attract a mass constituency by disseminating information favorable to themselves and damaging to their opponents, and they usually manage to do so without technically violating the official taboo on leaks by using symbolism or Aesopian language (*han sha she ying*—"holding sand and throwing shadows," or *zhi sang ma huai*—"pointing at the mulberry tree while cursing the locust"). Such communication transcends unit boundaries partly because high-level leaders are among the few whose careers have allowed them to assemble widespread "connections."³² Mao Zedong was particularly artful at discovering (or even planting) an obscure article criticizing some untouchable bigwig and then proceeding to inflate its significance to devastating proportions; the critique of Wu Han's play, *Hai Rui ba guan*, with which he launched the Cultural Revolution is, of course, the most famous example, but he used the same technique recurrently (e.g., he himself wrote the *People's Daily* commentary that launched the criticism of the film "Wu Xun" in the spring of 1951, and in October 1954 he stipulated publication of an obscure critique of Yu Pingbo's interpretation of *Red Chamber Dream*).

But he has had imitators on either side of the ideological spectrum. Thus when the radicals (with Mao's support) launched a campaign criticizing Confucius that implicated Zhou Enlai as the Duke of Zhou (*Zhou gong*), Zhou seems to have instigated the discovery that the late Lin Biao had been an avid collector of Confucian scrolls, thereby facilitating a rerouting of the campaign against Lin Biao and Confucius. The radicals attacked Deng in 1975 by way of denouncing the "capitulationist" Song Jiang in the novel *Water Margins*, and during the Tiananmen demonstrations a much older Deng was unflatteringly compared with the Empress Dowager; even the Great Helmsman was likened during his lifetime to the despotic Qin Shihuang.³³ Deng Xiaoping for his part made hard-hit-

---

31. *RR*, July 1, 1983, p. 3.
32. See my article, "Bases of Power in Chinese Politics: A Theory and an Analysis of the Fall of the 'Gang of Four,'" *World Politics*, 31:1 (October 1978), pp. 26–61.
33. See for example the famous big-character poster of Li Yizhe, posted in Canton in 1974; for a translation, see Li I-che, "Concerning Socialist Democracy and Legal System," *Issues and Studies*, 12:1 (January 1976), pp. 110–148.

ting speeches in the summer and fall of 1975 that were then relayed by uncomplimentary "rumors" concerning Jiang Qing's poor handing of culture and propaganda. Again, in early 1991 Deng published pseudonymous articles in a Shanghai newspaper on behalf of faster reform and tried to get them reprinted; when this failed, he undertook his trip to the South the following year (Chen Yun also went to Shanghai in 1992, endorsing Pudong but warning against "blindly copying" the model of other SEZs).[34] When two or more sides engage in this type of manipulation, rival vertical coalitions are formed, each with its own informal communications network.

2. There are both national and local rumors. The former subsist on leaks from the central political apparatus, given the center's monopolization of national political information. Because they are limited to word-of-mouth transmission, national rumors are usually limited to the capital, although during mass movements intercity messengers (*chuanlian*) and telephones create a national grapevine. Local rumors, or gossip (*xiaodao xiaoxi*), form a pervasive informal communications network within each unit, from which few secrets are proof. Intra-unit rumor networks, though tiny, provide more opportunity for mass feedback than the public sector; thus, whereas the big-character poster has appeared beyond unit compounds only episodically, and then accompanied by considerable turmoil, members of the unit have been rather more consistently permitted to write and post posters on a unit bulletin board for internal consumption. The rhetoric of "class struggle" has never fit well within the unit, where harmony is a functional requisite; beyond the unit, in contrast, lies a jungle, where civil culture easily breaks down.

3. CCP leaders have consistently supplied direction to the masses through a combination of symbolism and relatively ad hoc organizational techniques known as the "mass movement."[35] Mass mobilization was deemed especially useful in implementing new policies that marked a radical departure from the status quo, which required active community commitment in order to foster an atmosphere conducive to deviation from traditional norms and commitment to new policies. But the CCP was perhaps unique among Communist movements in the resourcefulness with which it found new uses for the mass movement. Throughout the 1950s the mass movement played a major role in the transformation of the Chinese political landscape: Mass movements

---

34. *Zheng ming*, June 1992, p. 11; Deng had said in a January 25, 1992, visit to Zhuhai that the province Guangdong and its SEZs should be a model for China's economic development.

35. For a relatively systematic attempt to analyze mass mobilization, see Charles Cell, *Revolution at Work: Mobilization Campaigns in China* (New York: Basic Books, 1977).

socialized the means of production, ostracized and punished enemies of the "people," rectified the world of ideas and culture, and even facilitated public sanitation efforts. Despite considerable diversity, mass campaigns have tended to have a populist, anti-elitist, and specifically anti-intellectual animus. Between 1949 and 1966, some sixteen nationwide campaigns were launched, at least eight of which singled out intellectuals as targets.[36] By thus pitting the masses against the intellectuals most inclined to a critical perspective, the regime has kept a tighter reign on dissent than, say, the Soviet Union.[37] In any event, mass movements typically provided an outlet for various and sundry mass grievances in the form of a human target, or scapegoat, who was juxtaposed against a more positive policy or value the regime wished to induce the masses to embrace.[38]

The "public sphere" is thus seen on closer examination to be segmented into relatively self-contained groupings, consisting of vertical hierarchies, or systems, at the top and units on the bottom. Although these are not without "windows," consisting of the mass media and certain crosscutting communications (such as *Reference News*), communication within each unit or system is much more ample than communication between them. Only during campaigns or leadership disputes is this cellularity normally breached, creating a festive spirit of emancipation often quite at odds with the ostensible purpose of the movement. At this time people can vacate narrowly circumscribed concerns and engage on a voyage of mutual discovery, finding in the "great public" the gloriously

---

36. These began with the criticism of the film "Wu Xun" (and its producers) in the spring of 1951; criticism of Yu Pinbo's "Studies on the novel *Dream of the Red Chamber*" (October 1954); criticism of the historian Shang Yue; criticism of the thought of Liang Shuming (May–November 1955); criticism of Hu Shi (December 1955); criticism of the Hu Feng counterrevolutionary group (February 1956); criticism of the anti-Party group of Ding Ling and Chen Qixia (1957); and criticism of the novel *Liu Zhiden* (September 1962). After the Eighth Plenum of the Eighth CC in 1962 when Mao emphasized class struggle, a series of criticisms of prominent intellectuals and their work was put forth, including Shao Quanlin, Zhou Gucheng (art and literature), Yang Xianzhen, Feng Ding (philosophy), Sun Yefang (economics), Jian Bozan (history), and a great many films and dramas. Other campaigns targeted mainly against intellectuals include the thought reform campaign from fall 1951 to fall 1952, the antirightist campaign in 1957, the 1958 campaign to "remove the white flag" (*ba bai qi*), designed to impugn White experts and encourage mass innovation in the Great Leap (which helped precipitate the withdrawal of Soviet advisors), and, of course, the Cultural Revolution.

37. Thus there have been no underground newspapers or samizdat, no mass political organizations in China (except during brief breakdowns of public control, such as the Cultural Revolution). Underground periodicals existed in the USSR during the eighteen years of the Brezhnev era, and there are currently 30,000 popular organizations there, including fishing and hunting clubs. Liu Binyan, *China's Crisis*, p. 24.

38. For an analysis of the logic of mass criticism, see Lowell Dittmer, *Liu Shaoqi and the Chinese Cultural Revolution* (Berkeley: University of California Press, 1974).

abstract and anonymous collective purpose not found in workaday bureaucratic or unit routines.

The Impact of Reform

Albeit best known for legitimating a more generous accommodation of the private sector of the economy, Deng's reform program also envisaged increasing political transparency. Deng might be said to have sustained Mao's commitment to Kang Youwei's slogan, "all public, no private," albeit via quite different tactics. Whereas Mao's public was communitarian and ideologically totalistic (*yiyuantang*—a one-voice hall), Deng strove for formalization and secularization. Considerable progress was achieved in both directions until the late 1980s, when the consequences of these trends precipitated a cleavage in the reform alignment and forced a retreat. Deng Xiaoping and his supporters at this point reverted to the tactics they had been seeking to leave behind, ensuring their personal survival but raising large questions about the future direction of the reforms they had inaugurated.

Secularization included, in the first instance, a fairly systematic demolition of the cult of Mao, as a way of undermining both a source of dogmatic resistance to policy innovation (the so-called "two whatevers") and the chief ideological pillar buttressing Deng's political nemesis, Hua Guofeng.[39] The cult was replaced at the elite level by the principle of collective leadership, whereas its role in the public sphere as a sort of universal a priori criterion of Truth was replaced by more empirical criteria under the slogans Practice as the Sole Criterion of Truth, Emancipation of the Mind, Crossing the River by Groping for Stones, and so forth. The implication of this line of thinking, if pushed to its logical conclusion, was that "practice" existed independently of any guiding revolutionary theory, that "facts" were value-free, and that Mao's Thought was applicable only to the historical milieu in which it was articulated. The new regime publicly condemned the imposition of a single political doctrine over every sphere of activity as "fetishism"[40] and, under the rubric

---

39. The "two whatevers" are "whatever decisions made by Chairman Mao, we must resolutely uphold; [and] whatever directives were issued by Chairman Mao, we must follow without fail." They were introduced by Hua in a draft of a January 1977 speech and appeared the following month in the joint editorial of *Renmin ribao*, *Hongqi*, and *Jiefang junbao* (Liberation Army Daily), thanks to (Hua ally) Wang Dongxing. Jin Zhiming, "Should Hua Guofeng Be Allowed to Remain as Party Chairman?" *Dong xi fang* (East and West) (Hong Kong), no. 24 (December 10, 1980), pp. 24–28.

40. Shi Zhu, "To Be Arbitrary with Regard to Practice Is to Fear Truth," *Guangming ribao*, October 5, 1978, p. 4. For example, one article drew implicit parallels between the European Inquisition and thought control in China during the period of the Gang of Four. Yan Jiaqi, "Religion, Rationality, and Practice: Visiting Three 'Law Courts' on the Question of Truth in Different Eras," *Guangming ribao*, September 14, 1978, pp. 3–4.

of "objective laws" (of economics, physics, etc.), endorsed limited functional autonomy for various scientific and professional activities; thus various forums were sponsored (as in the early 1960s) to elicit the opinions of professionals on matters relevant to their areas of expertise.

Inasmuch as the cult had formed the fountainhead of ideology (Mao's personal infallibility implied the universal validity of his Thought), demolition of the cult led to a general derogation of the role of ideology, making more room for pragmatic flexibility and innovation. The connection was most explicitly drawn in the "Resolution on Some Historical Questions in Our Party Since the Establishment of the Country," published by the Sixth Plenum of the Eleventh Party Congress in June 1981, which condemned Mao for "mistakes" (*cuowu*) in launching the Great Leap Forward and the Cultural Revolution (but not "serious mistakes," or *yanzhongdi cuowu*, as in the original draft—scratched out by Deng Xiaoping), repudiated the theory of "continuing the revolution under the dictatorship of the proletariat" with which Mao had been closely identified, and redefined his Thought to make it compatible with the Party's unfolding modernization program (e.g., no mention of "class struggle"—Mao's "key link"). Whereas in the last decade of his life Mao had placed particular emphasis on the role of the ideological superstructure as an independent variable in historical change,[41] the post–Mao interpretation returned to a reflectionist interpretation: The driving force in history was the forces of production, to which the relations of production must inevitably conform; the ideological superstructure in turn reflected the relations and forces of production.[42]

Economics, above all, moved into the empty spotlight left by ideology. Whereas during the Maoist era economics received very superficial (and often euphemistically inaccurate) attention,[43] it now began to take pride of place. The flagship *People's Daily*, expanded in January 1980 from four to eight pages, allotted more coverage to economic news. In January 1980, of the twenty-nine news stories that were given greatest

---

41. Tang Tsou, *The Cultural Revolution and Post-Mao Reforms: A Historical Perspective* (Chicago: University of Chicago Press, 1986), pp. 112–143.

42. See Brantly Womack, "Politics and Epistemology in China Since Mao," *CQ*, no. 80 (December 1979), pp. 768–792; also Charles Burton, *Political and Social Change in China Since 1978* (New York: Greenwood Press, 1990).

43. In the early 1950s, only two newspapers were assigned by the government to cover economic news: *Dagong bao* (Workers' Daily) (Beijing) and *Xinwen ribao* (News Daily) (Shanghai). But in 1960, *Xinwen ribao* merged with *Jiefang ribao*, leaving only one specialized economic newspaper in the country. And its coverage was not particularly "economic," tending to focus more and more attention on current political and international news. Bangtai Xu, "Press Freedom in China: A Case Study of *World Economic Herald* Before 1989," (Unpublished M.A. Thesis, Asian Studies, University of California at Berkeley, 1989).

Emergence of a Public Sphere? 127

prominence on the front page, twenty-one were economic reports. In the corresponding month of 1979, only three out of twenty-seven front-page headline stories focused on economics.[44] Reporting in other fields—politics, science, education, art, and literature—also tended to reflect the inherent logic or "objective laws" of those fields, rather than superimposing an extraneous ideological standard. Besides economics, there has been a bewildering variety of specialized publications of all types: 56.7 percent of China's 1,777 registered newspapers have started publication since 1978, a total of 1,008 new titles in less than five years; from 1980 to 1990, the number of magazine titles has grown from 900 to 6,005.[45] Evening newspapers, less constrained in the reportage of local news and "human interest" stories, have seen their circulation mount rapidly.[46] The number of radio receivers has increased rapidly during reform and the number of television sets still more rapidly, as China became the world's leading TV set manufacturer.[47] Though there are no underground media per se, a kind of parallel media have sprung up, colloquially referred to as "the second channel" (*di er qudao*); a publisher of, say, a *gungfu* novel, will negotiate the purchase of a license number from a state publishing house to publish a book and have it distributed through private bookstalls (*shutan*).[48]

"Formalization" refers to a shift from factional intrigue in either officially sponsored or clandestine forums to regularly scheduled meetings by officially constituted political organs. Under reform, policymaking bodies were all placed on a more routinized schedule, meeting more frequently and in longer sessions. Beginning with larger forums such as the

---

44. Of the total of 151 stories apppearing on the first page of the same paper in January 1979, only 49 were economic reports; in January 1980, the corresponding figures were 173 economic stories out of a total of 312. Xun Zhankun, "How to Reform Economic News Reporting?" *Veteran Journalists on News Coverage*, p. 298, as cited in Bangtai Xu, "Press Freedom."

45. *RR*, January 23, 1986, p. 3; September 3, 1990, p. 4; as cited in Alan Liu, "Communications and Development in Post-Mao Mainland China," *Issues and Studies*, 27:12 (December 1991), p. 75.

46. By 1986, there were 31 such papers in China, with a combined daily circulation of 7 million. *Zhongguo xinwen nianjian 1987* (China News Yearbook 1987) (Xingtai: Chinese Academy of Social Sciences Publishing House, 1987), p. 3; as cited in Alan Liu, "Communications," p. 75.

47. Estimates indicate that between 1981 and 1985, the number of radios increased from 130 million to 210 million, or 205 per thousand people. The number of TV sets increased from 10 million in March 1982 to 116 million, or 110 per thousand people, by late 1988. *RR*, February 16, 1981, p. 3, and October 7, 1988, p. 3; *Ming bao* (Hong Kong), March 6, 1982, p. 1; as cited in Alan Liu, "Communications," p. 76.

48. Marlowe Hood, "All the News Not Fit to Print: China's Internal Media," *China Forum*, 2:5 (May 1992), p. 3.

NPC plenary sessions, these organs began to open themselves to greater press coverage. As far as information policy is concerned, this entailed making the production of news more regular and "transparent" (*gongkaixing,* the Chinese equivalent of glasnost). News conferences began to be held for the first time with some regularity. In 1983, the ministries and municipal bodies designated English-speaking spokespersons whose job it was to answer questions and handle requests for interviews; it was also at this time that the system of weekly news briefings was set up so that reporters would have a chance every week to ask questions of Chinese officials.[49]

Whereas formal institutions of public relations won official approval, the government energetically proceeded against unofficial avenues of news disclosure. The big-character poster, a spontaneous emanation from the masses during the Hundred Flowers movement that Mao had endorsed, was first to go.[50] Immediately after the Third Plenum of the Eleventh CC, Deng introduced the Four Cardinal Principles (*si xiang jiben yuanzi*), which set firm limits on public debate. Although Hua Guofeng's downfall was facilitated by informal leaks and rumor mongering, it was the last elite power struggle to do so. In January 1980, Deng Xiaoping, in a speech to 20,000 CCP officials, announced that the clause in the constitution allowing the "four big" (i.e., big-character posters, the rights to speak out freely, air views fully, and hold great debates) should be removed because the rights had been abused; the NPC approved a constitutional amendment to that effect the following September. Accordingly, tabloid newspapers were shut down; street activists were thrown into labor camps or prison.[51] When the introduction of multicandidate voting in 1980–1981 unexpectedly permitted the advent of candidate-organized campaign committees, publication of pamphlets, and convening of rallies, Deng Xiaoping made a speech denouncing such tendencies, and the electoral law was subsequently amended to preclude their recurrence. (The elections held for the following term, in 1984, proceeded without incident.) In 1982 the right to strike was removed from the constitution— under socialism, where the workers own the means of production, strikes are unnecessary. To counter leaks by cadre children to Hong Kong

---

49. Frank Ching, "China's Second Opening to the West," in Chin-chuan Lee, ed., *Voices of China,* p. 17 et passim.

50. In July 1957 Mao said, "The big-character poster is a good thing. Let us take it over.... The more of them, the better. The big-character poster is classless, like language.... The big-character poster, as a form, is a light weapon like rifles, pistols, or machine guns. Newspapers like *Wen hui bao* or *Guangming ribao* are like planes and artillery." *Wansui* (1969), vol. 2, p. 115.

51. See Roger Garside, *Coming Alive: China After Mao* (New York: McGraw-Hill, 1981); see also David Goodman, *Beijing Street Voices: The Poetry and Politics of China's Democracy Movement* (London: Marion Boyars, 1981).

news media, the offical secrets act was reemphasized and the more prominent overseas journals embargoed from import. By "formalization," what the government clearly had in mind was an authoritatively controlled, top-down network.

It is easy to forget that the Deng Xiaoping reform program achieved many of its objectives. Public life was relieved of some of its pervasive ideological taboos, attention shifted from the almost inquisitorial quest for ideological purity to economic construction, and private life became more secure. Although it is hard to point to a precise causal connection, the economy prospered, as did the professional and educational sectors, despite complaints. Yet certain unintended consequences soon became apparent. The attempt to publicize the political sector achieved impressive results, but only so long as the economy kept surging forward in relatively trouble-free fashion; when crises and leadership splits began to afflict the regime in the late 1980s—at precisely those times when greater public openness might have had the greatest payoff in alleviating tension—politics was reprivatized. Thus the January 1987 decision to accept Hu Yaobang's resignation as secretary general of the CCP and to crack down on bourgeois liberalism was made in an "expanded" meeting, as were the decisions in May 1989 to impose martial law, to use troops to clear Tiananmen square, and, finally, to purge Zhao Ziyang (see Chapter 3).

Secondly, by secularizing the personality cult, minimizing the causal role of the ideological superstructure vis-à-vis the economic base, and otherwise promoting "deradicalization," the leadership soon discovered it had undermined its own legitimacy and divested itself of what had been a powerful instrument for enforcing conformity with its policies. Thus, immediately after the elimination of Hua Guofeng and the "small gang of four," public criticism of Mao Zedong and his Thought was suspended. Introduction of the concept of spiritual pollution (and its less notorious positive corollary, "Socialist spiritual civilization")—which allegedly had an existence independent of the forces and relations of production—represented an attempt to retreat from the advocacy of Emancipation of the Mind to a more controlled public sector. The return to such ideological "models" as Lei Feng, who was prominently featured in rectification campaigns after 1989, represents an attempt to reconsecrate the public realm and bar the intrusion of heterodox ideas.

Yet efforts to reverse ideological secularization were hamstrung by opposition from forces the reforms had unleashed. The intellectuals who comprised an important part of the reform movement's early core constituency had become attached to the Hundred Flowers as an end in itself and resisted any encroachments on this freedom even when such action became somewhat hazardous. The increasingly profit-sensitive mass media discovered a material interest in having an expanded range of subject matter to exploit commercially and have (usually passively) resisted attempts to repurify the public realm. Thus when ideology was resuscitated in the late 1980s to shore up the regime's sagging legitimacy, this had to be done without the intellectual resources on which the regime could previously rely—as was apparent in the crudeness of the formulations.

At the mass level, ideological secularization of the public realm provoked two different but related reactions. The first was a growing diversion from public to private concerns, including family, occupational, or avocational interests. Though seemingly consistent with the secularization the regime had encouraged, this ideologically anesthetized outlook troubled many of the old revolutionaries, who complained of a "money is everything" (*wang qian kan*) mentality. Ideological secularization soon resulted in a thriving and increasingly apolitical associational life. Despite the continuing taboo against extra-Party organization, a host of autonomous or quasi-autonomous associations sprang into being, such as trade associations, learned societies, and recreational clubs.[52] The growth of polling by both journalists and academic researchers provided indirect evidence that public opinion had acquired a certain independence.[53]

The second, countervailing reaction was a search for the lost "meaning of life," which invited voluntary submissions from the grass roots, or at any rate from outside the official hierarchy. During periods of relative intellectual openness, the intellectuals responded with ideas drawn from existentialism, Western Marxism (*xima*), structuralism, market economics, psychoanalysis, and Western democratic theory; although the Party disapproved, in the context of an economic opening to the outside world and avid promotion of Western tourism, it became somewhat awkward to bar such intellectual imports. The media became more autonomous, not through some declaration of independence or even

---

52. According to one press account, by 1989 there were 1,000 such autonomous associations operating nationally, and 100,000 at the local level. *China Daily*, September 2, 1989, p. 4, as cited in Whyte, "Urban China"; see also Alan Liu, "Communications."

53. The interest in public opinion was instigated by a change in media policy announced by Zhao Ziyang at the Thirteenth CCP Congress, when he outlined three functions for the media: to oversee public officials, to report on important events, and to reflect debate on key political issues. Public opinion should play a "supervisory role" in Party and government work. In 1986–1988 numerous centers for public opinion were established (at least fifteen in Beijing), and their findings were often published in the official press. For a more comprehensive report, see Stanley Rosen, "Public Opinion and Reform in the People's Republic of China," *Studies in Comparative Communism*, 22:2–3 (Summer–Fall 1989), pp. 153–170; see also Jianhua Zhu, Xinshu Zhao, and Hairong Li, "Public Political Consciousness in China: An Empirical Profile," *Asian Survey*, 30:10 (October 1990), pp. 992–1006.

through adoption of the press law on which a few dedicated people lavished considerable time and care, but in a sort of creeping de facto privatization, as local editors took advantage of administrative decentralization and circulation-based revenues to invent their own editorial policies.[54]

This combination of an apparently apolitical but vibrant associational life and the resurgence of political activism in the intellectual centers was to prove an explosive one. Though many had assumed that apolitical associational activity would be a distraction from political activism, when a crisis arose the two turned out to be mutually reinforcing (for example, the study "salons," or forums, that formed on university campuses in 1988 became nodal points in the organization of the protests). In the absence of authoritatively sponsored mass movements consonant with the entrepreneurial spirit that was still driving the most dynamic sector of the economy, political activists seized upon public occasions offering a plausible pretext for public entrepreneurship to incite a series of spontaneous movements, beginning with the fall 1985 campaign against the Japanese commercial invasion, followed by the December 1986 demonstrations in support of reform, and culminating in the enormous April–May 1989 demonstrations against corruption and in favor of democratization. The activists found a public realm that a security-obsessed secularization and formalization had left desiccated—and proceeded to fill it with life.

Spontaneous Political Activism

To understand the upheaval that swept all of urban China in the spring of 1989, it is necessary to return momentarily to the origin of this type of spontaneous uprising, the Cultural Revolution. The Cultural Revolution represents a historic shift from elite-sponsored mass movements to spontaneous mass mobilization, splitting the CCP between those who supported this development (the upwardly mobile) and those who were dead set against it (the victims). The post-Mao era represents the revenge of the latter (led by Deng Xiaoping) against the former. At the watershed Third Plenum of the Eleventh Party Congress where the reform program was launched, the leadership promised an end to campaigns. Yet things did not work out as planned.

---

54. Thus newspapers such as *Shenzhen Youth Daily* and Shanghai's *World Economic Herald* took considerable liberties. During the spring 1987 campaign against bourgeois liberalization, the former was shut down, but Beijing's *China Youth Daily* became extremely liberal just at that time. Liu Binyan, *China's Crisis*, pp. 89–95; see also "Press Freedom: Particles in the Air," in Joseph Man Chan and Chin-Chuan Lee, eds., *Mass Media and Political Transition: The Hong Kong Press in China's Orbit* (New York: Guilford Press, 1991), pp. 132–139.

The reform era has been repeatedly roiled by mass movements, of two increasingly divergent types: those sponsored by the leadership, and those spontaneously generated from below. The former have come a cropper, either because they proved unable to mobilize the masses (as in the case of the campaign to build "socialist spiritual civilization," or the post-Tiananmen campaign against "bourgeois liberalization"), or because if they did rouse the masses, their activity quickly tended to spin out of control and threaten the reforms or the reformers (as in the case of the 1980–1981 electoral campaign, or the 1983 campaign against "spiritual pollution"). Despite the inherent contradiction between mass mobilization and the stability deemed essential for economic prosperity, the CCP leadership does not seem to have found a functional substitute to mobilization to implement those policies that require mass consensus, so it continues to rely on campaigns—but with declining effectiveness and frequency.

In the absence of meaningful political activity in the public arena, voluntary political entrepreneurs have begun launching spontaneous movements around popular grievances. These movements stand in direct line of descent from the Cultural Revolution. To say this is not to damn them completely, for the Cultural Revolution made significant headway toward the establishment of a "civil culture" in the Chinese public sphere, notwithstanding its egregious faults. Thus the obvious task of subsequent spontaneous movements was to expand upon that progress while overcoming its faults. Its contribution was toward greater spontaneity, realized via an ability to launch a movement that could spread like a "prairie fire" on a wave of popular political grievances and demands. A spontaneous initial impulse does not necessarily imply full autonomy, as we shall see, though subsequent movements were to expand on this bridgehead.

The Cultural Revolution was subject to three types of fault. The first was the movement's dependency on the central leadership or on a decisive faction thereof; this did not necessarily imply a leadership split (though this often materialized), but it did require some sign (perhaps partly imagined) that at least part of the leadership was sympathetic to the goals of the demonstrators.[55] This is disadvantageous because it sacri-

---

55. At this point an elite split was a necessary but *not sufficient* condition for mobilization, which would reduce the Cultural Revolution to a publicly amplified power struggle and purge. Actually Mao had been trying for many months to instigate widespread, comprehensive criticism of the "capitalist road," but not until the spring of 1966 did he hit on the themes enabling him to do so. By the Eleventh Plenum (August 1966) Mao's personnel shifts had already been achieved, and, if anything, subsequent mass activity destabilized his new succession lineup. Similarly, although elite factionalism persists in the post-Mao era, it is usually resolved without mass involvement (e.g., the disposal of the "small gang of four" and the "petroleum faction").

fices a movement's autonomy to forces beyond its control. The second fault was the highly uncivil form of demand articulation we call a "breakthrough mentality," consisting of the polemical polarization of the world into the forces of light and the forces of darkness, people and monsters, red and black, proletariat and bourgeoisie, and so forth, calling for smashing the barrier dividing the two realms.[56] In its most extreme form this mentality leads to revolutionary vandalism and the infliction of pain or death upon the "enemy." This, of course, makes a movement extremely destructive and almost impossible to harness to any socially useful purpose. The third type of (closely related) fault was organizational anarchy and factionalism, which made it impossible to coordinate mass activities toward a set of common goals.

These three faults were clearly evinced in the Cultural Revolution. Even Cultural Revolution supporters acknowledged them to be serious liabilities; according to Deng: "In the two years before his death Chairman Mao said that the Cultural Revolution was wrong in two respects: For one thing, people wanted to 'overthrow everything,' for the other it resulted in a 'comprehensive civil war.'"[57] Because these faults were acknowledged to be drawbacks, sponsors of subsequent movements have attempted to eliminate them, whereas movement opponents like Deng have continued to capitalize on the movements' heritage and similarity to discredit them. Let us first review the major spontaneous movements of the Maoist era (viz., the Cultural Revolution, and the 1976 and 1978 protests) and then take a closer look at the progressively more ambitious 1985, 1986, and 1989 cases.

The Cultural Revolution, 1966–1976

In the case of the Cultural Revolution, though spontaneity was unquestionably present, it was highly qualified, wheras the three faults were most clearly manifested. With regard to central leadership, Mao Zedong, again unquestionably, was the prime mover of the campaign, without whom it could not have been launched, though he chose to work initially through such agents as Jiang Qing, Chen Boda, and Kang Sheng.[58] Subse-

---

56. See Lowell Dittmer, *China's Continuous Revolution: The Post-Liberation Epoch, 1949–1981* (Berkeley: University of California Press, 1987), chap. 4.

57. Deng, "Interview with Oriana Fallaci," (August 21 and 23, 1980), trans. in Helmut Martin, ed., in *Die Reform der Revolution: Ein Milliarde Menschen auf dem Weg* (Berlin: Siedler Verlag, 1988), p. 65.

58. E.g., according to recently divulged information, Kang Sheng was the first to insinuate to Mao that the essence of *Hai Rui's Dismissal* was "dismissal"—i.e., that the play was implicitly criticizing Mao for having sacked Peng Dehuai in 1959. Previously Mao is on record as having praised Hai Rui and even recommending him as a model. Zi Ling and Zi Zhen, "Wu Han yu *Hai Rui ba guan*," (Wu Han and *Hai Rui's Dismissal*) in Lin Haoji, ed., *Wen ge mi shi* (Secret History of the Cultural Revolution) (Taibei: Guoji wenti yanjiu so, 1986), p. 8.

quent research has revealed that Kang Sheng and Chen Boda played particularly active roles as provocateurs, meeting frequently with dissidents such as Nie Yuanzi to encourage defiance of the work team–generated consensus.

Finding such "backstage" (*houtai*) efforts insufficient, Mao finally stepped forward personally with open signals of support: first on June 1, when he ordered the broadcast of the first big-character poster; then in late July, when he returned to Beijing and countermanded the previous leadership of the movement and ordered the work teams withdrawn; then on August 18, by inviting Red Guards to mount the Tiananmen reviewing gate with him (at the conclusion of the Eleventh Plenum of the Eighth Party Congress, in the first of eleven mass rallies), publicly donning their brassard. These gestures were dramatically effective in mobilizing the masses, and meanwhile his "cult" had lifted him beyond Party disciplinary sanctions from Politburo members who disapproved.[59] Thereafter Mao shared leadership of the movement with a small band of intellectuals, to whom he gave quasiformal status as the Central Cultural Revolution Group (formed May 16, 1966). This leadership core, or "center," in effect displaced the Central Committee and its Politburo for the duration of the movement.

Mao provided direction to the movement by selecting its criticism targets, and he set up his targets through entrapment. He used similar tactics in the cases of Peng Zhen and Liu Shaoqi. In both cases he first set up the target by assigning him responsibility for the campaign, moved quietly to instigate a seemingly spontaneous revolutionary upsurge within the target's jurisdiction, then waited, cryptically observing the target as he attempted to handle the disturbance[60] (stoking the fire if it failed to escalate), revealing his hand and openly intervening only when the

---

59. For a somewhat sardonic but not inaccurate discussion of the "cult" see George Urban, *The Miracles of Chairman Mao* (London: Tom Stacey, 1971).

60. In the case of Liu and Deng, Mao was particularly inscrutable. When the former were facing the chaotic situation in Beijing, they were unsure how to react; they quickly boarded a plane to Hangzhou to report on the situation to Mao and to plead with him to return and take charge as soon as possible. Mao replied that he presently had no plans to return to Beijing and authorized Liu and Deng to handle the situation according to circumstances in the meantime. The latter flew back to Beijing and immediately called an expanded meeting of the Politburo Standing Committee (which the radicals Chen Boda and Kang Sheng also attended) to discuss how to deal with the unrest. After discussion, agreement was reached to send "work teams" to control the movement and maintain order. After the meeting, Liu telexed the decision to dispatch work teams to Mao in Hangzhou. Mao sent back a reply agreeing with the decision. Upon his return to Beijing in late July, however, he changed his mind and called for immediate withdrawal of work teams. Yan Jiaqi and Gao Gao, *Zhongguo "wen ge" shi nian shi* (The ten-year history of the Chinese Cultural Revolution) (Hong Kong: Da gong bao, 1986), pp. 26–27.

target had sufficiently incriminated himself to warrant censure and purge.[61] Peng was thus assigned to the five-member Cultural Revolution Group (Kang Sheng was on the committee as a "mole") when Mao demanded a criticism campaign of the author of *Hai Rui*, which, for Peng, would have involved dismantling his own political base (viz., the Beijing Municipal Party committee).[62] Following the purge of Peng and his followers, Liu and Deng were assigned to lead a movement now gyrating out of control, while Mao became incommunicado at his Hangzhou vacation resort. Upon his return to the capital fifty days later, Mao

---

61. The key informal role of the radicals in fomenting the uprising has now been documented. Kang Sheng later boasted that the famous big-character poster by Nie Yuanzi that initiated the campaign "was out of my efforts," which does not seem overstated. He and his wife had several secret talks with Nie (a lecturer in the philosophy department) in early May 1966, proofreading three revisions of her poster. Upon its appearance, the leadership under Liu Shaoqi, Zhou Enlai, and Deng Xiaoping endorsed its suppression by the majority of students on campus. Kang Sheng went around them and reported the poster to Mao, who promptly endorsed its broadcast on the nationwide radio network. Lin Haoji, *Wen ge*, pp. 16–17, 21–23, 36. After the May 16 Circular was passed by an expanded session of the Politburo, the Central Cultural Revolution Group, knowing about the tense relations between Nie and (Peking University president) Lu Ping, worked out a strategy of "setting fire from Beida and letting it burn upward." Yan Jiaqi and Gao Gao, *Zhongguo*, p. 21; Hei Yannan, *Shi nian dong luan* (Hong Kong: Xingchen, 1988), p. 46.

62. Mao appointed Peng Zhen to chair a "group of five" as early as 1964 to review the entire field of art and literature. In view of Peng's position as patron of those Beijing literati most active in the Aesopian criticism of Mao in the early 1960s (e.g., vice-mayor Wu Han, vice-mayor Deng Tuo, Liao Mosha, and the rest), Mao's motives seem transparent. For a while Peng's leadership of cultural rectification provided no pretext for censure, as in 1964 he led successive criticism campaigns against the playwright Tian Han and the critic Shao Quanlin, the philosopher Yang Xianzhen, and others. Yet Mao kept raising the ante. When Jiang Qing began to assemble her own group of followers in pursuit of a more radical transformation of culture without clearing her initiatives with Peng's Group, Mao encouraged her. Beginning in June–July 1965 this group collaborated with principal author Yao Wenyuan in drafting a sharp critique of Wu Han's play, *Hai Rui's Dismissal* (already withdrawn from circulation in 1962). With this project in mind, Mao proposed to a September–October 1965 central work conference that Wu Han be criticized. Scarcely two weeks later, he reviewed Yao's article and approved it for publication, without letting others within the leadership see it. "Speech to Foreign Visitors" (August 1967), in "Mao Zedong de yanjiang chuanwen" (Mao Zedong's complete speeches), *Ming bao*, July 5, 1968, p. 1. The article stimulated a controversy, but did not immediately achieve the desired breakthrough, partly due to Peng's skilled parrying of the criticism, partly because Mao concealed his own involvement. Controversy continued in an Aesopian vein through the early winter, culminating in a cautious self-criticism by Wu Han, then gathering momentum in the spring as criticism expanded to include the "three family village" (*san jia cun*). Not until May 1966 were Peng Zhen and his coterie finally purged, on the undoubtedly accurate charge of having resisted the escalation of a campaign obviously designed to destroy them. Thus the incident contains ample evidence of the elite intrigues behind the purge, primarily involving Mao and his supporters but also including Peng Zhen, who must have known who was behind the steadily mounting criticisms.

condemned his targets for using standard organizational sanctions to restore discipline, subjected them to two years of mass criticism, and eventually had them purged.[63]

These elite initiatives were, however, played out in a context of considerable mass spontaneity. Movement entrepreneurs like Kuai Dafu capitalized on social strains arising from the way the Party had arranged elite-mass and mass-mass (both vertical cleavages and horizontal segmentation) relations in the course of the previous seventeen years.[64] This included "contradictions" between skilled, unionized workers and nonunionized temporary workers (or between workers and management) in industry, between children of "good" and "bad" class backgrounds in the schools, between soldiers and civilians, and between localities, and it involved a pervasive resentment of the Party elite among various classes and groups.[65] Mass initiative was manifested in the targeting of "capitalist roaders," the organization and leadership of factional bands, the posting of big-character posters, as well as the editing of tabloid newspapers. Surviving central leaders would tour the country trying to coordinate Red Guard activities, but as soon as the most salient elite targets had been "toppled" in the "power seizures" of 1967 the various factions tended to turn on each other. The use of hyperbolic polemics was initiated very early in the campaign and quickly spun out of control, resulting in the violence, anarchy, and factionalism that resulted in the wholesale "rustication" of Red Guards in the summer of 1968.

In the Tiananmen Incident of April 5, 1976, China's Qingming festival,

---

63. As Party committees in various schools and work units became deluged with proliferating big-character posters during the "Fifty Days" between publication of the first big-character poster on June 2 and Mao Zedong's return to Beijing in late July, they turned for help to the center, and the center responded by sending CCP work teams. There is no reason to doubt that the Party was simply following standard operating procedure; as Liu put it, the dispatch of work teams "had been recognized as the proper means of organization in every movement since the Liberation in 1949." In an editorial note to his 1956 article, "Socialist Upsurge in China's Countryside," Mao even approved the dispatch of work teams: "Work teams must be sent, but it must be stated very clearly that they are being sent to help local Party organizations, not replace them." Stuart Schram, ed., *The Political Thought of Mao Tsetung* (New York: Praeger, 1963), p. 321. These work teams were able to restore order and reimpose firm Party leadership over all units to which they were dispatched, using fairly brutal but nonlethal crowd-control tactics to quell dissent. They were able to do so even in the face of what Party officials at the time considered unusually tenacious opposition. According to eyewitness accounts, by mid-July the situation in Beijing had quieted down considerably. Jean Daubier, *Histoire de la Revolution Culturelle Proletarienne en Chine*, 2 vols. (Paris: Francois Maspero, 1971), vol. 1, pp. 81, 84–85. Daubier was in Beijing at the time.

64. See Audrey Donnithorne, "China's Cellular Economy: Trends Since the Cultural Revolution," *CQ*, no. 52 (October–December 1972), p. 617.

65. See Hong Yung Lee, *The Politics of the Chinese Cultural Revolution* (Berkeley: University of California Press, 1976).

or memorial day, we likewise find indications of clandestine elite support for this brief upsurge of mass unrest: The moderates in the central ministries set up "wreath-making factories" and passed out leaflets to support commemoration of the late Zhou Enlai (and, implicitly, absolution of his protégé, Deng Xiaoping). Albeit too short-lived to result in the range of disruption that characterized the Cultural Revolution, the Incident did result in localized vandalism and violence. Although Deng bore the onus for this at the time, he was eventually able to turn the Incident to his advantage in building an antiradical constituency.

In the Democracy Wall movement of 1978, Deng expressed support for the young activists (who supported, inter alia, a reversal of verdicts on Mao's indictment of the first Tiananmen Incident), allowing interviews with Western or Japanese visitors in which he reaffirmed the constitutional right to post wall posters to be "leaked."[66] After such indications of mass support had been successfully exploited at the Third Plenum, "Democracy Wall" became a liability. The movement spiraled out of control in public protest marches and an orgy of publications lauding economic pragmatism,[67] the "rule of law,"[68] the scientific spirit as an antidote to charismatic dogmatism,[69] and a widespread "blooming" of poetry, short stories, plays (*huaju*), and other literary "flowers" (of uneven quality), and even a reconsideration of the criteria of Marxist literary criticism.[70] The elite's response was the invocation of the Four Cardinal Principles (*si xiang jiben yuanzi*), passage of a constitutional amendment revoking the right to post big-character posters and the right

---

66. These interviews were leaked or even transmitted through official channels, later relayed to the masses via the central document system and in VOA broadcasts: "We have no right to deny this or to criticize the masses for making use of democracy," he said. "If the masses feel some anger, let them express it." Unsurprisingly, the views of the protesters were on the whole sympathetic to Deng Xiaoping and critical of his opponents: Posters implicating Wu De and even Hua Guofeng for their role in suppressing the Tiananmen demonstrators were appearing opposite the entrance to the Beijing municipal Party committee at the time. See John Frazer, *The Chinese: Portrait of a People* (New York: Summit Books, 1980).

67. Commentator, "On Collective Ownership and Its Future," *Siwu luntan* (April fifth forum), no. 12 (September 9, 1979), pp. 1–8, trans. in *Joint Publications Research Service*, no. 74909 (January 11, 1980), pp. 22–35.

68. Qiu Mu, "Why Laws Are Made but Difficult to Enforce," *Tansuo* (Exploration), September 9, 1979, pp. 9–14.

69. See for example He Zuoxiu, Zhao Hongzhou, and Guo Hanying, "Criticize the 'Science and Technology Superstructure Theory of the Gang of Four,'" *Zhexue yanjiu* (Philosophical Studies), no. 4 (1979), pp. 13–22. This more favorable evaluation of science was endorsed by Deng in his "Speech at the National Science Conference" (March 18, 1978), in *FBIS-China*, March 21, 1978.

70. Anon., "On Human Rights," *Qimeng* (Enlightenment), no. 3 (January 1, 1979), pp. 11–27; see also, in the official press, Tao Delin, "A Hundred Schools of Thought Contending and 'Two Schools of Thought' Contending," *Guangming ribao*, September 19, 1979, p. 3.

to strike, and a raft of other legislation restricting the right to publication or public demonstrations. The clampdown began in early 1979, but it was not until mid–1981 that the last of the "people's publications" was shut down.[71]

Protesting Japan, 1985

The protest against Japanese commercial imperialism was the first major such spontaneous mobilization since Democracy Wall (and the first of any sort since the short-lived anti–spiritual pollution movement). The thrust of the campaign was implicitly antireform and specifically anti–Hu Yaobang, who had cultivated Sino-Japanese ties, and there were rumors that the protesters had behind-the-scenes backing from "princes and princesses" (*taizi*) of "overthrown high-ranking cadres"—who might certainly have had such a motive. The first wave of protests coincided with the convening of a special National Party Conference (September 18–23) and with plenums of the Twelfth CC held immediately before and afterward, so they could not have been better timed to get the leadership's attention (recall that this was the time when Hu was pressing ahead with his plan to retire senior cadres). The economy was booming, although the protest coincided with a ballooning imbalance of trade with Japan (China's largest trade partner at the time) that seems to have triggered underlying nationalistic resentment.[72]

This was the most spontaneous demonstration to date and the first to have been so skillfully designed to take advantage of officially sanctioned opportunities for mass initiative. September 18 was the anniversary of the Mukden Incident, a provocation fabricated by the Imperial Kwantung Army in 1931 as a pretext to seize Manchuria. It came shortly after Prime Minister Yasuhiro Nakasone's precedent-shattering official visit to honor Japanese war dead (including a number of convicted war criminals) at the Yasukuni Shrine (on August 15, the fortieth anniversary of the end of World War II). More than 1,000 students took part in the September 18 march, proceeding to the Monument to People's Heroes in Tiananmen Square, carrying floral wreaths on their shoulders. The police did not attempt to suppress the demonstration once in progress, but vid-

---

71. See Roger Garside, *Coming Alive: China After Mao* (New York: McGraw-Hill, 1981), and David Goodman, *Beijing Street Voices: The Poetry and Politics of China's Democracy Movement* (London: Marion Boyars, 1981).

72. China had an overall trade imbalance that drew down foreign exchange reserves from more than $14 billion at the end of 1984 to less than one-half that figure. The largest deficit was with Japan: In 1983, China recorded a negative balance with Japan of $1.6 billion, which continued to spiral to $2 billion in 1984 and to $2.7 billion in the first seven months of 1985.

eotaped the proceedings for "future reference." Meanwhile big-character posters (which had become illegal) began appearing all over the Peking University campus, spreading rapidly to Beijing's other major institutions of higher learning; although primarily concerned with "Japanese militarism," some posters complained about specifically student problems—poor food in the canteens, crowded dormitories, and so forth. The authorities tore down the posters, but more were posted, usually at night. Two of Deng's newly appointed Politburo members, Hu Qili and Li Peng, met with a delegation of students on September 28 at Zhongnanhai, the central Party headquarters, and asked them to desist. After the meeting, CCP authorities sent "work teams" to explain Sino-Japanese economic relations and track down backstage "bad elements."

That seemed to solve the problem in Beijing, but students sent letters and cables to other cities, and the protests spread. Within a few weeks, demonstrations were held in at least three other major urban centers. In Xi'an (capital of Shaanxi province), thousands of students staged campus demonstrations during the week of China's Independence holiday (September 30–October 2). Demonstrations were also reported in Wuhan (in Hubei province) and Chengdu (in Sichuan province—never even occupied by Japanese troops). On the evening of October 15 in Chengdu, several hundred young people marched through the city's leading schools and then several thousand converged in the center of the city at People's Square, beneath a statue of Mao Zedong. Some protesters smashed Japanese-made radios and tape recorders, damaged Toyota taxis, and smashed at least one Japanese motorcycle outside a local hotel.

Authorities reacted to the demonstrations quickly and quite effectively, without resort to violence. Former Ambassador to Japan Hu Hao was sent on an "appeasement mission" to Xi'an, where he addressed a meeting of some 30,000 students, and to other cities in which he put Sino-Japanese relations in a more favorable light. In Chengdu, the public security department briefly took an unspecified number of demonstrators (including one college student) into custody, and six youths were sentenced to labor reform. Meanwhile, the Japanese also sent conciliatory signals. Foreign Minister Shintaro Abe visited Deng Xiaoping and other top Chinese officials to help smooth over the problem, and Prime Minister Nakasone on November 8 expressed his understanding of Chinese criticisms of his visit to Yasukuni. He also promised that Japanese defense spending would not exceed 1 percent of GNP for fiscal year 1986. With that, the crisis seemed, for the time being, to be over.

Demanding Political Reform, December 1986

Beginning at around the time of the introduction of the second, urban phase of the reform program at the Third Plenum of the Twelfth CC in

October 1984, China experienced a second "Great Leap Forward"—albeit under quite different ideological auspices than the first. Industrial output increased by 14 percent in 1984, accelerating to 23 percent in the first half of 1985, to 17.2 percent in the third quarter, and to 10.2 percent in the fourth. The net increase in Chinese industrial output over the 1983–1985 period (ca. $35–40 billion) was equal to the entire annual industrial output of South Korea! Yet the leap had escaped from the control of the planners: Enterprises took advantage of retained profits and easy money to overinvest,[73] while uncontrolled growth in the money supply (partly due to mismanagement in China's newly organized banking system) precipitated then unprecedented inflation rates.[74] In 1985 China incurred its largest trade deficit since Liberation.[75] Corruption was rife. Thus in early 1985 the leadership imposed retrenchment: The banking system cut the money supply, imports were curtailed, and investment was brought under central control. Industrial growth fell to 10.2 percent in the fourth quarter of 1985, and in the first half of 1986 it plunged by 18.2 percent against the corresponding period of 1985. The collective sector grew only 9.5 percent in the first half of 1986, or less than one-quarter of its rate during the same period in 1985; the private sector actually shrank for the first time since 1978.

The reform grouping, temporarily bereft of its standard of economic reform, turned to political reform to regain momentum. Led by the statements of Hu Yaobang and his "Youth League faction" (Hu Qili, Zhu Houzi), but also by Deng Xiaoping himself (in a June 28 speech to the Standing Committee of the Politburo), the regime revived the Double Hundred policy, with a specific mandate to discuss political reform.[76] The intellectuals responded with alacrity. The ideas set forth were wide-ranging, with the Party journal *Red Flag* consistently upholding doctrinal orthodoxy and *People's Daily* permitting more venturesome proposals; the mainstream press remained relatively cautious. The relations of pro-

---

73. Whereas state budgetary allocations had accounted for 90 percent of capital construction investment in 1957 and 83 percent in 1978, by 1984 the state budget's share of investment had shrunk to 54.4 percent, dropping to 40–45 percent the following year.

74. The retail price index rose by more than 11 percent in urban areas and by 6.4 percent in rural areas in 1985, compared to an average price increase of 2.8 percent in 1978–1984, and a mere 0.5 percent from 1957 to 1978.

75. *Far Eastern Economic Review*, February 6, 1986, p. 55. The previous record deficit was $2 billion in 1980, which contributed to the undoing of Hua Guofeng.

76. Hu Yaobang's speech, delivered on April 9, 1986, was published in summary form as "On the Problem of Correct Handling of the Two Different Kinds of Contradiction Within the Party," in *RR*, July 1, 1986. See also Zhou Houzi, "Several Points to Ponder About Ideological and Cultural Questions," *RR*, August 11, 1986, p. 7, trans. in *FBIS-China*, August 28, 1986, p. K8.

duction were redefined to allow the issuance of nonnegotiable debentures, and small stock exchanges were founded in Shanghai and Shenzhen.[77] Some advocated extending the policy of "opening to the outside world" to the realm of ideology and culture.[78] A young lecturer in the philosophy department of Nanjing University named Song Longxiang published a blockbuster article (under the alias Ma Ding) in which he argued that "Chinese economists must free themselves from Marxist books, starting not from dogma but from living fact." Liu Binyan, a well-known investigative reporter, spoke out against the repressive impact of the Four Cardinal Principles in a November 1986 speech that has not, however, been published in full. With specific regard to political reform, Wan Li made an important speech that called for the use of "soft science" to improve feedback and overall political efficiency.[79] Many called for further electoral reforms.[80] There were calls for freedom of the press, for pushing ahead with a publication and press law (Hu Jiwei had reportedly been engaged in drafting one since 1983), and even for the authorization of private publishing organs.

While this "blooming" was in progress, the CCP leadership was holding its annual "retreat" at Beidaiho, where the presence of the elders was particularly marked. In this ambit Deng Xiaoping, who had (however vaguely) authorized political reform on June 28, seems to have recanted. The Sixth Plenum of the Twelfth CC, held in Beijing in September, adopted a "Resolution of the CC of the CCP on the Guiding Principles for Building a Socialist Society with an Advanced Culture and Ideology," which upheld the importance of a "socialist spiritual civilization"; when Lu Dingyi protested this document's attack on "bourgeois liberalization," he was refuted by none other than Deng Xiaoping. The upshot was not entirely negative from the perspective of the reformers, as the plenum reaffirmed the Double Hundred policy and the "opening to the outside world," but political reform was relegated to a committee for further "study."

It was in this context—raised expectations from the summer's "blooming" followed by dashed hopes at the plenum—that the student

---

77. See Sheng Xuanli, "A Discussion on the Question of 'Ownership System Reform and Structural Readjustment,'" *RR*, September 1, 1986, p. 1, trans. in *FBIS-China*, September 11, pp. K12–17.

78. Yi Qiu, "Renewal of Traditional Culture and Opening to the Outside World," *Gongren ribao* (Worker's Daily) (Beijing), June 13, 1986, p. 3.

79. Chen Chujia and Wu Ming, "Wan Li Addresses National Soft Science Symposium," Xinhua (Beijing), July 31, 1986, in *FBIS-China*, August 4, pp. K8–11.

80. Fang Lizhi gave several speeches on the general issue of democratic reform during this period, one of which has been translated in *Washington Post*, January 18, 1987, pp. C1–4.

protest demonstrations of December 1986 took place. This was the first protest in which activists began turning away from the Party to non-Party elites, viz., intellectuals. The immediate stimulus was supplied by an astrophysicist of radical-liberal political leanings named Fang Lizhi,[81] who, in a November public debate, challenged Vice-Premier Wan Li's assumption that democracy consists of the CCP allowing the masses to speak, deeming this to be a natural human right.[82] In speeches to students at his home campus (the University of Science and Technology in Hefei) and Wuhan, he encouraged their interest in politics and specifically in the district elections then being held (thanks to his intercession in the nominating process, one student and Fang himself were actually elected).

The largest demonstrations to shake China in some ten years began on December 5 and 9 on college campuses in Hefei and Wuhan, as students used the pretext of the anniversary of the December Ninth (1935) Movement to stage a march on government headquarters. Over the next two weeks, despite the official news blackout, demonstrations, often accompanied by big-character posters, spread to about seventeen additional cities and more than one hundred and fifty campuses, sometimes conflating various local grievances (in Shenzhen students protested a tuition fee issue and in Changsha they demonstrated on behalf of a teacher who had been beaten in a housing dispute) with more general, political demands. In contrast to the smaller and briefer demonstrations in the fall of 1985, which could be interpreted as opposing the opening policy, the 1986 protests clearly espoused the ideals of democracy and political reform. The protesters had learned the advantages of co-opting official rhetoric.

As the momentum mounted, as workers began to join with the students, and as demonstrations finally spread to the capital, disrupting traffic and (according to police) resulting in violence and destruction of property, the authorities became aroused. Sidestepping constitutional guarantees according Chinese citizens the right to protest, Shanghai, Beijing, and other cities passed local ordinances making that right contingent on various procedural formalities that left ample discretion for refusal. Newspapers broke their silence to write denunciatory editorials. Police started to take pictures of protesters, infiltrate their ranks, and "detain" ringleaders. Still, consecutive marches in Shanghai on

---

81. Though Li was most notorious, two other intellectuals were also expelled from the Party for incitement: writer Wang Ruowang, and investigative journalist Liu Binyan. In August 1987, five more were punished (punishments ranging from job dismissal to expulsion from the Party): playwright Wu Zuguang, and Marxist theorists Wang Ruoshui, Su Shaozhi, Sun Changjiang, and Zhang Xianyang.

82. *Washington Post*, January 18, 1987, pp. C1, C4.

December 19–21 drew from 50,000–70,000 participants, according to eyewitnesses.

At this point the breakthrough mentality made its resurgence, resulting in two capsized cars and scores of police injuries in the Shanghai marches. The wave of protests came to a head when several thousand students and their supporters assembled in Tiananmen on the morning of New Year's Day, despite a ban on unauthorized demonstrations and stern warnings in the official press. About three hundred people broke through a police cordon, shouting slogans and unfolding banners in support of democracy, press freedom, and reform. In their explicit defiance of the authority of the CCP and their co-optation of central symbols to demand immediate and sweeping reforms, these young people seemed to Party veterans an unpleasant echo of the Red Guards of a previous generation, and they adopted a harder line. A New Year's Day *People's Daily* commentary raised the issue of "bourgeois liberalization," which an editorial in the same paper five days later blamed for student unrest. Gone was the media pluralism that had reigned throughout the summer, as all newspapers joined in lambasting "bourgeois liberalization" and demanding adherence to the Four Cardinal Principles.

The political upshot, as noted in Chapter 3, is that Hu Yaobang was blamed for mollycoddling the protesters and demoted from his position as general secretary of the CCP (and as Deng's heir apparent). Although the evidence of Hu's active leadership of the protests is thin indeed, the fact that the protests ceased so abruptly when Hu was blamed for them suggests that he was a passive (and perhaps unwitting) accomplice.

Occupying Tiananmen, April 15–June 4, 1989

The background to the Tiananmen protests was one of deflation from the suspended reforms and the "overheated" business cycle of 1988. The June–July 1988 attempt at price reform had been economically disastrous over the short run, and the leadership resolved not to wait for the long run but to reverse course and blame things on the reformers. Zhao Ziyang, the leading reformer, emerged from the Beidaiho meetings and the ensuing Third Plenum of the Thirteenth CC (held in September in Beijing) a political cripple—without any reform programs he could push, obliged to support a retrenchment program he did not believe in that threatened the interests of his bureaucratic and mass constituency. Having been divested of his economic portfolio and forced to make a self-criticism, Zhao lapsed perforce into a passive position. But with or without his permission, the reform forces soon sought to regroup, rejoining the fray on cultural turf (thus repeating the pattern of transiting issue areas to sustain momentum we first noted in 1986).

For the first time since Hu's demotion, the intellectual constituency that Zhao had inherited (from Hu) reprised the issue of political reform. In December 1989, Hu Qili, Wang Renzhi, and Hu Sheng jointly planned and convened a seminar of reform intellectuals to commemorate the decennial of the famous Third Plenum of the Eleventh CC that had inaugurated the reforms. More than three hundred participants appeared, including Yu Guangyuan, Wang Ruoshui, Yan Jiaqi, Su Shaozhi, Tong Dalin, and other reform intellectuals. Su Shaozhi made a bold speech in which he attacked the campaigns against spiritual pollution and bourgeois liberalism and called for a reversal of verdicts on one of their leading victims, Wang Ruoshui. At around the same time, an editorial writer published an article contending that "there is a need courageously to draw lessons" from "modern democratic forms" that "have developed in Western capitalism" in building socialist democracy.[83] In February and March 1989, the issue shifted to human rights, as the regime imposed martial law on Tibet for the first time since 1959; this led international human rights organizations to censure China and domestic intellectuals to echo their concerns.[84] Three petitions were written by groups of high-ranking intellectuals in the early spring of 1989 calling for release of former Democracy Wall activist Wei Jingsheng and all "political prisoners" (the regime categorically denies their existence).

These protests put Zhao in a difficult position, for he wished to inherit Hu's mantle (and constituency) as leader of the reform movement but was highly vulnerable at this time to "leftist" indignation and needed Deng's support to survive. That support was, however, contingent upon repudiation of any form of mass participation that even remotely reminded Deng of the Cultural Revolution. Zhao was vulnerable not only because of the hyperinflation of the past summer but also because as Deng's heir apparent and the leading reformer he became the next logical target of all who held misgivings about the reform course or harbored their own ambitions for the succession. Throughout the spring of 1989, the "older cadres with great prestige" formed a coalition with younger clients, who had ambitions of their own, to assail Zhao's stewardship, now adding to their complaints of economic mismanagement a critique

---

83. "New Realm in the Emancipation of Thinking," *Guangming Ribao* (Beijing), December 29, 1988.

84. Martial law was imposed in Lhasa in March following the violent suppression of riots touched off when the police opened fire on a small group of monks involved in a peaceful demonstration in favor of Tibetan autonomy. Some 60,000 PLA troops were brought in to help the police with mass arrests and house-to-house searches.

of his lack of vigorous ideological leadership.[85] These complaints culminated in Li Xiannian's flight to Shanghai for secret consultations with Deng, in which he urged that Zhao be required to make self-criticism for his errors and step down at the Fourth Plenum; Li Peng might then move into the general secretary's slot, while Yao Yilin would become premier, with Zou Jiahua (another Soviet-returned student) to replace Yao; Zhao might stay on for six months as vice-chair of the CMC as a sop. Due to the controversy, the Fourth Plenum, originally set to convene immediately before the NPC and CPPCC sessions, was postponed—Deng wanted no reshuffle until after the Sino-Soviet summit in mid-May.

Zhao, impaled on the horns of a dilemma—whether to fight for his constituency or placate his high-level critics—equivocated, taking a tough rhetorical stance while holding the line against sanctions with teeth in them.[86] Only thus could he retain the patronage of Deng, who shared his interest in salvaging reform achievements (e.g., Deng gave a speech on January 19 castigating the "trend toward taking the road back"). Although the Propaganda Department compiled a list of targets for public criticism, at the last minute Zhao said, "Just ignore it and there is no need for us to handle the case." On the other hand, Zhao convened the Politburo several times in the wake of the Bush visit to denounce Fang Lizhi (whom the Chinese had gone out of their way to exclude from an embassy reception), and he impugned the various petition drives as tools of international human rights organizations; at a March 5 enlarged Politburo meeting, he gave an "important speech" lambasting critics of China's Tibetan policy. The State Council's Education Commission was encouraged to send work teams to various college campuses to see what the students were up to and prevent signature-gathering petitions, inflammatory wall posters, and protest movements.

---

85. E.g., around the turn of the year, Chen Yun circulated "Eight Opinions," which held Zhao responsible for "failure to do public opinion, ideological and theoretical work properly," claiming that "the entire ideological front is occupied by the bourgeoisie and nothing proletarian is left." See Dittmer, "China in 1988," in *Asian Survey* 29:1 (January 1989), pp. 12–29; and Dittmer, "China in 1989," *Asian Survey* 30:1 (January 1990), pp. 25–42. Bo Yibo, who had prepared the indictment of Hu Yaobang in January 1987, submitted a "letter of appeal" to Deng Xiaoping focusing on the recent decennial conference (which he characterized as an "attack on the Party CC") and calling for suspension of the *Herald* and for public criticism of its editor (Qin Benli). Wang Zhen and Bo Yibo reportedly proposed three times to Deng that Zhao make a self-criticism for his mistakes in work.

86. Thus Zhao decreed that Chen Yun's Eight Opinions (see note 85, above) need not be "transmitted throughout the country" as Chen had stipulated, and he remarked with regard to Bo Yibo's protest, "Intellectuals have their own understanding of problems. What is there to be surprised at?" See Dittmer, "The Tiananmen Massacre," *Problems of Communism* 38:5 (September–October 1989), pp. 2–17.

Meanwhile, Hu Yaobang picked this inauspicious moment to launch his comeback. Still a full member of the Politburo, though he had taken no part in Party life since his demotion, Hu returned to Beijing from a place of convalescence in Nanning to attend the NPC and CPPCC sessions, where his brief appearance raised a stir. Yet his real debut came on April 8, when the CC convened an enlarged Politburo meeting to discuss problems in education. For the first time since his demotion, Hu registered not only to attend but to speak in the meeting. There he reportedly delivered an impassioned plea for greater support for education. But some forty minutes into the meeting (according to rumor, in an altercation with his old nemesis, Bo Yibo), Hu was stricken with a heart attack and obliged to depart on a stretcher. On April 15, 1989, Hu died of a heart infarction at the hospital. In a conversation with Li Rui shortly before his death, he expressed his regret at having submitted a self-criticism in January 1989 in which he had criticized others.[87]

Hu's dramatic reappearance and untimely death struck the spark that set the prairie fire. First, the two events split the leadership. In preparation for his memorial service, the leadership divided over two questions: How Hu's resignation should be assessed (i.e., could there be a reversal of verdicts?), and whether Hu could be deemed a "great Marxist." The antireform coalition that had deposed the late general secretary opposed any verdict reversal, which would obviously place coalition members in a bad light. Seeking compromise, Zhao suggested that Hu might be praised as a "great Marxist" but that the issue of his forced resignation should be shelved. Deng at first seemed to agree, but some of the other elders had reservations and the memorial speech had to go through many drafts before winning approval.

Second, the Hu issue provided an opportunity for mobilization of the students, who had become Hu's most ardent admirers since his fall from grace for having failed to crack down hard on the 1986 protests. Protesters began to gather even before the funeral: On the evening of April 19, about 10,000 students gathered in Tiananmen Square, where they staged a sit-in and demanded the right to "petition" Party leaders—this demonstration was forcibly dispersed by armed police. Although demonstrators were prohibited from entering Tiananmen on April 22, when the memorial service was held in the Great Hall of the People, they staged a sit-in in the square all through the night of April 21 and remained there in defiance of the ban. On April 24, students declared a strike of classes of indefinite duration and established the National

---

87. See *Jing bao* (Mirror), no. 144 (July 10, 1989), pp. 42–48, and *Zheng ming*, no. 139 (May 1, 1989), pp. 11–12.

Students' Federation Preparatory Committee—the first step toward establishing autonomous student and labor unions (obviously modeled on Solidarity). Meanwhile, Zhao Ziyang departed on a week-long trip to North Korea (April 23–30), leaving only vague instructions on how to cope with the situation.

Upon Zhao's departure, the hard-liners fastened upon the nonviolent but mushrooming protests as a national emergency and hunkered down in a crisis decisionmaking mode. Li Peng convened an expanded session of the Politburo Standing Committee on April 24 to discuss the situation, and he and Yang Shangkun reported to Deng the next day. Deng fully reciprocated their sense of urgency, saying, "We must take a clear-cut stand and forceful measures to oppose and stop the upheaval. . . . Don't be afraid of students, because we still have several million troops."[88] A tacit consensus may have been reached at this time to use troops if the demonstrators did not respond to warning, but a warning was issued first. Based largely on Deng's comments, a lead editorial was published in *People's Daily* on April 26 which characterized the protests as a "turmoil" (*dongluan*) that "was organized" by a "tiny handful of people" with ulterior motives opposed to the interests of the Party and the nation. Prohibiting any further disorder, the editorial warned that "troops will be dispatched when necessary." In explicit defiance of this ultimatum, the students launched their largest march the following day (many took the precaution of writing their wills). Security forces made only token efforts to halt some 100,000 students from marching for seventeen hours through the streets of Beijing, finally breaking through police lines to surge into Tiananmen Square; police restraint avoided immediate bloodshed, but may have given the protesters an illusory sense of invulnerability. In deference to the warning, the protests remained peaceful and, in fact, were tightly disciplined, interlarding the acts of protest with patriotic songs and slogans and forming a human chain on either side of the march to maintain order and prevent outsiders, whom they could not control, from joining in.

Although Zhao Ziyang had approved the April 26 editorial by telegraph from Pyongyang, upon his return he took a few days to reassess the situation. The leadership had become polarized between those urging a crackdown and those favoring a more conciliatory stance, and most of Zhao's constituency gravitated to the latter position. Taking advantage of his discovery that the editorial had been altered in several respects before publication, Zhao decided now that it had been too "strident." He then

---

88. See "A Document Circulated Among Senior Party and Government Officials Earlier This Month [April 25, 1989]," as reprinted in Michel Oksenberg, Lawrence Sullivan, and Mark Lambert, eds., *Beijing Spring, 1989* (Armonk, N.Y.: M. E. Sharpe, 1990), pp. 203–206.

made a special trip to Beidaiho to apprise Deng of his feelings. Deng, perhaps chastened by the miscarriage of his own preferred solution, seems to have provisionally approved a shift of course. On this basis, Zhao made an impromptu speech to representatives of the Asian Development Bank in which he set forth a new, soft line: The students were well-intentioned and patriotic; their input might contribute to the furtherance of the reforms.

For the next two weeks, Zhao's line was in effect: There was no attempt to crack down, and, in fact, on May 6 Zhao permitted the Chinese media to cover the protests, which they proceeded to do with considerable accuracy, even sympathy. Although Zhao was able to make no further concrete concessions, the withdrawal of regime opposition seems to have undermined the protest, as the movement experienced a lull. At student request, several dialogues were held between various regime officials and selected protest delegations, usually ending inconclusively.[89] Student demands tended to shift but eventually focused on a repudiation of the April 26 editorial (which would imply amnesty for all participants), on some liberalization of speech and press rights, and on action against corruption. Regime spokesmen were conciliatory but noncommittal.

In mid-May, both the mass movement and the regime response changed course, for at least three reasons. First, the protesters escalated tactics, adopting mass hunger strikes beginning on May 13; this raised the stakes and enhanced their credibility, attracting much more widespread support. Second, the Gorbachev summit visit attracted international media to Beijing, and the protesters realized they could share this limelight with minimal danger of violence, at least during the visit. Both of these factors caused the number of participants in the Tiananmen sit-in to burgeon, and as the international media began to report on the protests and beam the news back into China via British Broadcasting Corporation (BBC) and Voice of America (VOA) broadcasts, protest metastasized, spreading to most provincial capitals and college towns. Finally, it was during this visit that the leadership resolved to crack down hard on the protesters (no doubt partly because the protesters had embarrassed the regime before outsiders, though partly because the protest was gathering momentum). This, however, exposed to public scrutiny a leadership breach hitherto veiled by Party discipline, which in turn had a polarizing effect on the protest.

The decisionmaking dynamics within the leadership at the time are

---

89. See Corinna-Barbara Francis, "The Progress of Protest in China: The Spring of 1989," *Asian Survey*, 29:9 (September 1989), pp. 898–915.

still somewhat unclear, but enough has leaked out to be able to make some fairly strong inferences. As far as the hard-liners were concerned, Zhao's soft line had by now demonstrated its bankruptcy, and the only possible solution was armed force. Zhao probably argued that his approach had never really been given a chance. The dispute came down to a choice between the April 26 editorial, which Zhao argued should be rescinded as per student demand, and Zhao's May 4 speech, which Li Peng argued was an unauthorized deviation from the Party line as represented in the April 26 editorial. Zhao's proposal (to rescind the editorial, taking personal responsibility for any "error," along with certain other concessions) was rejected by the Politburo Standing Committee on May 16, reportedly by a vote of four to one, when it was also decided to invoke martial law.

It seems to have been at this point that Zhao's strategy, hitherto a search for compromise between hard-liner and student demands, subtly shifted. He exploited his public appearance with Gorbachev later the same day (which must have dumbfounded the latter) to unveil the arrangement whereby Deng retained ultimate veto power over Politburo decisions. This must have infuriated Deng: Not only was Zhao fingering him for failure to make concessions, he was also confirming suspicions of backstage manipulation that made a mockery of formal structure. From attempting to engineer the protesters' departure from the square, Zhao seems to have shifted to supporting—hence encouraging—their demands. Thus he made several personal visits to the square after his intra-Party defeat, for rather emotional heart-to-heart talks with protest leaders. The hard-liners viewed his actions as being in clear violation of the rules of democratic centralism, designed to mobilize the protesters against the Politburo majority. Be that as it may, his tactics were not dissimilar to Deng's exploitation of Democracy Wall protests to facilitate his own displacement of Hua Guofeng in December 1978.

In the course of the ensuing week, Deng Xiaoping, Yang Shangkun, Li Peng, and others made preparations for the requisite transfer of troops, with Deng Xiaoping apparently playing a decisive role both in pushing through the decision and in persuading regional military commanders to comply. On May 19, martial law was proclaimed, in a public meeting that clearly exposed the cleavage within the leadership: Zhao Ziyang failed to appear—although he had retracted his resignation, he claimed illness. The Politburo moved to strip Zhao of his power, rescinding his right to transfer troops (Zhao was still nominal vice-chair of the CMC) and placing him under virtual house arrest. Yet in contrast to 1986, the purge of the general secretary did not break the back of the protest movement. To the contrary, when troops set out for Tiananmen Square on the morning of May 20, they were impeded by an outpouring of support from the citizenry, as an estimated two million people clogged the streets and prevented their advance to the square.

For the next two weeks, the leaders seemed flummoxed. After forcing Zhao to step aside for failing to resolve the crisis, they seemed equally powerless to end it. The students remained camped on the square (although their numbers were dwindling), still spurning compromise but also carefully avoiding any pretext for a crackdown. In making preparations for the postponed Fourth Plenum, now necessary to formalize the leadership reshuffle, the Deng–Li–Yang troika found it difficult to persuade a majority that Zhao was guilty of "crimes," and the latter's refusal to submit a self-criticism or resign left the issue in doubt. In fact, there was an unprecedented defection rate from the Party line, as over a hundred military officers (led by several generals) signed a petition to the CMC calling on troops not to fight civilians, and some 57 members of the 135-seat NPC Standing Committee called for an emergency session of the NPC—which had the constitutional right to revoke martial law and even to dismiss Li Peng. If things were to go on in this way, leaving the outlawed demonstrators to gradually disperse from the square at their own pace while politics took its course through constitutional channels, the hard-liners might well be forced to compromise or even lose on this issue. Thus the leadership decision to crack down with military force, in which Deng Xiaoping, Yang Shangkun, and Li Peng again played leading roles, seems to have been motivated by two factors. First, if martial law, contrary to all expectations, could be blunted by massive passive resistance, this was truly a crisis of authority demanding sterner measures. Second, to criminalize the Democracy Movement by invoking such severe sanctions would also discredit and intimidate Zhaoist sympathizers within the CC.

As is now well known, this decision was carried out with lavish brutality on the night of June 3–4, resulting in the deaths of several hundred people, most of whom were nonstudents who had interceded to block the troop advance or simply happened to be in the vicinity. The Tiananmen massacre was followed by a brief hiatus during which few members of the central leadership were to be seen. Then on June 9 Deng made a surprise TV appearance, his first since the Gorbachev summit, together with other senior officials and military officers gathering to pay tribute to the soldiers who had been "martyred" defending the capital from anarchy. His speech at that time, though delivered with some evidence of failing health, has been quoted more extensively than any such document since the days of Chairman Mao. As in 1987, the crackdown was immediately generalized throughout the country, accompanied by a skillfully edited propaganda film depicting the protest as a "counterrevolutionary revolt." The number of officially reported arrests as of early July exceeded 2,500, though unofficial estimates put it at over 10,000. The official count of those executed was around 27, most of whom were workers rather than students. Secret lists of intellectuals whose thinking was considered to be a source of the protesters' misdeeds were compiled for criticism and purge, and an "underground railroad" soon sprang up through which a number of fugitives managed to flee through Hong Kong to the West. Most former protesters proceeded to France, where they were welcomed on the second centennial of the French Revolution, to establish a Chinese Democracy Federation.

The Fourth Plenum of the Thirteenth Central Committee was finally convened on June 23; despite intensive propaganda preparation, more than fifty members and alternate members asked for sick leave or leave of absence, but they could easily be dispensed with as the leadership "packed" the session with nonmembers. The formal disposition of the general secretary was the main item on the agenda. Zhao had requested an opportunity to speak at the plenum; this request was denied, but an expanded Politburo meeting was convened preceding the plenum (on June 14), where he made a statement in his defense. "First, I did not make a mistake," he asserted. "Second, I still hold that the starting point of the student movement was good. They were patriotic."[90] In direct defiance of the victorious majority, he insisted that the April 26 editorial was mistaken, that there was no social basis for "turmoil" in China, but that those who imposed martial law should be held accountable for intensifying contradictions. Arguing that there was no Zhaoist anti-Party clique in the Party, he sought to protect the "large numbers of innocent, good comrades" who had gotten involved.[91] Fittingly enough, Zhao's indictment was made in a report by Li Peng, on behalf of the Politburo, to the Fourth CC. Zhao was expelled from all posts in the Party and (later) government, and a special group was established to "look further into his case," suggesting that he might later be evicted from the Party and placed on trial (the former is prerequisite to the latter). Despite recurrent criticisms by Peng Zhen, Li Xiannian, Song Ping, and Wang Zhen, the investigation group, however, found no reliable proof that Zhao had participated directly in the protest movement or had led an anti-Party group in the Party—more to the point, Deng apparently felt that any further prosecution of Zhao might endanger remaining reforms. Chen Yun agreed that controversies over problems at the top levels should be shelved for two or three years.[92]

---

90. *Bai xing ban yue kan* (Bai Xing Semimonthly) (Hong Kong), no. 203 (November 1, 1989), pp. 18–24.
91. *Zheng ming*, no. 142 (August 1, 1989), pp. 9–10.
92. *Zheng ming*, no. 142 (August 1, 1989), pp. 6–7, and no. 144 (October 1, 1989), pp. 6–8.

Despite Zhao's efforts on their behalf, those closely associated with him also suffered political demotions. Hu Qili was purged from the Politburo, though he did retain a seat in the CC. Removed from the Secretariat with the general secretary were Rui Xingwen, formerly in charge of ideology, and united front chief Yan Mingfu, who had overall responsibility for negotiations with the demonstrators. Also apparently out were Wang Jiabao (head of the CC's General Affairs Department), Du Rensheng (director of the CC's Rural Policy Research Center), An Zhiwen (vice-minister of the State Commission for Reform of the Economic Structure), and Bao Tong (head of the Institute for Reform of the Political Structure, who alone among high-level cadres was placed under arrest). Minister of Culture Wang Meng was obliged to resign. Beneficiaries of these purges included new Politburo members Song Ping, the (then) seventy-two-year-old former vice-minister, who became minister of the State Planning Commission (a Cultural Revolution survivor and protégé of Chen Yun); Li Ruihuan, fifty-five, an energetic ex-mayor of Tianjin (rumored son-in-law of Wan Li), who was given the propaganda portfolio (and promptly initiated a purge of the *People's Daily* staff); and hard–line Beijing Party Secretary Li Ximing.

In the selection of a new general secretary, Chen Yun reportedly nominated Yao Yilin, while Peng Zhen recommended Qiao Shi, resulting in a stalemate, which Deng broke with his nomination of compromise candidate Jiang Zemin, former party secretary of Shanghai. Jiang had studied electrical engineering in Moscow in the early 1950s (where he was probably a classmate of Li Peng) and is also close to Li Xiannian (a relationship reportedly analogous to Li Peng's with Zhou Enlai). When the vote was taken, Jiang managed to eke out only seven votes more than the total cast for others, for a scant majority. As a former minister of the electronics industry, he is believed to understand the need for new technology and is reputed to have supported urban economic reforms in Shanghai. He came to Deng's attention, however, for the hard line he took against *World Economic Herald* (firing editor Qin Benli when he published minutes from a restricted briefing on Hu Yaobang in late April) and for his successful yet low-profile suppression of Shanghai's democracy movement. His helicopter-like ascent is sometimes attributed to Deng's desire to add an advocate of reform to counterbalance a hard-line majority on the Politburo Standing Committee (which consists, in addition to Jiang, of Li Peng; Li Ruihuan; Organization Department Head Song Ping; Qiao Shi, who is still in charge of the Central Disciplinary Inspection Committee and also runs the Central Party School and the Party's theoretical journal, *Seeking Truth*; and Yao Yilin, a Chen Yun protégé who has been in charge of economic retrenchment since 1988).

The immediate and almost unanimous international repudiation of the well-publicized June bloodbath may, ironically, have eased the leadership's reassertion of political control, as it provided a convenient pretext for quarantining China from the "bourgeois liberal" countries whose contact they held responsible (in part correctly) for the protesters' libertarian aspirations. Thus censorship of international mail was reimposed, fax ties cut or placed under surveillance, and Chinese-language VOA and BBC broadcasts were electronically jammed; needless to say, the liberalization of domestic media that Zhao introduced in early May ended with the career of its sponsor. Yet the leadership managed to reaffirm the policy of "opening to the outside world" even when it was least credible, and the decline in tourism, economic aid, commerce, and investment that accompanied China's ostracism from the international community—motivated in part by moral scruples, though more by business prudence—has not proved irrevocable. As in the case of the Soviet crackdowns on Hungary in 1956 and on Czechoslovakia in 1968, the West has shown itself to be quite tolerant so long as its material interests are not threatened. By August, foreign commercial banks had quietly resumed making new loans to Chinese institutions, albeit small and short-term ones; a major breakthrough occurred at the July 1990 meeting of the Group of Seven, when Japan announced a resumption of loans. Again by August, most bilateral or multilateral international sanctions had been suspended.

Conclusions

Progress toward a "civil society" in China began from a very different starting point than it did in the West.[93] Before the Cultural Revolution the public sphere did not really exist; there was, rather, a thoroughly compartmentalized gridwork of "systems" and "units," served by relatively comprehensive intramural communications but embedded in a public realm of bland generalities and "revolutionary" values semidetached from their empirical referents. Above this honeycomb was the central apparatus; it alone had the capability to bridge interstitial walls, which it did from time to time via invasive "mass movements." These campaigns proved highly successful in the early years of the regime in transforming the political status quo and mobilizing popular support around a new order. After the use of the campaign as a redistributive vehicle had been exhausted, however, it became increasingly difficult to find constructive uses for mass movements or collective incentives for their participants.

---

93. See also Rowe, "Public Sphere," and David Strand, "Protest in Beijing: Civil Society and Public Sphere in China," *Problems of Communism*, 34:3 (May–June 1990), pp. 1–19.

The Cultural Revolution represented the final exhaustion of the mass movement and the transition to a new type of spontaneous mobilization from the bottom up—a transition most in the established leadership could not successfully negotiate. Indeed, few could, as the movement became a self-cannibalizing dynamo difficult to turn to anyone's political advantage, not only endangering the elites who started it but also spawning factions like dragon's teeth that turned on each other. Mao's nostalgic attempt to revive the Chinese revolution and to "steel" China's youth in its "cauldron" imbued the movement with an anarchic, heaven storming, breakthrough mentality that made it difficult to put to any constructive use. Yet, all the same, it marked at least the beginning of a true civil society in Chinese politics by breaking the claim of the CCP to monopolize leadership of the public sector and by creating a network of quasi-autonomous alternative media.

The reform era represents a struggle to come to terms with the legacy of the Cultural Revolution and to salvage its positive contributions in the context of constant friction between pell-mell economic growth and a fierce elite determination to maintain existing political structures. As we have seen, efforts to create a public sphere soon veered onto two diverging tracks: one an attempt to build a civil culture, from the top down; and the other an attempt to build a mass culture, from the bottom up. From the top down the focus was on formalization and secularization, with a strong emphasis on procedure. At first the assumption seemed to be that if civil procedures were adhered to, the content could take care of itself, but over time the leadership became increasingly concerned about the incursion of bourgeois values and other forms of spiritual pollution and devoted increasing attention to substance. The substance they offered was, however, an ungainly mix of pre–Cultural Revolution era Mao Zedong Thought and traditional Confucian values, capable of engendering enthusiastic support only from those whose political interests were imperiled by change.

The instigators of the various spontaneous protest movements, in contrast, were concerned almost exclusively with substantive issues—now, however, with liberal and reformist, rather than revolutionary, values. And their early protests bore the earmarks of their Cultural Revolution legacy, tending to degenerate into vandalism and inflammatory, irresponsible polemics. With a string of repeated suppressions, however, came a slowly dawning awareness of the importance of civil procedure: The 1989 protest in this respect represented a great leap forward compared to 1976 or even 1986.

By May 1989, as a result of these crosscurrents of cultural tradition and political change, the reform leadership found itself confronting a transitional, chameleon-like phenomenon, in which different actors per-

Emergence of a Public Sphere?   155

ceived different tendencies. How to deal with it became so controversial that it shattered a leadership already embroiled in controversy over reform and succession issues. To Zhao and his following, the new public realm was essentially patriotic, civil, and proreform and hence capable of being exploited to salvage both Zhao's own ailing career and the programs he supported. To Deng and the hard-liners, these were Red Guard–style radicals mouthing reform slogans to ward off punishment but actually just trying to create a big commotion and make names for themselves. To the American media public, this was a prototype of Western civil society, complete with a Goddess of Democracy, apparently modeled after the Statue of Liberty.

In fact, it was none of these things, though it shared characteristics with each of them. Although ostensibly in favor of Zhao and his reform grouping, the demonstrators were of no political use to Zhao because they could not be persuaded to leave once their point had been made, insisting on remaining until their illegal presence became an embarrassment to their alleged patron. Although they employed certain Cultural Revolution tactics (such as public criticism of selected central leaders) until they lost control of the situation in the final hours, they adhered to nonviolent tactics with impressive self-discipline. Though clearly entranced with Western democracy (and seemingly with everything Western, including fashion, music, and consumer technology), they were none too sure what it was, as indicated by the fact that they could make no decision concerning their own movement unless absolute consensus was obtained, with the result that marching orders were repeatedly dictated by their most extreme contingent.[94] In Isaiah Berlin's terms, the demonstrators understood democracy in terms of "freedom from," not "freedom to." Having dared to be free, they seemed paralyzed by the next step.

Some of these idiosyncrasies can be accounted for by the fact that the movement's acts and the regime's reactions still took place within a distinctively Chinese political cultural space. The public sector was defined substantively, with a strong emphasis on selflessness. Thus everyone engaged in the confrontation became ennobled, from the students (whose sincerity was most convincingly demonstrated by the hunger strike—willingness to fast to the death struck a chord among food-obsessed Chinese)[95] to the highest leadership (where even Li Peng professed his solicitude for the students). It was perhaps in part due to the ennobling

---

94. See Dorothy J. Solinger, "Democracy with Chinese Characteristics," *World Policy Journal*, 6:4 (Fall 1989), pp. 621–632.

95. According to Sun Longqi, in *Zhongguo wenhua de "shenceng jiegou"* (The "deep structure" of Chinese culture) (Taibei: Gufeng, 1986).

cast of the public spotlight that it proved so difficult to leave the stage: Public negotiations were demanded and sometimes granted; the students would quibble about whether the right persons had been selected as negotiating partners, complain about lack of television coverage, and so forth; by their own admission nothing was settled at these sessions, but new sessions were repeatedly demanded. It was easy for the hard-liners to conclude that negotiations would continue as long as there was an audience. For its part, the regime's failure to show "human feeling" (*renqing wei*) when it excluded students from Hu Yaobang's state funeral was a serious public relations blunder, as was Li Peng's wooden performance throughout the negotiations; Zhao Ziyang's emotional rendezvous with hunger strikers on the night of May 19 was better (if "too late," as he conceded). Although leaks per se were avoided, elite-mass links were tacitly formed via the nuances of public rhetoric, most notably when Zhao used his televised audience with Gorbachev to announce that Deng had made secret arrangements giving him veto power over all central decisions. Thus a horizontal cleavage quickly became transformed into a vertical one, as both sides sought constituencies for their position (the hard-liners turned to the PLA).[96]

The emergent public sphere had, however, changed considerably in the course of reform. Whereas both the Cultural Revolution and the Tiananmen demonstrations were marked by the jubilant, festive atmosphere that came from this mutual baptism in selflessness, there was a contrast in tone between the peace-loving, flower child innocence of the Tiananmen demonstrators and the incendiary rhetoric of the Red Guards, who wanted to "overthrow the king of hell and free all the little devils." This may have been at least partly tactical—whereas the Red Guards had Mao on their side from 1966 to 1968, in 1989 the demonstrators were quite aware that the country's military strength would be arrayed against them if brought into the fray. Despite the relative sympathy for Zhao, elite-mass links were quite loose: The vertical coalition with Zhao was effectuated only at the point when Zhao had become politically defunct, and even the hard-liners seem to have had difficulty assembling the military units used to clear the square. The ban on informal lateral communications media once again broke down completely, with

---

96. "It was clear that Zhao was trying to betray Deng in public," wrote one eyewitness. "The response was enormous—on 17 May, more than one million people, consisting of Chinese of all walks of life as well as students, demonstrated. For the first time, slogans in great numbers were directed at Deng, demanding his retirement." King K. Tsao, "Civil Disobedience and Dissent Against the Party-State: An Eyewitness Account of the 1989 Chinese Student Movement," in Peter Li, Steven Mark, and Marjorie Hi Li, eds., *Culture and Politics in China: An Anatomy of Tiananmen Square* (New Brunswick, N.J.: Transaction, 1991), pp. 153–171.

intercity *chuanlian* (linkups) now augmented by more advanced communication techniques—the telephone or fax machine was used between cities and with overseas supporters; students used beepers, walkie-talkies, megaphones, motor scooter couriers, and even cellular telephones to facilitate local communications. When media censorship was lifted by the moderates during the first two weeks of May, the Chinese press functioned as an effective nationwide mobilization network, and the international media, particularly those with a Chinese audience (VOA and BBC), functioned in this capacity until transmissions were jammed.

A serious weakness was the movement's continuing dependence on leadership patronage.[97] Since Democracy Wall, the center had maintained an effective embargo against elite collusion with mass agitators. The leadership's premise that the masses must accept CCP dictatorship or there would be chaos was a self-fulfilling prophecy: The iron prohibition against political deviation prompted protesters to project a link with elite sponsors even when none existed. The first member of the leadership to be thus co-opted was Hu Yaobang, whose death—demonstrating ultimate selflessness—provided the original catalyst. Zhao Ziyang then seemed available, but the students were initially suspicious of Zhao, due partly to the fact that his family was tainted by the corruption they were protesting against and partly to Zhao's role in bringing down the martyr whose death they were mourning; so the linkage was not formed until it was too late to do either side any good. Meanwhile, the circulation of authority within the movement leadership made it impossible to generate feasible strategies when the authorities stood pat.[98] Why responsible leadership failed to arise to persuade the movement to evacuate the square and try again later when conditions were ripe is a good question—it is conceivable that those able to foresee the peril ahead were still laboring under the Maoist delusion that the masses are always right. In any case, the movement was sufficiently "democratic" that it drifted away from anyone who would not lead it where it wished to go. Without effective official patronage or an internal leadership capable of seizing the initiative, the movement stubbornly, passively awaited its own destruction.

One of the underlying reasons for the continuing dependency of the Chinese public sphere is undoubtedly economic. An autonomous public

---

97. See Lee Feigon, *China Rising: The Meaning of Tiananmen* (Chicago: I. I. Dee, 1990).

98. Internecine factionalism was not a problem and the movement made unprecedented strides in creating a central coordinating body, but there was not one but several such confederations (e.g., the Autonomous Student Union of Beijing Universities, the Beijing University Students' Group for Dialogue, the Headquarters for Defending the Square), each subdivided into factions, with a tendency for authority to wander haphazardly. See Francis, "Progress of Protest," pp. 898–915.

sphere presupposes an independent middle class capable of supporting it.[99] Although the loosening of controls over the economy in the course of reform had given rise to distinct tendencies in this direction,[100] both the publicly owned but administratively decentralized and relatively autonomous enterprises (such as Shanghai's *World Economic Herald*) and the collectively or privately owned enterprises (such as the Stone Corporation) retained formal or informal ties to the regime. When the chips were down, the regime demonstrated that it was prepared to "recall" the autonomy it had "lent" (e.g., progress toward press autonomy was quickly quashed once martial law was imposed).[101] Yet the regime also discovered that to do so it had to pay a price.

What might the future hold for the Chinese public realm? After a vigorous reassertion of central power during the retrenchment campaign, economic reform seems to have revived, permitting the market sector least dependent on the central apparatus to resume vigorous growth—the sector whose interests coincide most closely with an autonomous public sphere. Tiananmen was the first grass-roots movement to have attempted to generate a coherent internal leadership, and, although that attempt ultimately failed, future political entrepreneurs may learn from their forebears. Great progress was achieved at Tiananmen in the cultivation of civility, although there does seem to have been some breakdown of discipline.[102] With the passage from the scene of Deng Xiaoping and his generation of revolutionary veterans, the succeeding leadership may be a bit less paranoid about public activities not immediately threatening to its interests, a bit more reluctant to expend the political capital needed to crack down. It may even have sufficient need for public support to be willing to make concessions or offer leadership. Under such circumstances, previous experience suggests that a full-blown civil society—albeit still with distinctive Chinese cultural characteristics—is apt to emerge as quickly as bamboo shoots after a spring rain.

---

99. Habermas, *Strukturwandlung*, passim.

100. Mayfair Mei-hui Yang, "Between State and Society: The Construction of Corporateness in a Chinese Socialist Factory," *Australian Journal of Chinese Affairs*, no. 22 (July 1989), pp. 35–40, 55.

101. Seth Faison, "The Changing Role of the Chinese Media," in Tony Saich, ed., *The Chinese People's Movement: Perspectives on Spring 1989* (Armonk, N.Y.: M. E. Sharpe, 1990), pp. 145–164.

102. There were mass-initiated incidents of violence concurrent with the Beijing demonstrations in Xi'an and Changsha on April 22, which may have excited hardliners, biased in any case against the demonstrations, and may have aggravated a growing confrontational trend in Beijing the week after the declaration of martial law (e.g., posters calling for purge of the hardliners), resulting in a determined show of defiance after the Beijing crackdown in Hangzhou and Shanghai. See the chapters by Tony Saich, Joseph Esherick, Andrea Worden, Keith Forster, and Shelley Warner, in Jonathan Unger, ed., *The Pro-Democracy Protests in China: Reports from the Provinces* (Armonk, N.Y.: M. E. Sharpe, 1991).

5

Domestic Reform and International Adaptation

As the largest and most potentially significant of the new Party-states to join the international Communist movement in the aftermath of World War II, the People's Republic of China took Marxism-Leninism's revolutionary challenge to the Westphalian nation-state system more seriously than most. After all, China had traditionally viewed itself not as one nation-state among sovereign equals but as an imperial center of a world surrounded by less civilized peoples,[1] and its introduction to the international system in the nineteenth century had been a rather rude awakening. Thus Communist China enthusiastically embraced a new vision of the world that gave pride of place to a transnational vanguard class as vehicle of a new order of universalistic values.

The nation-state did not entirely disappear from the picture, however, as the CCP also used nationalism and multiclass united front arrangements ("national liberation wars") with great political skill and apparent conviction. Instead of ignoring the nation-state, the new leadership crafted a conceptual hybrid: International class solidarity existed as embodied by nation-states, which could be characterized in class terms based on whether their national behavior (*biaoxian*) conformed to ideological role requirements. Thus there were "bourgeois reactionary" nation-states and "proletarian revolutionary" nation-states, and still other nation-states were mixed cases (not because they were afflicted by

---

1. For an explanation of the geomantic logic of China's central position (and Beijing's centrality within China), see Jeffrey Meyer, *The Dragons of Tiananmen: Beijing as a Sacred City* (Columbia: University of South Carolina Press, 1991).

domestic class struggle, for that was universally the case and only to be expected, but because their *international* role was ambiguous, in that they oppressed some nation-states but were oppressed by others).

Post-Liberation China thus sought to reconcile a variety of impulses in crafting a foreign policy to navigate the tempestuous postwar international currents. On the one hand, as a proud new nation that had "stood up," China wished to lay full claim to the great power status the Kuomintang had begun to assert successfully in the course of World War II[2] and lost little time in claiming traditional irredenta, such as Mongolia, Manchuria, Xinjiang (where the Soviet Union had been making inroads), Tibet, Hainan Island, Hong Kong, and Taiwan. China's involvement in the Korean and the Vietnamese conflicts was to some extent motivated by national interests, as was the costly split with its erstwhile mentor, the Soviet Union.

On the other hand, the PRC also wished to dissociate itself from the "feudal" foreign policy traditions of its imperial antecedents, which symbolized narrow-minded self-interest, weakness, and passivity, and to make the Chinese experience meaningful and valid to other nation-states of the same "class" (i.e., economically underdeveloped new nations, exploited and oppressed by the North Atlantic metropole). Not only would world revolution vindicate the historical inevitability of the Chinese experience, but until that revolution had been triumphantly concluded the security of the PRC itself would remain uncertain—a lesson about security had been underscored by the prompt imposition of an American blockade after Liberation.

In effect, the People's Republic thus constructed a two-tiered foreign policy, consisting of "international" and "transnational" tiers. On the international level, China practiced power politics as one among many sovereign nation-states. On the transnational level, the PRC transcended the framework of international diplomacy and functioned as a (self-appointed) symbolic representative of the international proletariat.[3] We hence consider China's transnational relations and its interstate relations seriatim.

Transnational Relations

The transnational dimension was initially conceived as an undifferentiated extension of the worldwide proletarian revolution, which had been given an organizational headquarters and logistic support by the "camp"

---

2. Compare Robert E. Bedeski, *State-building in Modern China: The Kuomintang in the Prewar Period* (Berkeley: Center for Chinese Studies, China Research Monograph no. 18, 1981).
3. For an informative discussion of the theoretical background, compare J. Kubalkova and A. A. Cruikshank, *Marxism and International Relations* (New York: Clarendon Press, 1985).

of nation-states where the revolution had first prevailed. Yet it soon became evident to Chinese Marxists that there was no international proletariat to speak of functioning independently of nation-states. The constituency of the proletarian revolution was hence a grouping of nation-states, which China came to identify as international "reference groups." At first conflated, this broad grouping gradually evolved into two discrete categories: the so-called Communist bloc countries, led by the Soviet Union (USSR); and the less-developed countries, eventually referred to as the Third World. To see how China adjusted its transnational policies in the course of the reform era, we shall first look at the PRC's interactions with the Third World and then at its relations with "fraternal" communist party-states in the bloc.

The Third World

China was among the first to recognize the revolutionary potential of the decolonizing new nations. As early as 1946, the CCP put them in a separate theoretical category as a nonhostile buffer zone rather than as part of the capitalist encirclement in Zhdanov's "two-camps" model.[4] As the first among these "less-developed countries" (LDCs) to carry through a socialist revolution, China deemed itself a missionary to the others as well as their natural leader, able to guide them through industrialization to the inevitable postindustrial utopia. And China's diplomacy along these lines was not without its signal successes, notably in the Chinese contribution to the self-definition of the Third World as a "neutral belt of states [and] as the 'zone of peace' between the Western coalition and China."[5] In its role as cofounder of the Nonaligned Movement, China formulated the Five Principles of Peaceful Coexistence during talks with Indian, Burmese, and Indonesian leaders in 1954–1955; the Five Principles have since been generalized to cover all facets of Chinese foreign policy.

Yet when the USSR (with far more ample material resources) moved

---

4. Liu Shaoqi, then the CCP's leading theorist, called attention to the relevance of the Chinese interpretation of Marxism to the new nations as early as 1945, in his report to the Seventh Party Congress. Four years later, he asserted that "the path taken by the Chinese people in defeating imperialism and its lackeys and in founding the People's Republic is the path that should be taken by the people of various colonial and semi-colonial countries in their fight for national independence and people's democracy." Liu Shao-ch'i, *On the Party* (Peking: Foreign Languages Press, 1951), p. 31; *Xinhua* (Peking), November 23, 1949; on the politics of how to categorize the new nations within the Comintern, see Roger E. Kanet, ed., *The Soviet Union and the Developing Nations* (Baltimore, Md.: Johns Hopkins University Press, 1974), pp. 1–26.

5. Kuo-kang Shao, "Chou En-lai's Diplomatic Approach to Nonaligned States in Asia: 1953–60," *China Quarterly*, no. 78 (June 1979), p. 324.

to co-opt the Chinese role as socialism's ambassador to the Third World, most LDCs were prepared to shift their ideological allegiance (to Beijing's chagrin). And money was not necessarily the only motive: China's revolutionary experience included a strain of revolutionary brutality that many in the Third World felt it best to avoid, or at least deemphasize, turning rather to Khrushchev's "peaceful evolution" or Nehru's pacificism. Mao, however, refused to recant his commitment to "struggle," which he formalized at the end of the 1950s in the "theory of continuous revolution" and evinced in periodic confrontations with the United States in the Taiwan Strait, in border clashes with India, and in moral (and some material) support for national liberation wars throughout the Third World (not to mention the well-publicized Great Proletarian Cultural Revolution). The China-India-Egypt alignment gave way to the so-called Beijing-Jakarta-Hanoi-Pyongyang axis, as the Chinese shifted from the policy they had introduced in 1955–1957, but now repudiated as "class collaboration," to international class war; Chinese aid found its way to guerrilla movements in Thailand, Burma, Indonesia, Malaya, the Philippines, and even beyond Asia to Algeria, Guinea-Bissau, Angola, Mozambique, the African National Congress, and the Palestine Liberation Organization.

The militant revolutionary phase of Chinese Third World policy, during which Beijing spurned both superpowers and most of the moderate leadership of the Nonaligned Movement as well to focus on the violent radical fringe, lasted from the late 1960s through the Cultural Revolution (abating somewhat after the opening of the Sino-American contacts in the early 1970s). The theoretical significance of this part of the world steadily escalated, first in the "intermediate zone theory" (first articulated by Mao in 1946), which included all countries between the two camps that were still in contention, and then in the 1963 subdivision of this zone into a "first intermediate zone" consisting of the developing countries, and a "second intermediate zone" consisting of nonhegemonial developed countries such as France, Canada, Japan, and Australia. In April 1974, this sort of "zonal" partition was replaced by the Theory of Three Worlds, as articulated by Deng Xiaoping (reflecting, however, comments by Mao in a conversation with a foreign head of state made in February 1974) in a speech to a special session of the United Nations (UN) General Assembly.

According to this theory, the socialist "camp" was no longer in existence (to the shocked dismay of China's Albanian allies), for the Soviet Union had degenerated into "socialist imperialism." The two superpowers were equated as members of the First World, sharing an insatiable greed for "hegemony," i.e., exploiting and oppressing the Third World and "bullying" other developed countries. The Second World exploited developing countries but its members were in turn exploited and bullied by the First World. The Third World, where China now ranked itself, had assumed the messianic role of the proletariat: With three-fourths of the world's population, three-fifths of its area, and a large share of its natural resources, markets, and investment opportunities, these countries "constitute a revolutionary motive force propelling the wheels of world history and are the main force combatting colonialism, imperialism, and particularly the superpowers."[6]

With the introduction of Deng Xiaoping's reform program in late 1978, China's Third World rhetoric began to be played out in various international forums, where it was useful to facilitate international coalition building.[7] It was, after all, chiefly Third World support that made Beijing's entry into the United Nations possible in 1971, in a resolution that simultaneously evicted Taiwan and gave the PRC a permanent seat on the Security Council; that in turn opened the way to admission to the World Bank and International Monetary Fund (IMF), organizations that controlled the flow of international developmental aid. Although Beijing has usually voted with the United States on Security Council resolutions (in extreme cases abstaining, as in the Gulf War), in roll call votes in the General Assembly (where the Third World now holds a clear majority) China has more often opposed U.S. positions than not. At the Cancun conference in October 1981, Zhao Ziyang made an ambitious proposal for creation of a new international economic order (NIEO), according to which developing countries should have full access to Western markets without protectionist barriers or disadvantageous terms of trade, although still retaining "full and eternal sovereignty" over their own natural resources. And in 1982, China publicly associated itself with the basic principles espoused by the Group of 77. Although its support for the NIEO then flagged for several years, Beijing returned to the issue in an October 1988 call by Deng Xiaoping for a new international political and economic order based on the Five Principles of Peaceful Coexistence, which the Chinese delegation presented to the UN General Assembly in 1990.

---

6. Quoted from Deng's statement of the Three Worlds Theory at the UN General Assembly in April 1974, in Richard J. Walsh, *Change, Continuity, and Commitment: China's Adaptive Foreign Policy* (Lanham, Md.: University Press of America, 1988), pp. 90–104 et passim.

7. From near-total exclusion at the beginning of the 1970s, Chinese membership in international governmental organizations (IGOs) increased from 1 to 21 from 1971 to 1976, increasing further from 21 to 37 from 1977 to 1989; its membership in international nongovernmental organizations (INGOs) jumped from 71 to 677 in the post-Mao period (1977–1989). Samuel S. Kim, "International Organizational Behavior," in Thomas Robinson and David Shambaugh, eds., *Ideas and Interpretations in Chinese Foreign Policy* (New York: Oxford University Press, 1993).

During the reform era, China's rhetoric in support of the Third World has remained staunch; as Deng put it in 1984:

> The foreign policy of China in the 1980s, the 1990s, until the 21st century can be summed up in two sentences: First, we fight against hegemony, to preserve world peace. Second, China will always belong to the Third World, that is the foundation of our foreign policy. ... Even when China's development has brought wealth and power it will belong to the Third World, because China will never strive for hegemony or to intimidate others.[8]

True, some questioned the sincerity of such statements as the PRC's foreign developmental assistance dwindled relative to the Maoist era. But after Tiananmen, as in previous periods when China's relations with the great powers frayed (e.g., the 1960s), Beijing has returned to the Third World for purposes of legitimation. Identification with the developing countries was far less threatening than the opening to the West in terms of the international demonstration effect (what the CCP calls "spiritual pollution"), and none voiced human rights concerns or imposed sanctions. Thus a mid-1989 Politburo directive on foreign policy announced that "from now on China will put more effort into resuming and developing relations with old friends (in Africa) and Third World countries."[9] Deng Xiaoping ruminated in the course of his sojourn at Beidaiho in the summer of 1990:

> In the past several years we have concentrated too much on one part of the world and neglected the other. ... The USA and other Western nations invoked sanctions against us but those who are truly sympathetic and support us are some old friends in the developing countries. ... This course (the pro–Third World policy) may not be altered for 20 years.[10]

African countries have been intensively cultivated since Tiananmen through visits and invitations: In July 1989, Foreign Minister Qian Qichen visited Botswana, Zimbabwe, Angola, Zambia, Mozambique, and Lesotho, while Deputy Foreign Minister Yang Fucheng visited five other African countries. Li Peng made his first official visit after Tiananmen to Nepal, Bangladesh, and Pakistan, promising new aid; President Yang

---

8. Deng, in a statement dated May 29, 1984, in "Bases of Our Foreign Policy: Neither the American nor the Soviet Card," as trans. in Helmut Martin, ed., *Die Reform der Revolution: Eine Milliarde Menschen auf dem Weg* (Berlin: Siedler Verlag, 1988), p. 158.

9. *Foreign Broadcast Information Service-China*, October 3, 1989, p. 3.

10. *Zheng ming*, August 1990, p. 15.

Shangkun visited Egypt and other Arab countries in 1989 and made the first visit to Latin America by a Chinese chief of state in May 1990. China has taken a more flexible stance toward Third World countries with which it had no formal relations, such as Israel (with whom relations were normalized in January 1992). The Thai prime minister made an official visit in 1989, and both Saudi Arabia and Indonesia established diplomatic ties in 1990 (countering the impact of Taiwan's recognition by six small Third World countries the previous year).

The Chinese also launched a vigorous defense of Third World countries' right to immunity from superpower intervention, evidently hoping to build a united front, anticipating China's resistance to Western sanctions under the auspices of "human rights"; for example, a UN condemnation of the American invasion of Panama is lauded as an expression of Third World unity. In Chinese eyes, this admirable solidarity was also reflected in November 1989, when the UN General Assembly (with strong Third World backing) defeated a resolution on freedom of the press proposed by the West, which the Chinese claim was "designed to interfere in the internal affairs of Third World countries."[11] This appeal has not gone without echo in Third World capitals disquieted by the neglect and self-absorption of the First and Second worlds.

Yet despite this most recent rhetorical revival, Beijing's support for the Third World has been oddly halfhearted. Despite rhetorical support, China has consistently refused to join Third World organizations: It has not joined the Group of 77, the Organization of Petroleum Exporting Countries (OPEC), or the Nonaligned Movement, and in the IMF and World Bank it refused to join the Group of 24.[12] Even within the mainstream IGOs to which it does belong, China's support for Third World positions has been more symbolic than substantive, with a pattern of participating in debates on general principles but shying away from many of the functional committees and subsidiary bodies where business is transacted.[13] Even China's rhetorical support has been inconstant: The Theory of Three Worlds went into relative eclipse in the 1980s, overshadowed by a vision of world peace and economically interdependent development; not until Tiananmen was Beijing moved to reassert its commitment to

---

11. Chen Jiabao, "Third World's Role in International Affairs," *Beijing Review*, 33:4 (January 22–28, 1990), pp. 14–16.

12. The Intergovernmental Group of 24 on Monetary Affairs was formed in 1971 by finance ministers from the Third World member states of the IMF. Harry Harding, *A Fragile Relationship: The United States and China Since 1972* (Washington, D.C.: Brookings, 1992), p. 338 ff.

13. Kim, "International Organizational Behavior," p. 9.

Third World positions (such as the NIEO)—at a time when the developed countries were imposing sanctions for human rights violations and international financial organizations were closing their loan windows.

China's waning commitment to the Third World may have something to do with its own economic interests, which have shifted as its developmental efforts began to bear fruit. The PRC now, in fact, competes with the Third World in its quest for export markets, foreign investment, and international aid, and it has acquired an economic interest in the well-being of the developed countries that are its best customers and sources of capital and technology.[14] Under the circumstances, Beijing's bona fides as leader of a bloc of have-not countries with a revolutionary international agenda has limited credibility. To all appearances, Beijing no longer has any serious intention of sponsoring revolutionary activity in the developing countries; China's role in the post-Mao era has rather been that of regional policeman, resorting to violence either in defense of the geopolitical status quo (e.g., in Afghanistan or Cambodia) or on behalf of conventional national interests (Tibet, the Spratleys)—not in pursuit of revolutionary class war. China's "fifth column" abroad is typically not the proletariat but the bourgeoisie (compare the role of foreign trade and investment policy in appealing to business elites in Hong Kong, Taiwan, and South Korea). This nationalist, and generally defensive, foreign policy posture was reinforced by Tiananmen and the ensuing collapse of the Communist bloc.

China, after all, now has a considerable stake in the global economic order. Whereas during the period of Maoist "self-reliance" (1957–1977) China's foreign trade amounted to not more than 4 percent of GNP, during the reform decade external trade rose by an average of more than 20 percent per annum, twice the rate of GNP growth and faster than that of any other centrally planned economy;[15] by 1987 the country's trade dependency ratio was 27.9 percent, higher than that of Japan or the United States.[16] With involvement has come debt: China's foreign debt load in-

---

14. At about the same stage of industrial development as Southeast Asia's proto-NICs (e.g., Malaysia, Thailand), China must compete with these countries for access to the shrinking American market and Japanese investment dollars. China has become one of the largest recipients of concessional interest-free loans from the World Bank's soft-loan window, the International Development Agency.

15. John C. Hsu, *China's Foreign Trade Reforms: Impact on Growth and Stability* (New York: Cambridge University Press, 1989), pp. 1–2. There has been a 63 percent increase in the flow of foreign capital into China from the first to the second half of the 1980s, destined chiefly for the five SEZs and fourteen open coastal cities.

16. Between 1978 and 1987, China doubled its share of world trade (from 0.8 percent to 1.6 percent), rising from twenty-eighth to twelfth place in the list of the world's biggest traders. Peter Ferdinand, "Regionalism," in Gerald Segal, ed., *Chinese Politics and Foreign Policy Reform* (London: Kegan Paul, 1990), pp. 135–158.

creased from zero in 1979 to $16 billion in 1985, to $40 billion in 1988, $50 billion in 1990, $60 billion in 1991, and $69.3 billion by the end of 1992.[17] The Japanese External Trade Organization (JETRO) estimated China's debt service for 1990 at $7 billion, a sizable increase from $2 billion in 1988; debt service peaked in 1992 at circa $10 billion.[18] Inasmuch as the United States continues to function as gatekeeper to the IMF, World Bank, and even to some extent to Japanese bilateral aid, the PRC will continue to need American help for access to credit to keep up debt payments, notwithstanding Chinese denunciations of American ideological interference.

Identification with the Third World will strengthen China's standing in the UN General Assembly and may even garner some support vis-à-vis human rights organizations, but this is not likely to be of much use in strengthening the CCP regime's legitimacy—in the wake of the bloc's collapse, communism is also a spent force in the Third World. During the heyday of China's commitment to the Third World, the latter played a role analogous to the proletariat in domestic class struggle in a fairly coherent Marxist-Leninist-Maoist theory of world development and future salvation. Identification with that role gave theoretical voice to China's old, post–Opium War sense of outrage at being scorned and taken advantage of by the powers. But China's very real progress over the past three decades (and especially during the reform period, when the most rapid progress of all was achieved in casual disregard for sacred ideological tenets) seems to have made such identification retrogressive or at least irrelevant. And the Third World itself has become something of a fiction: Divided as perhaps never before by diverse economic wherewithals, developmental prospects, and ideological proclivities, it has been left to splay out in all directions by the collapse of bipolarity.

The Communist Bloc

China's identification with the Communist bloc was a way of adopting an international patron, developmental model, and support group: Mao remarked at the time that "the Soviet Union's today is China's tomorrow." And certainly the identification was useful, and perhaps essential, to the nation's survival during its early years, when the country was

---

17. *Economist*, March 24, 1990, p. 35; Reuters, April 25, 1993.
18. Kojima Sueo, in *China Newsletter*, no. 81 (July–August 1989), p. 1. China is now in the middle of a peak repayment period. By its own estimate, "China will have to spend about $10 billion a year for five years or more to pay back foreign debt principal and interest, starting in 1992." *China Daily* (Beijing), December 16, 1989, p. 2. Thanks to the healthy growth of exports, however, China's debt service ratio will remain below 20 percent, the internationally recognized safety level.

placed under U.S. naval blockade and threatened more than once with nuclear attack. Yet the identification was ultimately felt to be so stultifying to China's own foreign policy interests and, indeed, to its discovery of its distinctive national identity that it was repudiated. Repudiation was not a simple, swift break, but an agonizing separation that had to be justified publicly in penetrating mutual theoretical critiques. Once finalized in the mid-1960s in Mao's denial that the bloc even existed, the assumption was widespread that the breach would never heal.

That conventional wisdom was wrong. Once China had taken the time to sort out its own distinct identity (not without internal convulsions), it gradually became possible to come to terms with the nemesis of the North. Sino-Soviet policy actually underwent the first stages of "reform" during Mao's late years, making this the first policy arena to undergo such rationalization.[19] This was partly due to the good offices of the moderate Zhou Enlai, perhaps, but even more to the fact that the nation's sovereignty, and even its survival, was put at risk, obliging policymakers to subordinate ideology to *raison d'état*. When the ideological polemics of the 1960s precipitated the mutual buildup of border forces that culminated in a Chinese-initiated border clash at Zhenbao (Damansky) Island on the Chinese side of the main channel of the Wusuli (Ussuri) River on March 2, 1969, the Russians not only retaliated massively (resulting, according to recent revelations, in thousands of Chinese casualties),[20] but also subjected the Chinese to a sustained siege of diplomacy by force. For the next half year they provoked a series of clashes along the entire length of the border, augmented by both veiled and public warnings to the effect that the USSR was considering a preemptive nuclear strike against the nascent Chinese first-strike force.[21] Meanwhile, the American conflict with Vietnam was still at a delicate stage, when U.S.

---

19. As Deng Xiaoping himself put it in defense of Maoist foreign policy achievements, "During the 'Cultural Revolution' great successes were achieved in our work in foreign affairs. Despite the domestic turmoil, internationally China's status as a great nation was recognized and its stature rose." "Remarks on Successive Drafts of the 'Resolution on Certain Questions in the History of Our Party Since the Founding of the PRC'" (March 1980–June 1981), in *Selected Works of Deng Xiaoping (1975–1982)* (Beijing: Foreign Languages Press, 1984), pp. 267–268.

20. Major General Vitaly Bubenin, who was a Border Guard lieutenant on the scene, recalled the clashes in an interview with the newspaper *Vostok Rossii* (Russia's East), attributing the March 2 clash to a Chinese ambush but admitting that on March 15 Soviet forces launched a calculated counterattack using huge salvos of rockets. James Flannery, reporting from Khabarovsk in a Reuters dispatch, June 3, 1992.

21. See Thomas Robinson, "China Confronts the Soviet Union: Warfare and Diplomacy on China's Inner Asian Frontiers," in Roderick MacFarquhar and John K. Fairbank, eds., *The Cambridge History of China, Vol. 15: The People's Republic, Part 2: Revolutions Within the Chinese Revolution, 1966–1982* (New York: Cambridge University Press, 1991), pp. 218–301.

strategic bombing of Hanoi and Haiphong and the "incursion" into Cambodia made the possibility of Chinese intervention quite real.

The PRC, finding itself on the brink of confrontation with both superpowers at once (in the context of which Moscow was suggesting Soviet-American collusion), was obliged to calculate its national interest very carefully. Under these circumstances the Soviets did succeed in driving the Chinese to the negotiating table—border talks began in Moscow in October 1969, alternating between capitals on a semiannual schedule for the next decade—though the Soviets did not win many concessions from them there. The Americans achieved a much more meaningful breakthrough, signaled by the February 1972 Nixon visit and the opening of trade, defense consultations, and implicit U.S.-extended deterrence from Soviet nuclear blackmail—in return for which China sharply scaled down its support for the Vietnam War. In point of fact, the Chinese leadership responded to this security dilemma by allowing considerations of national interest to override ideological considerations almost entirely.

Sino-Soviet relations were conducted during the reform decade within the framework of what has come to be known as the "strategic triangle," playing within parameters set during the late Maoist era. Triangularity meant that each bilateral relationship was contingent upon each participant's relations with the third. Although the logic of this relationship has already been elaborated elsewhere,[22] its essence was not simply "two against one," but one *playing* the other two (or two playing the third) in a variety of ways.[23] This was the insight behind the American "romantic triangle" inaugurated by the Nixon administration in the early 1970s, which played on the Sino-Soviet antagonism to cultivate better relations with both Moscow and Beijing than would otherwise have been feasible.

Whereas the Sino-Soviet antagonism could be successfully manipulated by Washington in the 1970s, during the early 1980s the revival of the Cold War made it possible for China to arrange its own romantic triangle. Reassured by the Reagan arms buildup, Beijing was able to reduce arms spending by about 7 percent per annum as a proportion of GNP from 1979 (year of the Vietnam invasion) to 1989. Meanwhile, the economic difficulties both superpowers began experiencing in the course of their confrontation (most acute in the Soviet case), due to overburdened arms budgets and neglected civilian economies, eventually led to a

---

22. For a more detailed exposition, see my *Sino-Soviet Normalization and Its International Implications, 1945–1990* (Seattle: University of Washington Press, 1992).

23. The first attempt to deal systematically with the logic of the triangle, Theodore Caplow's *Two Against One: Coalitions in Triads* (Englewood Cliffs, N.J.: Prentice-Hall, 1968), is strategically limited to this sort of balance-of-power weighting.

revival of Soviet-American détente, beginning with the Intermediate-range Nuclear Forces (INF) Treaty of December 1987 and continuing through the Conventional Forces (CFE) Treaty in Europe (December 1990), the Strategic Arms Reduction Treaties (START) I and II (successfully concluded in July 1991 and December 1992 respectively), and unilateral Soviet withdrawal from Eastern Europe. Meanwhile, Sino-Soviet normalization talks began in 1982, followed by a relatively steady growth of trade (particularly cross-border trade, which resumed in 1982). The process, held to a funereal tempo by a Chinese leadership intent upon wringing maximal concessions from both sides, culminated in "normalization" with Gorbachev's May 1989 visit to Beijing. However, although the disappearance of antagonistic relationships facilitated cooperation among all three players, it eviscerated the triangle of its leverage, and ultimately of its structure, and it collapsed as well.

Sino-Soviet relations from the May 1989 summit until the dissolution of the Soviet Union in December 1991 were thus concerned with placing the relationship on a new and more realistic footing. Surprisingly, despite secularization trends in both countries, ideology continued to play a major role, now in the form of reform socialism. This "postnormalization" period may be divided into four stages.

1. The Summit. The 1989 summit, arranged in accord with agreements reached during the December 1988 Qian Qichen visit to Moscow and the February 1989 Shevardnadze visit to Beijing, put a ceremonial capstone on a seven-year bilateral normalization process. Whereas in the early (1982–1986) phase of normalization the Chinese had seemed most forthcoming (by agreeing to talks and other exchanges in the absence of any Soviet response to Chinese demands), from 1986 to 1989 the Soviets made a series of tangible concessions: Gorbachev, in his July 28, 1986, speech in Vladivostok, agreed to settle the dispute over the Ussuri-Amur riverine boundary along the Thalweg (the deepest point of the channel); and beginning at the ninth round (October 6–14, 1986), the Soviet Union agreed to discuss Cambodia, thereafter entering into intensive discussions with the Chinese to resolve the issue (from September 1988 until they issued a joint statement in February 1989, Chinese and Soviet foreign ministers held no less than five rounds of talks on a Cambodian settlement). As the Chinese were unsatisfied by a 1988 Soviet pledge that Vietnam would withdraw all troops from Cambodia by 1990, in April 1989 Vietnam announced withdrawal of all remaining troops by the end of September regardless of whether a satisfactory political settlement had been achieved. Thus by May 1989 the so-called Three Obstacles to normalization (Afghanistan, Cambodia, and the Sino-Soviet border) had "essentially" been eliminated.

The Soviets, meanwhile, launched their own domestic reform program, which seemed at first to have been stimulated by the Chinese experience but soon veered off in a quite different direction, focusing on politics as a precondition for economic reform. The Soviet emphasis on political reform at its January 1987 Plenum indeed coincided with the CCP's decision, after a few rather tepid experiments, to foreclose that route—as symbolized by the suppression of the December 1986 student movement and the January demotion of General Secretary Hu Yaobang. Yet Gorbachev's political reform continued to inspire the Chinese journalistic and intellectual community. Thus the Tiananmen demonstrations were to some extent stimulated by the summit: Although the demonstrators refused to clear the square, they asked Gorbachev, a reform hero to whom Zhao Ziyang was then hopefully compared, to address them, and Gorbachev even asked permission to do so (the CCP leadership demurred).

The summit—which Deng heralded as "ending the past, opening up the future"—thus had both domestic and foreign policy ramifications. Gorbachev praised Deng's pragmatism, noting that neither Karl Marx nor Vladimir Lenin had the answer to today's problems for the USSR and the PRC. He also revealed some of the details of Soviet military cutbacks for Asia.[24] But what was most striking was how much the meeting was transformed by the mass movement and culminating massacre that framed it. Soviet disappointment was understandable: After all, Gorbachev had come to visit what was identified as a reform regime—indeed, perhaps the most successful exemplar of socialist reform in the world. Yet two weeks after he left the country China seemed to have forsaken that course by cracking down hard on vocal reform supporters.

The Soviet summiteers (Gorbachev, Foreign Minister Shevardnadze, and Gorbachev's personal foreign affairs adviser Aleksandr Yakovlev, as well as the China experts in the Communist Party of the Soviet Union [CPSU] Central Committee's International Department) were upset by the bloody denouement of the demonstrations they had witnessed[25] but

---

24. Most of the promised cuts were in border garrisons facing China, with far less change in the lineup against American-Japanese forces: Of the 12 divisions and 11 air force regiments to be withdrawn from the Soviet Far East by 1991 (totaling about 200,000 troops), 120,000 were to come from the border with China. In addition, 16 battleships were to be removed from the Red Pacific Banner Fleet. Already in progress was the removal of all SS-20 missiles from the Soviet Far East, as promised in the INF treaty, and the withdrawal of 75 percent of the ground forces in Mongolia. Going beyond these agreed-upon reductions, Gorbachev proposed the complete demilitarization of the border, the details of which would be arranged in the bilateral troop reduction talks under way at the vice–foreign ministerial level since February 1987.

25. According to an anonymous memoir by a senior Russian China specialist, as cited in *Far Eastern Economic Review,* June 11, 1992.

remained discreet in public, and, momentarily, it seemed that the Soviet Union might draw strategic dividends from China's ostracism. It is reported that in internal discussions, Politburo Standing Committee members Li Peng and Yao Yilin, both members of the growing pool of Soviet "returned students" in the emergent leadership (along with Jiang Zemin, Chen Yun, Yang Shangkun, and others), advocated the need to counterbalance China's economic relations with the capitalist world with closer economic cooperation with Socialist countries. Both planned and free (i.e., border) trade expanded: Total bilateral trade turnover was $3.95 billion for the year (an 18 percent hike over 1988's $3.26 billion), having increased 1.5 times in the past decade (1980–1990) and now amounting to 8 percent of China's total trade; the Soviet Union had become China's fifth-largest trade partner.[26]

2. The Winter of 1989–1990. During the winter of 1989–1990, old Chinese suspicions of Soviet tricks combined with new apprehensions about the upsetting repercussions of Soviet reform efforts to abruptly end the summer's honeymoon. China had, since the mid-1950s, recurrently criticized Soviet occupation of Eastern Europe, on the one hand hoping to build a united front against Moscow within the bloc, and on the other, fearing that the Brezhnev Doctrine might provide a precedent for a Soviet punitive expedition against China. Thus when Warsaw Pact forces invaded Czechoslovakia in 1968, the CCP joined the Kremlin's critics; China even publicly supported German reunification (on Bonn's terms, recognizing both Germanys) in the 1960s and 1970s. Yet in the wake of Tiananmen the CCP leadership had second thoughts. At a small discussion group with Yang Shangkun, Wan Li, and the six formal members of the Politburo Standing Committee during the four-day Fifth Plenum of the Thirteenth CC in early November, Deng Xiaoping attacked Gorbachev's "new thinking," accusing him of pursuing a path "not in conformity with true Marxism-Leninism." In November 1989, Politburo member Qiao Shi attended the Fourteenth Congress of the Romanian Communist Party; in his talks with Ceausescu and with newly appointed General Secretary of the Bulgarian Communist Party Mladenov, the Chinese security chief stressed the maintenance of strict ideological orthodoxy. When Gorbachev condemned both the Czech invasion and the Brezhnev Doctrine in Italy in early December 1989, the CCP took an evasive stand.

Such expressions of unease in response to the collapse of ruling communist parties along the northern tier escalated sharply in early Decem-

---

26. Gu Guanfu and Chun-tu Hsueh, "Sino-Soviet Ties Grow Steadily," *Beijing Review*, 36 (September 3–9, 1990), pp. 8–12. Total trade for the five years from 1986 to 1990 amounted to 22 billion Swiss francs and double that for the entire decade of the 1970s.

ber, when the Bucharest regime collapsed despite waging desperate resistance (and notwithstanding Qiao Shi's recent visit, when he advised the leadership on how to implement the "Chinese solution"). The ensuing execution of the Ceausescus threw elderly CCP veterans into great consternation. Deferring earlier plans to lift martial law by Christmas eve, the PLA placed troops on first-degree alert in late December 1989, and steps were taken to monitor student activity.

The CCP convened a series of high-level meetings in December and January at which Deng, Li Peng, and Jiang Zemin vied in denouncing Gorbachev and forecasting his imminent political demise. After the February 1990 Soviet CC Plenum that renounced the CPSU's monopoly of power and opened the way to a multiparty parliament, an expanded CCP Politburo meeting was held in which a directive on Sino-Soviet relations was approved for dissemination through the ranks; this document called for "thoroughly educating" CCP members on the true nature of Soviet "revisionism." Retreating from a post-Tiananmen statement by Vice-Premier Yao Yilin that China should develop relations with the USSR as a "counterbalance" to Western sanctions, foreign trade units were instructed by the central government to be "more cautious" in developing trade and economic relations with Soviet companies.[27]

Deng nevertheless resisted the advice of such hard-liners as Deng Liqun, who proposed a revival of public polemics: "First of all we should mobilize the entire Party to do our own work well," he said. "I do not favor issuing documents like the 'first to ninth commentaries on the CPSU'" (written in the early 1960s).[28] In response to the defection of Eastern Europe, Deng predicted Gorbachev's replacement and sanctioned a rapprochement with Vietnam in December 1989, sending Jiang Zemin to Pyongyang in the spring of 1990 to cement that alliance: "The three socialist countries of Asia must protect and uphold the flag of socialism."[29] Yet he advised Jiang against trying to assume a leading role in the international Communist movement. Three factors seem to have been uppermost in his thinking: First, the Soviets dispatched several emissaries to Beijing, asking them not to do anything that might damage bilateral relations. Second, Gorbachev himself made two statements during the February 1990 CPSU CC Plenum that had a redeeming impact: He reaffirmed his commitment to socialism; and he spurned calls by reformist supporters to resign as CPSU general secretary. Third, Taiwan was at this

---

27. *South China Morning Post* (*SCMP*) (Hong Kong), February 17, 1990, p. 12; Lo Ping, "Notes on a Northern Journey," *Zheng ming*, no. 150 (April 1, 1990), pp. 6–8.
28. Quoted in Lo Ping, "Notes on a Northern Journey," *Zheng ming*, no. 150 (April 1, 1990), pp. 6–8.
29. "Deng Forecasts Gorbachev Downfall," *SCMP*, January 25, 1990, p. 1.

time energetically pursuing dollar diplomacy in pursuit of diplomatic recognition, and as the former Soviet satellites lost no time recognizing South Korea upon their self-generated emancipation, it was clear that they might also recognize Taiwan unless the PRC quickly buried the ideological hatchet.

3. Thawing Relations. From the spring of 1990 through the summer of 1991, the CCP continued its internal critique of the Soviet reform program in an effort to deter possible Chinese emulators, but at the same time diplomatic and commercial relations warmed considerably. It had become clear that the overthrow of communism in Eastern Europe would not necessarily endanger the CCP regime, as neither democracy nor capitalism would prove to be a quick panacea for any of these countries.

Meanwhile, in Moscow, as Gorbachev's difficulties with Lithuania and other would-be breakaway states mounted in the spring amid growing popular discontent with perestroika, Gorbachev began to surround himself with military-security types filled with admiration for China and to curb his liberal wing (e.g., on April 10 the CPSU Central Committee published an open letter criticizing reformers within the Party)—moves the CCP leadership, concerned about splitting tendencies in their own Autonomous Regions, heartily welcomed. Gorbachev's pilgrimage to the economically dynamic Pacific Rim, after a promising beginning heralded by the recognition of South Korea on January 1, suffered a sharp setback in his April 1991 visit to Tokyo, where he met with little flexibility on the issue of Japan's "northern territories" (four Soviet-occupied islands claimed by Japan). China seemed his best chance in Asia.

Thus the relationship began to thaw in the warmth of an ideological affinity redefined in terms of "reform socialism." Li Peng's visit to Moscow (April 23–26, 1990) was a major icebreaker, resulting in six important agreements, including the "Agreement on Strengthening Trust in the Military Realm as a Guiding Principle," which made provision for "confidence-building measures" and renewed military cooperation. Hitherto China's military modernization efforts had relied on Western technology, but in the wake of U.S. sanctions the Chinese saw a chance to both teach Washington a lesson and make some bargain arms acquisitions. A series of exchanges by high-level military officials began in the spring of 1990, bearing fruit in a fall 1990 deal to purchase twenty-four troop-carrying Soviet helicopters capable of operating in high-altitude climates (the United States had refused to permit sale of such weapons systems because they might be used in Tibet) and some two dozen Mach 2 Sukhov SU-27 fighters, at a "friendship" price ($700 million), with an option to buy an additional forty-eight, reversing a mutual thirty-year freeze on arms sales (meanwhile Beijing canceled its $550 million purchase of U.S. avionics to upgrade Chinese F-8 fighters). There was also tentative agreement on Chinese coproduction of MiG-31s and "widespread reports" of Chinese interest in buying Soviet T-72 tanks, IL-76 transport planes, an aircraft carrier, and refueling technology to give its bombers a range of more than 1,000 miles. Beijing expressed interest in Soviet space technology, and the Soviets expressed interest in China's success in converting military factories to civilian production.[30] Beginning in the second half of 1991, China planned to send military personnel to study in the Soviet Union; a number of pilots were gathered for concentrated preparations for studies in the USSR in June, where they would undergo a training course of one to one and one-half years.

Meanwhile economic, cultural, and educational exchanges continued to forge ahead. Although total Soviet foreign trade dropped 6.4 percent for the year, Sino-Soviet trade volume increased to $5.3 billion in 1990, one-quarter of which was border trade, topping the 1989 record level by 26 percent, as the USSR overtook Germany as China's fourth-largest trade partner. The State Council approved the designation of Heihe City in northern Heilongjiang, which overlooks Blagoveshchensk (the third-largest city in the Soviet Far East) across the Amur/Heilong River, as a special economic district.[31] Some 200 cooperative projects were initiated between localities of the two countries, and China dispatched 15,000 citizens to the Soviet Far East for labor service; twenty Sino-Soviet joint ventures were established in the USSR and a few in China—personnel from the Soviet Union became engaged in cocoa production on Hainan Island. There were 300 exchanges of scientific and technological delegations in 1990. The Soviet Union sent 809 exchange students to China between 1988 and 1990, and 1,307 Chinese postgraduate students went to study in the USSR.[32]

Stimulated by the unexpectedly swift resolution of the Gulf crisis and the prospective emergence of a unipolar "new world order" that would have sidelined socialism in favor of bourgeois democracy ("Bushism"), Sino-Soviet détente shifted into high gear in early 1991. In February, Deng Xiaoping gave a speech in which he said China should try to create a five-power socialist alliance consisting of the Soviet Union, North

---

30. Since summer 1991, China has successfully recruited a few hundred senior Soviet scientists to work on new weapons technology, offering them a monthly salary of 1,200 yuan in addition to free housing and a paid annual home leave. Guocang Huan, "The New Relationship with the Former Soviet Union," *Current History*, 91:566 (September 1992), pp. 253–256.

31. *SCMP*, September 3, 1990, p. 12. In 1990, Heihe negotiated trade contracts worth about $140 million in 1990.

32. *Zhongguo qingnian bao* (China youth daily), May 13, 1991, p. 2.

Korea, Mongolia, and Vietnam, within which a "friendly Sino-Soviet relationship should take a central position."[33] Although the Chinese were less than enthusiastic about Gorbachev, Chineses Kremlinologists found no viable alternative: Ligachev was ideologically preferable but had virtually no following, and the influence of Yeltsin (who was anathema) was waxing.[34]

Thus the CCP began to publicize Sino-Soviet friendship, praising Soviet fraternal assistance in the 1950s. Over twenty Soviet novels of that vintage, censored until 1990, suddenly became required reading material for political education, including *How Steel Is Tempered* and *An Iron Torrent*; a flock of Soviet feature films was released. During his trip to Beijing in early May 1991, Soviet Defense Minister Yazov suggested a Sino-Soviet strategic alliance against the West. A week later Jiang Zemin finally reciprocated Gorbachev's 1989 visit; greeted in Moscow with bear hugs and much talk about "socialism," Jiang nostalgically (but noncommitally) discussed reviving the spirit of the 1950s.[35] Jiang and Gorbachev signed an agreement on the eastern borders, in which China gained sovereignty of the symbolically significant one-square-mile Damansky/ Chenbao Island (where the 1969 clash had started) and a few other river islands on the Chinese side of the channel (though the fate of Heixia/ Black Bear Island remained moot). Meanwhile (pursuant to agreements made during Li Peng's visit), trade shifted on January 1, 1991, from escrow to cash settlement; the lack of foreign exchange in both countries entailed a decline in trade to $3.9 billion in 1991 (though border trade, still on a barter basis, continued to boom).

4. Normalization. The relationship took its final twist in August 1991, when a coup by Soviet hard-liners seemed momentarily to offer CCP leaders a new option with which they could be more ideologically comfortable, only to snatch it away. Notwithstanding their sensitivity to diplomatic protocol, the Chinese had never shrunk from promoting those Soviet options most compatible with their own interests. Jiang Zemin's April visit was meant to signal support for Gorbachev, and he also held a private meeting with Vice President Yanaev, later a key figure in the coup, but spurned Yeltsin's request for a meeting. Upset by the margin of Yeltsin's victory in the June 1991 election (in which he emerged as president of the Russian Republic), the PRC invited his hard-line opponent, Ivan Polozkov, a member of the CPSU Politburo and chair of the Russian

---

33. *Zheng ming*, June 1, 1991.
34. Liu Zhixun, *Guang jiao jing* (Wide angle), June 16, 1991, pp. 20–23.
35. "We intend to return to the state of relations we had in the 1950s," Jiang said. "These are the relations among allies." *Christian Science Monitor*, May 27, 1991.

Republic's Party Committee, to Beijing for a ten-day visit at precisely the time of Yeltsin's talks with President Bush in the United States.[36] From May through August, three top CCP leaders, including not only Jiang but also Li Peng and PLA Chief of Staff Chi Haotian, visited the Soviet Union on separate occasions.

This stepped-up diplomatic activity[37] naturally gave rise to suspicions that Chinese leaders had acquired advance notice or even had colluded with the Soviet conspirators—rumors that have been subsequently denied by both countries. The inside story is that CCP leaders were delighted by the coup and dismayed by its swift collapse, which left them no time to intervene. The CCP quickly geared up for emergency decision-making and issued a rapid flurry of top-priority circulars in the course of the coup's seventy-hour lifespan. The first circular appeared on August 19, the day of the coup, when Deng Xiaoping and other leaders rushed back to Beijing (from Beidaiho, where they were enjoying their summer vacation) to hear Chi Haotian report on his talks with Yazov. Chi urged the CCP to express its support openly for the State of Emergency Committee (SEC) immediately, but Deng advised to "remain composed and watch what happens." The coup was certainly a "good thing," he added; we must "not be visibly pleased but only be delighted at the bottom of our hearts."[38]

But before a document could be issued publicizing the CCP's endorsement, the leadership got word (on the evening of August 21) that the coup had collapsed. A second emergency enlarged Politburo meeting was convened. The Politburo confined itself to noting publicly that Gorbachev had resumed his duties (congratulations were clearly not in order) and proposed readjusting relations with the Soviet Union on the basis of noninterference in each other's internal affairs. The SEC ("the real Marxists") had regrettably committed various tactical blunders, such as naively relying on legal procedures (e.g., waiting for a parliamentary session to endorse their putsch) and failing to take "resolute measures" to quell protests, arrest Yeltsin, or control the army. The CCP should draw a lesson from the Soviet experience and guard against similar events in China—these guidelines were conveyed orally to all State

---

36. *SCMP*, June 20, 1991, p. 9.

37. It is true, for example, that Chi's visit preceded the coup by only a week (August 7–12) and that it included secret talks with Yanaev and Yazov. There are also reports that Yazov inquired (during his May visit) whether the PRC would supply grain and foodstuffs to the USSR if some incident should lead to a suspension of Western aid (to which he received an affirmative answer). But there is no evidence of any collusion on the coup itself.

38. V. Cai Yong Mei article in *Kaifang* (Opening) (Hong Kong), no. 15 (September 15, 1991), pp. 22–24.

Council ministries and to all Party, government, and PLA organs on August 22. The PLA was placed on first-degree combat alert; all troops on leave (particularly border troops) were ordered to return and stand by.

The final blow had yet to fall: On August 24, Yeltsin ordered the disbandment of the Russian CPSU, and Gorbachev "voluntarily" resigned from his post as general secretary. By December, the secession of the republics that the coup was meant to forestall could no longer be contained, and the Soviet Union was replaced by the Commonwealth of Independent States (CIS). This unleashed another wave of indignation among CCP hard-liners. Bo Yibo's apopleptic reaction to this "disaster" is typical:

> The Soviet Union was a military and economic superpower in the 1970s and 1980s, but it has now disintegrated as a state. All Soviet officials, from the president of the Soviet Union to the president of the Russian Republic and government ministers, have been sent to the United States, Western Europe and Japan to beg for economic aid and grains so that they can get through their difficulties this cold winter.[39]

The immediate upshot was to bolster inner-Party opposition to further reform. Thus the CCP proclaimed its "five upholds and five oppositions": Uphold the Party's leadership, the Party's absolute control of the army, the people's democratic dicatorship, the socialist road, and the economic-legal system based on public ownership; oppose any multiparty system, the PLA's involvement in politics, the parliamentary system, social democracy, and privatization. Yang Shangkun argued during the meeting that Soviet developments proved that the measures taken by the CCP during June 3–4, 1989, were correct.

The premium on loyalty also gave at least temporary sanction to nepotistic tendencies. Chen Yun proclaimed, "This is not only a life-and-death situation concerning our Party and State but also a life-and-death question concerning our wives, children, and ourselves."[40] The leadership agreed that the collapse of the coup could be attributed to the lack of a "core force" of veteran proletarian revolutionaries and a poor choice of successors. "Do not be afraid of opinions against groups and strata of young princes," Deng inferred. "The root cause of the problem in the CPSU was that their choice of succeeding leadership was bad and impre-

---

39. The speech was excerpted in an internal document issued by the CC's General Office on November 1, 1991, and reprinted in *Zheng ming*, no. 170 (December 1, 1991), pp. 22–23.

40. Lo Ping, in *Zheng ming*, no. 167 (September 1, 1991), pp. 6, 8; He Boshi, in *Dang dai* (Contemporary), no. 6 (September 15, 1991), pp. 8–12.

cise and hence allowed bourgeois individualistic careerists to grasp political power." The CC Organization Department notified localities that they should not deliberately exclude children of cadres in choosing cadre candidates and that they should choose cadres with a strong Party spirit and sense of political responsibility at the second and third echelons, allowing a long period to observe and test them.

Meanwhile, the Party conducted an internal campaign to strike home the lesson that the ultimate consequences of Gorbachev-style reform were disastrous, citing plenty of objective evidence to bolster their case. Whereas the public media focused on how hard life had become for the common people, the internal media stressed the travails befalling leaders and cadres—Erich Honecker and Markus Wolf facing trials in German courts, a former prime minister serving as train conductor, some high cadres becoming peddlers or homeless people, all losing jobs and perquisites of office.[41] Although the USSR's collapse may have been in China's national interest, members of the CCP leadership so fully identified with the CPSU regime that its fate filled them with a "sense of crisis" (*weiji gan*).

One offsetting gain in what CCP elites view as a generally catastrophic development is that for the first time since the early 1950s there is no ideological strain between the PRC's identification with the socialist bloc and its identification with the Third World. In the vacuum left by Moscow, Beijing has evinced some interest in moving into a position of leadership vis-à-vis what remains of the international Communist movement, which now encompasses only developing countries. China thus agreed to extend $715 million in concessionary credits to the Soviet Union for the purchase of badly needed Chinese agricultural commodities in March 1991[42] and to donate aid to Cuba to compensate for termination of Soviet aid—Cuban workers have begun plying the streets on bicycles imported from China in place of motorized vehicles formerly propelled by subsidized Soviet fuel, and Vice President Rodriquez made a hegira to Beijing in early July 1991.

Although the appeal of socialism has always been greater for the less-developed than for the more advanced countries, China's role as savior of international communism was doomed even before the collapse of the Soviet Union, for at least two reasons. First, a revived bloc based on the goal of defending endangered socialist values bespeaks a conservative or even fundamentalist impulse that flies in the face of the momentum of

---

41. *Bai xing*, no. 248 (September 16, 1991), pp. 6–7; Jan Wong, *Globe and Mail* (Toronto), September 7, October 28, 1991; Yvonne Preston, in *The Age* (Melbourne), October 29, 1991.

42. Liu Guangjun and Chen Baojiu, "A New Change in China's Economic Relations and Trade with the Soviet Union," *Jingji cankao* (Economic Reference) (Beijing), July 5, 1990, p. 1.

reform, which moves in the direction of pragmatism, freer markets, more material incentives, and commercialization—in a word, toward change, experimentation, and innovation. A consistent "conservative Communist" position implies a *principiis obsta* (beware the beginnings) attitude toward political reform, and, if pursued to its logical conclusion, also entails curtailing any economic reforms that threaten to generate demands for political reform, and so forth—creating an infinite regress in which any change is seen as potentially destabilizing. The Deng Xiaoping solution—reforming the economy while exempting politics from change—is a recipe for eventually intolerable cognitive dissonance (which is not to say it cannot go on for some time). Ultimately the only logically consistent stance would be to return to economic as well as political orthodoxy. The problem with this solution, as the sponsors of the post-Tiananmen retrenchment effort have already discovered, is that no one seems to be able to make a centrally planned economy work efficiently any longer.[43] Nowhere was this more convincingly demonstrated than in the utter policy bankruptcy of the Soviet coup launchers upon their brief seizure of power. And if the economy cannot be made to maintain living standards and employment rates at existing levels, an explosive social situation could quickly materialize, given the presence of some 100 million migratory workers (the "blind floating population") camping in China's cities. Yet the regime's appetite for economic growth seems to increase rather than abate with success, as material prosperity only undermines the regime's supramundane legitimacy. This addiction to economic growth in turn drives the regime to marketize, privatize, and otherwise loosen its grip on the economy. In the face of this seemingly irresistible complex of factors pushing for further economic reform, the reassertion of an international socialist mission was ill-fated.

Second, foreign policy prospects for a return to Communist orthodoxy are no more auspicious. The PRC may pride itself on sending money and bicycles to Cuba, but this will bring no relief from Chinese economic difficulties. With the defection of European and Soviet communism, the bloc is so shrunken that any attempt to claim leadership is apt to offer limited ego gratification and less political utility. For practical purposes, the international Communist movement consists of four regimes, three of which are Asian and are led by aging, paranoid leaders intent upon preserving past gains, uneasily making expedient adaptations to pressing economic and political realities but lacking any ideo-

---

43. See Barry Naughton, "The Economy Emerges from a Rough Patch," *Current History*, 90:557 (September 1991), pp. 259–263, for an explanation of how and why the hard-line retrenchment efforts failed.

logically coherent program of their own for meeting the challenge of modernization.

In sum, China's self-definition in terms of transnational reference groups has been a useful device through which the country has drawn more universal relevance from its own revolution and subsequent nation-building experience, thereby magnifying its influence in the world significantly beyond what it might have claimed by dint of its national resources, strategic force-projection capabilities, or level of economic development alone. Whereas China has on the whole prospered, the lot of its chosen reference groups has been a less happy one. Identification with what is left of the bloc no longer places China in the world vanguard but leaves it on the outer fringes of the emerging international system, isolated and apprehensive of a second Cold War. To identify with the Third World is to look backward developmentally—to the extent that the concept has any coherent referents at all. Transnational identification with the old international reference groups seems likely to solve neither the dilemma of political legitimacy nor the question of China's role in the new world order—it only puts a temporary damper on liberalizing trends with which the regime seems otherwise unable to cope.[44]

Yet a regime needing international support may also seek new reference groups. There are powerful voices urging China to now adopt the Asian NICs for this role, although (perhaps because?) their developmental path has by general consensus positioned them on the opposite end of the ideological spectrum.[45] However, to pursue this model consistently will in the course of time bring China face to face with the same crisis of participation the NICs are now weathering.

International Relations

The eclipse of the transnational dimension of Chinese foreign policy implies, willy-nilly, a corresponding rise in the importance of the international dimension, where relations are determined on the basis of interests rather than conceptual projections. A corollary of this shift is that China's international ambit has contracted from the global field to which its aspirations were once projected to the area with which it has most frequent empirical interaction—meaning primarily the Asian Pacific region (e.g., Asia's share of China's total trade rose from 49 to 60 percent between 1983 and 1989, with the six Association of Southeast Asian Nations

---

44. See the insightful analysis by Jean-Luc Domenach, "Ideological Reform," in Segal, ed., *Chinese Politics*, pp. 19–36.

45. E.g., in Central Document no. 2, 1992, Deng Xiaoping said that the "four small tigers" of East Asia should be emulated, above all Singapore.

[ASEAN] countries becoming China's fifth-largest trade partner).[46] China's loss of leverage in the strategic triangle contributes to this downsizing, as does gradual superpower withdrawal from the region.

Since Tiananmen, China has thus accelerated its expenditure of diplomatic resources on regional fence mending, refusing to take sides as Indo-Pakistani tensions escalated over Kashmir, pledging to halt arms sales to the Khmer Rouge in Cambodia, refusing to increase military assistance to North Korea or help in its nuclear program. Beijing established relations with the three remaining holdouts of the six ASEAN countries (viz., Singapore, Indonesia, and Brunei) by 1991 and normalized relations with South Korea the following year. Although legitimacy anxieties have caused "greater China" (*vide* Hong Kong) policy to rigidify somewhat, the PRC took a slightly more flexible stance toward Taiwan (by permitting Taiwanese membership in the Asian Pacific Economic Community and the Asian Developmental Bank under a face-saving formula).

The term "region" is, however, large and imprecise. In terms of power politics, the strategic triangle has been replaced by an Asian Pacific quadrangle consisting of China, Russia, Japan, and the United States. Russia has transformed itself from being China's main security threat and ideological nemesis to being a functionally complementary business partner; the United States has lost its utility as an implicit nuclear guarantor but has become China's largest export market; Japan has emerged as China's banker, economic benefactor, and would-be patron. Let us examine Beijing's relations with each in turn.

Sino-Russian Relations

Despite a most inauspicious start, the new leadership of the Republic of Russia quickly made clear its intention to maintain amicable relations with China (as inheritor of the international commitments of the USSR), and the Chinese regime reciprocated. Carried upon the wave of momentum toward economic cooperation and strategic coordination set in motion during the Gorbachev era, the PRC promptly recognized both the eleven republics now constituting the CIS as well as the four that opted out (again, partly lest they recognize Taiwan; Latvia did establish consular relations with Taipei—an attempt at compromise that Beijing rejected, breaking relations). And trade has continued to wax, jumping from a

---

46. Paul Kreisberg, "China's Asia Policies," and Robert S. Ross, "China and Post-Cambodian Southeast Asia: Coping with Success," in Frank J. Macchiarola and Robert B. Oxnam, eds., *The China Challenge: American Policies in East Asia*, Proceedings of the Academy of Political Science, vol. 38, no. 2 (1991), pp. 75–86 and 52–66, respectively.

mere $960,000 as recently as 1985 to more than $6 billion in 1992, surpassing Russia's trade with Japan and returning China to the leading position in Russia's economic ties with the Pacific. Lack of hard currency has hampered program trade somewhat, but border trade has grown in explosive fashion (by 1991 it was 60 percent of all trade, projected to comprise 80 percent in 1992). By May 1992 three economic development zones (similar to the SEZs) were established in Urumqi, and in Shiheizi and Kuitun in Xinjiang to lure foreign capital, all sited on the Eurasia railway near inner Asian Islamic countries; similar arrangements were planned for Suifenhe in Heilongjiang, Huichun in Jilin, and Manzhouli in Inner Mongolia. Moscow finally dubbed Vladivostok an "open city" in early 1992, welcoming not only Chinese but also Korean and Japanese capital and technology. Chinese "special households" (*getihu*) have been permitted to travel to the adjoining republics with minimal restriction, and thousands of Chinese traders have been shuttling back and forth selling Chinese leather jackets, down coats, and wool sweaters in Siberia (trains from Beijing now arrive in Irkutsk three times weekly), small tractors in Kyrgyzstan and Kazakhstan, and so forth; these traders bring home tales of dismal economic conditions across the border that get great media play.[47] Russians, Ukrainians, and other post-Soviets also began flocking to China to sell their wares out of duffle bags and accumulate enough currency to purchase consumer goods to take home and resell at a profit: They came in such numbers that "Foreign Guest Special Business Counters" had to be set up at two Beijing markets (Hongqiao and Dongdaqiao) to "avoid disorder."[48] Local labor organizations in northern China hire out lumberjacks, vegetable farmers, and construction workers—by the summer of 1992, some 20,000 Chinese workers were working in Siberia, where they earned a reputation for discipline and hard work.

The various forums established under the aegis of normalization have continued to function smoothly. The first economic and trade agreement since the breakup of the Soviet Union was signed in early March 1992, and on March 16–17 Russian Foreign Minister Andrei Kozyrev visited China to discuss developing new channels between the two countries. In August, Russian Defense Minister Pavel Grachev met with Chinese Defense Minister Qin Jiwei in the first meeting between defense ministers since dissolution of the Soviet Union to discuss further military cooperation and arms sales. Yeltsin himself visited China in December 1992, and in April 1993 the commander in chief of the Chinese navy made an unprecedented visit to military enterprises in Moscow, St. Petersburg, and

---

47. David R. Schweisberg, United Press International (UPI), July 27, 1992; *Moscow Times*, September 17, 1992; Reuters, June 24, 1992.

48. UPI, June 10, 1992; Reuters, June 24, 1992.

the Far East.⁴⁹ Border talks resumed in October 1992, now complicated by the fact that China has borders not only with Russia but with Kazakhstan, Kyrgyzstan, and Tajikistan (Russia thus led a joint CIS delegation). China and the Soviet Union had fortunately already agreed on 93 percent of their 5,500-kilometer border (including nearly all of the eastern quadrant) prior to the USSR's dissolution. China is now pushing for revival of a hydroelectric power plan dating back to the days of Sino-Soviet friendship, which would include construction of twelve dams: seven very large ones on the Amur River (beginning from the Khingan gorge going upriver), and five more on its tributaries.⁵⁰ Most of the power would be sold to China. The two sides are now involved in joint patrolling of the Heilongjiang (Amur) Ussuri rivers, primarily to curtail smuggling. Hundreds of Russian scientists are now working in China (many in the defense industry, about which more later, but also on the design and operation of advanced nuclear reactors); and Chinese and Russian scientists are preparing a joint mission to explore Mars.

Such negotiations have been eased by the fact that the security dilemma seems to have virtually vanished. Russia has been steadily cutting troop levels in the strategic area abutting North China: In recent years troop levels in the region have been cut from more than 500,000 to roughly 200,000. Huge armaments factories in the Khabarovsk industrial region have been closed, precipitating unemployment rates nearing 30 percent in some towns. The Pacific Fleet, still the largest of the four, has been less affected by military retrenchment than have military forces in the West (where Russia lost key military bases, training facilities, housing, repair facilities, and industrial enterprises to Eastern Europe and the former Soviet republics), but budgetary constraints have forced it to curtail regional patrols and intelligence-gathering activities.⁵¹ In June 1992 the last remaining combat troops were withdrawn from Outer Mongolia (which hosted some 65,000 troops in the 1960s).⁵² This force reduction is driven by an economic crisis rivaling the Great Depression of the 1930s in the West in severity and rationalized by a reconception of national security that carries the logic of Gorbachev's "new thinking" to its radical conclusion—Brezhnev's obsession with security only in-

---

49. I owe this information to Professor Clay Moltz, assistant director of the Program for Nonproliferation Studies at the Monterey Institute of International Studies.

50. Daniel Sneider, in *Christian Science Monitor*, August 27, 1992.

51. James Clay Moltz, "The Russian Economic Crisis: Implications for Asian-Pacific Policy and Security" (Unpublished paper delivered at the Institute on Global Conflict and Cooperation [IGCC] Conference on The Asia Pacific Security Region, La Jolla, Calif., May 13–15, 1993).

52. See James Flannery in Reuters, June 3, 1992; also Reuters, June 17, 1992.

creased regional suspicions and diverted the Soviet economy from more productive investments: "Power politics swallowed up tremendous resources and weighed heavily on the country without paying any dividends. Not only did the threat to our security not diminish, it actually increased.... Meanwhile, the Soviet Far East lagged increasingly behind in economic development."[53]

Not only has the border issue been more or less neutralized (there are still reservations over the Chinese proposal for mutual withdrawal of troops one hundred miles from the border, which would place Russian troops behind the Trans-Siberian Railway) but the antagonism indirectly generated by Soviet alliances with China's southern neighbors has also been defused, leading to substantial improvements in Sino-Indian, Sino-Mongolian, and Sino-Vietnamese relations. Indeed, according to some Chinese analysts, China's security outlook has never been brighter since the Opium War.

Yet the policy implications are less clear. Though some have argued for further troop demobilization and retrenchments of military expenditures, the trend since 1989 has been in the other direction (from 1989 to 1992 Chinese military spending increased some 50 percent). China's rearmament program has made it a major customer for accelerating Russian arms sales, giving bilateral cooperation a somewhat more sinister cast.[54] The reasons for the buildup are no doubt largely domestic, for the regime needs a firm hand to compensate for its loss of ideological legitimacy while navigating between the aftermath of Tiananmen and an impending succession. Yet China has also sought to project power beyond its shores—by acquiring air-refueling capability for its fighter aircraft, by building a blue-water navy, and perhaps by acquiring an aircraft carrier.[55] Two lessons taught the PLA that it was unprepared to execute

---

53. Yegor Bazhanov, "Reflections on Soviet Policy in the Asia-Pacific Region," *Pravda*, January 16, 1990, p. 5, as trans. in *Current Digest of the Soviet Press*, 42:3 (1990), p. 10.

54. China is now taking delivery of seventy-two "fourth generation" Su-27 Flanker all-weather fighters; the price tag for the first twenty-four was $1 billion, one-third payable in hard currency, the rest in bartered goods. China has signed an agreement to buy 24 MiG-31 Foxhound high-altitude interceptors and is eager to manufacture up to 200 more in a factory in Shenyang. Beijing is said to be interested in the Tu-22M Backfire bomber, a quite formidable Mach-2 nuclear-strike bomber. It is also actively pursuing two of the Il-76 Mainstay Airborne Warning and Control aircraft, not to mention over-the-horizon radar, tactical ground-to-air missiles, and advanced missile guidance systems. David Jenkins, *The Sidney Morning Herald*, March 1, 1993.

55. Nicholas Kristof, "As China Looks at World Order, It Detects New Struggles Emerging," *New York Times*, April 21, 1992, pp. A1, A4; on the naval buildup, see David G. Muller, *China as a Maritime Power* (Boulder: Westview Press, 1983), and Rosita Dellios, *Modern Chinese Defense Strategy: Present Developments, Future Directions* (New York: St. Martin's Press, 1990).

local wars: China's 1979 border war with Vietnam (in which it sustained 30,000 casualties), and the success of high-technology weapons during the Falklands War and the Gulf War. To cope with future threats on its periphery, China thus emphasizes the creation and modernization of "special purpose" elite shock troops.[56] Whereas previously this could be rationalized in terms of the Soviet threat, Chinese territorial designs on a large region of islands and ocean in the South China Sea are now being viewed with greater concern.

The CCP elite's interpretation of Sino-Russian relations seems to have evolved over time. The initial reaction appears to have been that the Soviet disintegration reconfirmed the correctness of the Tiananmen hard-liners' "line" and the folly of any liberal alternative. Given the demonstrated bankruptcy of political reform (and Yeltsin's reforms are deemed far worse than Gorbachev's, execrated as "utopian capitalism"), China could only bank on redoubled economic efforts. "Only through our development can we convince disbelievers of the superiority of the socialist system," as Deng put it in late 1991. "They will be a bit more clear-headed when we have reached the level of small-scale prosperity by the end of the century. If, by the next century, we become a socialist country with a medium-level prosperity, the majority of the disbelievers will have realized their mistakes."[57]

Whereas in the immediate aftermath of the coup the hard-liners threatened to reverse economic as well as political reform in a sweeping campaign against "peaceful evolution" (*heping yanbian*), by fall 1990 Deng was able to create a pragmatic sanctuary for economic reform as a "core." By the summer of 1992, during Deng Xiaoping's trip to the South (or *nan xun*, a throwback to imperial terminology), in preparation for yet another comeback qua leader of the reform forces, a slightly revised interpretation appeared. According to this view, the disaster befalling the Soviet Union could be attributed not to reform itself but to the fact that the Brezhnev leadership had delayed reform for too long, walling the Soviet Union off from economic and technological developments in the outside world. The policy implications of this line of analysis were that further reform would be necessary to save China from the fate of the USSR.

What is most striking about Sino-Russian relations is not that there

---

56. See He Chong, "Let Some Units Modernize First," *Jiefangjun bao* (Liberation Army Daily), February 5, 1988, in *Joint Publications Research Service-CAR* (*JPRS-CAR*) , February 19, 1988, p. 85; as cited in Yitzhak Shichor, "Defense Policy Reform," in Segal, ed., *Chinese Politics*, pp. 77–99.

57. New China News Agency (NCNA), October 9, 1991; *Jingji ribao* (Economic Daily) (Beijing), November 22, 1991; see also *SCMP*, August 26 and December 14, 1991.

have been so many changes, given the profound domestic upheavals in both countries, but that the relationship has been able to survive and prosper despite them. Never has the ideological gap been wider—Kozyrev even raised human rights concerns during his March 1992 visit, to his hosts' dismayed surprise. In triangular terms the current relationship—one in which Moscow and Beijing have excellent relations with each other—should be threatening to the United States, yet the prospective pariah has evinced no sense of alarm. True, the strategic balance has shifted somewhat—but not, I would argue, enough to account for such a shift in triangular dynamics: Any reduction of Russian strategic forces in the Pacific has been offset by parallel American reductions, and in any case those forces continue to dwarf those of any conceivable East Asian competitor. China's strategic forces have meanwhile been expanding.

We have perhaps been misled by the ideological deradicalization that has unquestionably been taking place in both countries to prematurely assume that ideology meant nothing whatever, whereas the relationship's revival demonstrates that ideology means a great deal. If ideology played a larger part in the dispute than we had assumed, ideology is also among the factors facilitating its reconciliation. As long as ideology was still a lodestar for the Communist party elites of the two countries (where its credibility no doubt persisted much longer than among their mass publics), it created an expectation of transnational unity and solidarity that clashed with their respective national interests and created a certain irreducible cognitive dissonance and bilateral tension. We have seen this to be true even during the post-Tiananmen period when ideological commitment was declining in both systems.

In contrast, there is now no reason to expect any sort of privileged transnational relationship (i.e., "socialist fraternity"), making possible for the first time a truly "normal" relationship between two sovereign nation-states. This is mainly due to the Soviet disavowal of Marxism-Leninism, of course, but it is also because the CCP has discarded ideology as a basis for international class solidarity—China now endorses the Five Principles of Peaceful Coexistence as a basis for relations with socialist and nonsocialist countries alike. China's new relationship with Russia constitutes a useful bridge, allowing the nostalgic embers of shared transnational identification to warm up an otherwise businesslike exchange that will continue to be vital for complementary economic and geostrategic reasons.

Sino-American Relations

China's relations with the United States have undergone a transformation similar to Chinese relations with the Communist bloc, in the sense that what was once perceived less as a nation-state than as the national core of a transnational value system has gradually become shorn of its ideological nimbus. This process began with the Nixon opening at the beginning of the 1970s and accelerated during the reform period, even as the Chinese government backed away from its initial embrace at the time of diplomatic normalization (1979) to a more independent posture. Indeed, as Chinese communism proceeded in rather eclectic fashion to incorporate more and more market elements during the course of reform, many American friends of China perceived the two countries to be converging toward a common value system—an assumption many Chinese youth seem to have naively shared, as they made clear in their attitude toward Western media representatives and bystanders during the Tiananmen demonstrations.

Since Tiananmen, Sino-American relations have by general consensus fallen to their lowest point since the crisis over Taiwan arms sales in the early 1980s. There are at least two reasons for this. The first is triangular: The gradual improvement in Sino-Soviet relations in the 1980s began to undermine China's strategic utility as a counterweight to the Soviet Union, whereas the improvement in Soviet-American relations, beginning in 1986 at Reykjavik and culminating in a series of dramatic Soviet concessions, dealt it a lethal blow. Sino-American relations began to be detached from their supposed utility in an anti-Soviet united front and to be evaluated in purely bilateral terms. It was in this context that the second factor, the sudden break in value convergence symbolized by Tiananmen, was so disturbing. To the American public, the well-publicized six-week period of democracy marches and demonstrations provided evidence that political cultural convergence toward American values was taking place much more swiftly than anyone had dared hope. The violent suppression of this movement, symbolized for the American public by the smashing of the Goddess of Democracy, underlined the regime's determination to forestall any such convergence—which it subsequently execrated as "peaceful evolution" down a "capitalist road."

In the purge and rectification that followed, Beijing fleshed out its critique, according to which anything hailing from the West was deemed insidious and subversive. Even seemingly friendly gestures, such as those made by the Peace Corps and Fulbright scholars, were thought to be part of a cunning plot to penetrate and undermine socialist order and peddle bourgeois values.[58] The American public responded with considerable ire to this turn of events; even though the Bush administration took the lead in the imposition of sanctions (on June 5, 1989) and con-

---

58. Samuel S. Kim, "Chinese Foreign Policy After Tiananmen," *Current History*, 89:548 (September 1990), pp. 245–282.

tinued to maintain them longer than most of China's other trade partners, it took political heat domestically for not responding more harshly to Chinese human rights abuses.[59] In the aftermath of Tiananmen, China soon toned down its public critique of Western influence, but via competent reportage by foreign correspondents Western publics continued to be apprised of the ongoing domestic campaign against "bourgeois liberal" and "counterrevolutionary" influences.

Lacking a persuasive strategic or ideological rationale to cushion the relationship, an imbalance of trade and other policy irritants came to seem less tolerable than might have otherwise been the case. Although that imbalance (some $18 billion by 1992, according to U.S. figures) was not America's highest (and although historically the balance has been positive), the fact that the PRC reemphasized its status as a centrally planned economy made it more difficult for the regime to evade responsibility for its trade policy than in capitalist states, which can scapegoat their private sectors. And the trade imbalance has continued to grow in the years since Tiananmen in the face of American protests, as the United States became China's largest single export market in 1989—accounting for nearly 20 percent of China's foreign trade, whereas China accounted for only a bit more than 2 percent of U.S. trade. Moreover, the United States has been the major market for China's highest value-added goods, the products that will take the PRC down the road of "export-oriented industrialization."

The issue of arms sales also became more salient. Given the more explosive North-South polarity noted above, American attention shifted from newly dormant superpower relations to the risks of nuclear proliferation to regional powers, in which context China's refusal to observe sanctions on the export of missile or nuclear technology (or, according to U.S. intelligence, to honor promises once made) became more annoying than before.[60] Thus a nuclear cooperation program and process for liber-

---

59. As of 1991, about one-half of the economic sanctions adopted by the United States in 1989 remained in effect. China was ineligible for U.S. government and commercial weapons sales, exchanges of military personnel and other "high-level contacts," Overseas Private Insurance Corporation investment guarantees, or concessional trade financing through the Department of Commerce's Trade Development Program. The administration renewed China's eligibility for Export-Import Bank financing (in the spring of 1990, two loans totaling $33 million were extended to China) and permitted China to launch American-made satellites on Chinese rockets. Robert G. Sutter, "Tiananmen's Lingering Fallout on Sino-American Relations," *Current History*, 90:557 (September 1991), pp. 247–250.

60. Within a few years, China has become the world's fourth- or fifth-largest arms supplier. Chinese weapons sales have had considerable impact, due to the volume of weapons produced, short production time, lack of political restraints, and China's willingness to supply weapons to countries at war in highly sensitive regions (from the American perspective),

alizing U.S. controls on technology transfer remained frozen until 1992, when China finally agreed to abide by the Nuclear Non-Proliferation Treaty and (with conditions) the Missile Technology Control Regime regulating missile technology proliferation. China has also begun to participate somewhat more actively in multilateral arms control. Since 1984, the PRC has signed the Outer Space Treaty, joined the International Atomic Energy Agency, and endorsed the South Pacific Nuclear Free Zone. China has also become quite active in various UN organs dedicated to arms control and disarmament.[61]

From China's perspective, the relationship's deterioration has been a matter of dismay and some bewilderment. Two of the three levers that the PRC had used during the triangle to control this lopsided relationship seem to have become inoperative: The loss of the first, China's indispensability to counter the Soviet threat, was a corollary of the collapse of the triangle. The second, China's convergence with democratic and free market values, was cast into doubt by Tiananmen. Even the third lever, Beijing's aggrieved protest that the United States was interfering with China's legitimate nationalist aspirations, seems to have lost much of its cogency in the wake of the far more active diplomatic stance Taipei has taken on this issue in the last five years. By opening bilateral trade and tourism and proposing its own preconditions and timetable for unification, Taipei has signaled its determination to take responsibility for its own future. Lacking an alternative international patron, the loss of these three levers leaves the CCP regime in a more passive position, waiting as the United States ratchets up the pressure to make concessions that would (from the regime's perspective) further undermine its legitimacy.

In retrospect, Tiananmen may have served a useful function in dispelling unrealistic illusions of convergence on both sides and in placing the relationship on a sounder and more realistic footing. Since the crackdown, China has been making incremental adjustments to many of the

---

such as the sale of DF-3 intercontinental range ballistic missiles to Saudi Arabia. Due to the separation of foreign economic affairs from foreign policy and the devolution of decision-making on foreign trade to lower levels, the foreign ministry seems to have become detached from decisions regarding arms sales. Shichor, "Defense Policy," pp. 77–99. (To keep this in perspective, in 1991, the last year for which figures were available, the United States sold more arms to the Third World than all other nations combined.)

61. China, for example, joined the UN Conference on Disarmament, where it participated in an ad hoc working group on nuclear test bans, made technical contributions to the agenda, and played an active role in resolving procedural impediments. China also participated constructively in the UN First Committee, a group dealing with international security issues, and in March 1987 hosted a regional UN conference on international disarmament. Walsh, *Change, Continuity, and Commitment*, pp. 105–106.

policies that have created difficulties,[62] and the fledgling Clinton administration has backed off somewhat from campaign promises to punish the Beijing regime by revoking most favored nation status, though it must be said that the relationship is still in search of a new raison d'être. And it seems doubtful that China will discover one until it has resolved its leadership succession crisis. Given the continuing salience of the personal factor in Chinese politics, only after a new leadership has consolidated itself will it become fully clear what China's future developmental priorities are and what foreign policy arrangements it will choose to pursue to accommodate them.

Sino-Japanese Relations

Geographically propinquitous to China, Japan has, after a history of cultural emulation culminating in a bloody but ultimately vain stab at military conquest, surpassed its larger neighbor economically, leaving the relationship laden with guilt, admiration, resentment, and other complex feelings. Since the new beginning after World War II, with new regimes leading both countries, Japan has endeavored to place the relationship on a strictly businesslike footing despite Chinese efforts to keep the issue of the past alive. At American behest, Japan recognized Taipei rather than Beijing at the conclusion of the civil war, but Japanese interest in the China market led to the clandestine establishment of trade relations. As early as 1948, Prime Minister Shigeru Yoshida summed up Japan's attitude when he said: "I don't care whether China is red or green. China is a national market and it has become necessary for Japan to think about markets."[63] Sino-Japanese trade first became significant in the early 1960s in the wake of the Sino-Soviet schism, and by 1970 Japan had become China's primary trade partner (accounting for 20 percent of China's total trade). Yet the signing of the Long-Term Trade Agreement and the Peace and Friendship Treaty in 1978 set the stage for a new era. Trade rose from $5 billion in 1978 to $13 billion in 1984, $20 billion in 1985, $15.5 billion in

---

62. After initially denouncing human rights protests and unwarranted interference, China released Fang Lizhi and a host of other political prisoners, and in October 1991, and again in August 1992, Beijing issued a White Paper on prison conditions that systematically defended its policy. On nuclear proliferation, Beijing joined 140 other signatories of the Non-Proliferation Treaty at the end of 1991 and agreed to abide by the regimes governing missile sales. On trade, China sent a 100-member delegation to the United States to purchase some $700 million worth of American goods in 1991 and in the summer of 1992 signed a market access agreement after protracted negotiations.

63. Shigeru Yoshida, *The Yoshida Memoirs: The Story of Japan in Crisis*, trans. Kenichi Yoshida (London: Heinemann, 1961), pp. 127–131.

1986, and $19.6 billion by 1989 (the post-1986 decline was due to Chinese adoption of import controls, as well as to a fall in the price of oil). In the last half of the 1980s, Japan consistently ranked as China's second-largest trading partner (after Hong Kong) and its largest lender. There have been three major loans, in 1979, 1984, and 1988; the last, for $5.2 billion, was suspended in the wake of Tiananmen, as Japan joined other members of the Group of Seven (viz., the United States, Canada, Great Britain, France, Italy, and Germany) in condemning the crackdown. But immediately after the (July 7, 1990) Houston economic summit (where Prime Minister Toshiki Kaifu succeeded in moderating the Group's position on China in the final communique), Deputy Foreign Minister Hisashi Owada visited Beijing, assuring the Chinese of Tokyo's determination to resume the $5.5 billion loan despite Bush's request to go slowly, and in August 1991 Kaifu became the first leader of a major industrial democracy to visit China since the crackdown.[64] Since 1982, China has been the largest single recipient of Japanese developmental aid, which has come to represent more than 50 percent of the total assistance China receives from both bilateral and multilateral sources.[65]

But the relationship has had its ups and downs. The Chinese were initially overoptimistic about how fast they could increase their oil exports and expanded imports faster than they could generate foreign exchange to pay for them (trade doubled in less than three years during Hua Guofeng's "foreign leap forward," as China signed contracts worth several hundred million U.S. dollars). Thus in 1981, China unilaterally canceled about 1,000 of these projects, suspending contracts worth roughly 300 billion yuan, including the notorious Baoshan iron and steel plant; not until Japan agreed to provide 300 billion yuan in commodity loans could the project be brought to completion. In 1985, this cycle was repeated: Japanese exports incurred a trade deficit of $6.1 billion. Blaming the Japanese for inflicting a massive trade deficit on China, the PRC once again restricted or canceled a great many contracts with Japanese exporters, driving many of the small and medium-sized Japanese contractors into bankruptcy. In the fall of 1988, China again underwent drastic economic retrenchment following the bout of hyperinflation the

---

64. In the spring of 1992, CCP General Secretary Jiang Zemin reciprocated with a visit to Japan, followed by a visit from NPC Standing Committee Chair Wan Li later the same year.

65. Chinese aid amounted to $3.6 billion in 1982, $3.5 billion in 1983, and $3.8 billion in 1984 and 1985. Overseas Economic Cooperation Fund, *Kaigai keizai kyoroku binran*, 1987, p. 251, as cited in Sadako Ogata, "Regional and Political Security Issues: Sino–Japanese–United States Triangle" (Unpublished paper, Institute of East Asian Studies, University of California, Berkeley, n.d.). Japanese government institutions made or promised 3.3 trillion yen in loans to China from 1979 to 1992, equal to nearly $30 billion at 1993 exchange rates. *Wall Street Journal*, May 12, 1993.

foregoing summer, curtailing credit and placing restrictions on foreign exchange. This uncertain business climate, capped by Tiananmen and the threat of further political instability, prompted Japanese entrepreneurs to reduce their rate of investment in China.[66]

Grievances have by no means been limited to the Japanese side. Like the United States and many other countries, the PRC has complained about the trade imbalance: Japan has had a bilateral trade surplus almost every year from 1972 to 1989, except for 1981 and 1983. There have also been complaints about the quality of Japanese exports. China has faulted the terms of trade; inasmuch as China's exports to Japan are primarily raw materials and labor-intensive manufactured goods, whereas Japan's exports to China are mainly technologically advanced machinery and equipment, China is subject to the unfavorable terms of trade that plague most Third World exporters: Raw material prices fluctuate wildly in world markets, whereas prices for industrial products remain more stable. When Japan found itself with a suddenly enhanced surplus of foreign exchange in 1985–1986 after the so-called Plaza Accord forced a revaluation of the yen,[67] China expected to reap the lion's share of the expected boom in foreign direct investment. And indeed, Japanese FDI in China did rise from $100 million in 1985 to $1.2 billion in 1987. But most Japanese investment went to Southeast Asia (especially Thailand) or to the United States, and China complained that the ratio of investment to trade remained too low. From 1979 to 1987 there were only 395 Sino-Japanese joint ventures; in fiscal year 1986 the cumulative total Japanese investment of $600 million in China amounted to only 0.5 percent of total Japanese FDI, compared to nearly twice that amount in Taiwan. Since an investment protection agreement was concluded in August 1988 after seven years of negotiation, Japanese FDI in China increased somewhat more rapidly but still remained only one-half that of U.S. investment as of 1990. After Tiananmen, in the context of recentralizing trade controls, China imposed draconian import constraints, with the result that Japanese exports stagnated while Chinese imports continued to show steady growth, culminating in one of Japan's few trade deficits. Yet this also stimulated Japanese investment designed to overcome trade barriers.

---

66. Japanese foreign direct investment (FDI) on the mainland thus dropped from $515 million in 1988 to $356 million in 1989. Allen S. Whiting and Xin Jianfei, "Sino-Japanese Relations: Pragmatism and Passion," *World Policy Journal*, 8:1 (Winter 1990–1991), pp. 107–135.

67. An unanticipated upshot of the currency revaluation was that almost overnight Japan became one of the major financial powers. Since 1985 Japan has become the world's largest net creditor; from 1986 to 1989 Japan's net assets abroad nearly doubled, from $129.8 billion to $240.7 billion. All of the world's ten largest banks were Japanese by 1989; Japanese banks now supply 20 percent of all credit in California and control four of the top ten banks.

Thus, in fiscal 1992, Japanese investment doubled to about $1 billion, while Sino-Japanese trade (partly linked to its investment) also jumped 27 percent, to nearly $29 billion.[68]

Like South Korea and Taiwan, China also raises double-bind complaints about Japanese investment, claiming that it focuses on short-term, low-tech, high-profit enterprises, such as hotels and office space, and has little impact on improving production capacity. Whereas Chinese complain of Japanese refusal to transfer high technology, Japanese counter-criticisms of Chinese refusal to accept the "appropriate" technology for that country's current level of development unwittingly confirm China's grievance. Although the Chinese receive more aid from Japan than from any other country, they grouse that most of these funds are tied to the purchase of Japanese goods, technology, and industrial plants, creating substantial technology dependence (i.e., China's industry becomes tied to Japanese suppliers). The Chinese point out that more Japanese developmental aid is allocated to Southeast Asia than to China and criticize the donor for the hegemonic intent they attribute to such "gifts."[69]

Finally, China has bitterly and repeatedly raised the issue of Japanese war guilt: In 1982, 1984, and 1986, Japanese textbooks were assailed for failing to acknowledge Japanese indemnity for atrocities committed during the invasion of China. In 1985, Prime Minister Nakasone, together with members of his cabinet, made an official visit to the Yasukuni Shrine, where Japanese war criminals and other war dead are interred, triggering the first major Chinese student protest movement since Democracy Wall against the "second Japanese [commercial] invasion." China reacted indignantly to a series of insensitive statements about Japanese war guilt by leading politicians: In 1986, Minister of Education Masayuki Fujio stated publicly that the "rape" of Nanjing did not violate international law—people who complained about Japanese history books should first look back to see whether they had not committed such a thing in their own history; Nakasone dismissed him amid a storm of protest after he refused to resign. In 1987, ownership of a dormitory (Kokaryo) in Kyoto was disputed between Taiwan and China, and Taiwan won on legal grounds in the courts; China indignantly (but fruitlessly) demanded that the decision be overruled by the government. In May 1988, China was "shocked" by a series of statements by National Land Agency Director Seisuke Okuno, who contended that Japan had

---

68. *Wall Street Journal*, May 12, 1993, p. A1–8.
69. Japan now provides nearly two-thirds of the foreign aid received by Thailand, the Philippines, Malaysia, Indonesia, and Singapore, with the United States ranking a weak second.

not intended to invade China; Okuno was eventually forced to resign. Less than a year later, Takeshita himself, on the eve of the Emperor Showa's funeral, expressed uncertainty about Japanese responsibility for aggression in World War II and was even vague about whether Hitler's policies constituted aggression.[70] Meanwhile, the Chinese constructed a War of Resistance Against Japan Museum near Beijing (opened in 1987).

Sensitive Chinese reactions to such indications of selective national amnesia are understandable, but their timing suggests that they also serve a tactical function (viz., rhetorical ammunition). The first textbook protest in 1982 came on the heels of the Baoshan controversy, for example, and the 470 billion yen Nakasone loan package of 1984 helped soothe Chinese feelings. The 810 billion yen Takeshita aid package of 1988 was similarly intended to mollify the Chinese after the second textbook crisis, the Okuno affair, and the Kokaryo dormitory cause célèbre.[71]

Throughout the triangular era, Beijing's strategic stance vis-à-vis Tokyo seems to have been contingent on its relations with the two superpowers, as one would expect. During the 1950s, when China was aligned with the Soviet Union against the United States, China vehemently opposed the Japanese-American Mutual Security Treaty (MST); this opposition continued through the 1960s despite the rising salience of the Soviet threat, presumably due to continued Chinese preoccupation with the U.S. threat. In the wake of the Sino-Soviet border clash and the ensuing opening to the United States (followed by diplomatic normalization with Japan in September 1972, well ahead of the U.S.) China lapsed into silence on the MST and by the end of the decade was even encouraging Japan to increase its defense spending.[72] With the normalization process of Sino-Soviet relations back on track in 1982, China, however, reconsidered, once again coming to view Japanese arms spending with consternation. When, under Nakasone's leadership, the Japanese defense budget for 1987 exceeded 1 percent of GNP (by four-thousandths of one

---

70. Kenneth B. Pyle, *The Japanese Question: Power and Purpose in a New Era* (Washington, D.C.: AEI Press, 1992), p. 17.

71. The title to a student dormitory named Kokaryo, in Kyoto, was disputed between Taiwan and the PRC. Upon the decision by a Japanese court that the dormitory legally belonged to Taiwan, Beijing decried the decision for its implicit endorsement of a "two-Chinas policy" and demanded that the executive overrule the court. The Japanese leadership objected that this would violate the separation of powers in their system, an answer that China eventually had to abide with. See Walter Arnold, "Political and Economic Influences in Japan's Relations with China Since 1978," in Kathleen Newland, ed., *The International Relations of Japan* (New York: St. Martin's Press, 1991), pp. 121–146.

72. In 1980 China's deputy chief of general staff, Wu Xiuqian, intimated to Nakasone that Japan should increase its defense spending to 2 percent of GNP. Reinhard Drifte, *Japan's Foreign Policy* (New York: Council on Foreign Relations Press, 1990), p. 52.

percentage point, after protracted controversy), Deng Xiaoping criticized this as a sign of Japanese militarism (prompting a Japanese vice minister of foreign affairs's diagnosis that Deng was senile—a suggestion that earned the official an early retirement).[73] The Chinese have repeatedly pointed out that Japan ranks third in the world in absolute defense expenditures, without noting that this is a distant third (the amount was only $34 billion in 1992, compared with $292 billion for the United States and $52 billion for an economically afflicted Russia) or that estimates of Japan's expenditures vary with the exchange rate, so that a 20 percent rise in the value of the dollar would drop Japan back behind England and France.[74]

To what extent such complaints reflect serious Chinese concern—in view of the fact that China is the only Asian nation with an operational nuclear strike force and maintains the world's largest conventional army and air force—it is hard to say (Japan's well-equipped self-defense force [SDF] is only 240,000-strong). In any case, such statements have been carefully muted since Tiananmen. The June crackdown means that both countries now have skeletons in the closet, and Tokyo has proved itself a friend indeed, moving first to drop sanctions and restore loans and aid, leading the way to China's diplomatic rehabilitation in visits by Kaifu in 1991 and by Emperor Akihito himself in the fall of 1992. For its part, Tokyo needs friends, feeling sensitive about U.S. Japan-bashing but still suspicious of Russia, eager to assume greater international responsibility but nervous about arousing unpleasant memories. There is no question that the Chinese are chary of what they view as Japan's growing international assertiveness (though they welcome its growing autonomy from the United States), yet they avoided public criticism of Japan's hapless efforts to participate in the Gulf War and (so far) of its agonized decision to lend SDF troops to UN peacekeeping operations in Cambodia. The acid test of this new East Asian pas de deux will be China's stance on an anticipated proposal to expand the UN Security Council to include Japan and Germany as permanent members.

Conclusions

The PRC has, under the foreign policy adjustments of the reform era, reached its international apogee. By all empirical indicators, it has become one of the world's leading trading states, has gained a permanent

---

73. Under a political convention established "for the time being" by the cabinet of Prime Minister Takeo Miki in 1976, Japanese defense spending was not supposed to exceed 1 percent of GNP.

74. Whiting and Xin, "Sino-Japanese Relations," pp. 107–135.

seat on the UN Security Council and been seated on most other important international organizations, and has gained recognition from most other states in the world on terms accepting in principle its sovereignty over Hong Kong and Taiwan. We have witnessed in the course of reform an overall tendency to shift from the transnational to the international dimension, elsewhere referred to as an aspect of ideological "deradicalization."[75] Of course, part of the reason for this is that foreign policy is no longer viewed as a symbolic blank slate on which new visions of political salvation may be limned but is rather viewed as a commercial artery for access to economically remunerative technology or goods and for the transaction of other profitable business. Unfortunately, China's traditional international reference groups have not proven to be its best business partners. A rift has emerged between the "old friends" whereby the country is still prone to legitimate itself ideologically and the international "associates" on whom it has come to rely for commercial advantage and strategic security.

Like the nouveau riches that China seeks to become, the country has in the course of scaling the ladder of development become alienated from its revolutionary origins, evoking an occasional sense of bad faith. At a time of domestic legitimacy crisis (such as that represented by Tiananmen), such bad faith becomes politically intolerable, and there is a felt need to return to the communities logically linked to the idea system on which legitimacy was originally based. Thus, for at least the time being, identification with traditional transnational reference groups has enjoyed a brief revival—only to have one of these groups explode while the other could offer little coherence. Without triangular leverage and without the ability to use transnational appeals as a form of leverage to magnify its international impact, the PRC's influence has tended to shrink to a regional ambit. This may be but one facet of a more general trend toward economic regionalization in the post–Cold War world. Whether this is a transitory or more lasting phenomenon it is difficult to say, for the international system is still groping for a coherent new structure at this point. In any case, the Asian Pacific has emerged as perhaps the world's most economically vital region, and China's prospective role as regional "growth pole" is quite attractive.

Until Tiananmen prompted a revision of its national agenda, China seemed well on the way to successful adaptation to the newly emerging regional and international realities. Beijing had in the course of reform successfully reversed the garrison state priorities of the Maoist era (i.e.,

---

75. See Robert C. Tucker, "The Deradicalization of Marxist Movements," *American Political Science Review (APSR)*, 61 (June 1967), pp. 347–348; and Tang Tsou, "Letter to the Editor," *APSR*, 62 (December 1967), pp. 1101–1103.

economic autarky, large heavy industry and defense budgets, geographic location of investment based on strategic rather than economic criteria) and showed promise of becoming Asia's fifth and largest NIC. Chinese foreign policy seemed to have adapted very well to these new priorities, burying the hatchet with old and new adversaries and putting the country, for the first time, on good terms with nearly everyone. China's international status reached new heights, despite the country's still modest level of economic and technological advancement.

The crackdown at Tiananmen did not reverse as many domestic economic reforms as its supporters had hoped and its adversaries feared,[76] but it has contributed to a certain slippage in the international arena. The last-resort success of armed suppression seems to have restored a certain faith in the "barrel of a gun" more generally, resulting in a return to increasing arms expenditures and greater emphasis on police and military force,[77] which does not seem likely to be conducive to tourism or other aspects of economic interdependence. Greater reliance on suppression to keep the domestic population in line is also functionally conducive to an atmosphere of confrontation with an external scapegoat, and although the regime has tried to limit its xenophobic propaganda to domestic consumption, the new line has (together with the collapse of more potent ideological adversaries) aggravated friction with the West and with various international organizations committed to human rights. Finally, the regime is in an ambivalent position with respect to its economically successful policy of opening to the outside world, on the one hand, continuing to welcome further investment and trade, and, on the other hand, trying to interdict its cultural ramifications.

All of these policies seem apt to complicate, to a greater or lesser degree, China's successful adaptation to the new world order—though they do not seem likely to impede it altogether. China's longing for geostrategic great power status seems anachronistic in a post–Cold War era but may form part of a dialectic with its no-less-powerful drive toward economic prosperity to sustain national unity of purpose.

---

76. See Naughton, "The Economy Emerges," pp. 259–263.
77. Police strength increased to 800,000 in 1991, whereas that of the paramilitary People's Armed Police grew to more than 600,000, according to Public Security Minister Tao Siliu in a speech to the Eighteenth National Meeting on Public Security Work in Beijing. Tao also announced plans to boost investment in the national security apparatus in the coming decade. *SCMP*, November 6, 1991. After a decade of steady decline, military budgets have increased by more than 10 percent each year (at this writing) since the crackdown.

6

The Future of Socialist Reform

Over the past forty years there have been profound changes in the Chinese political system, begging the question of where these changes seem likely to lead. The most important overall pattern has been the shift from revolutionary change—wrought by breakthroughs and great leaps, and by breakthroughs involving charismatic leadership, elite-sponsored heaven storming, and revolutionary transnationalism—to reform, accomplished via disjointed incrementalism, entailing the disenchantment of ideology, the routinization of charisma, the establishment of a more calm and civil culture, and, in the international arena, the calculated pursuit of national interests.

Though there is still a certain amount of ambivalence about this shift, the disillusionment with radicalism that crested during the Cultural Revolution has fostered an overall consensus that reform is the most prudent way to make historical "progress." For elites, the chief advantage of reform is greater career security, offering a fixed and rational set of "rules of the game" whereby officials can exert greater control over their life chances. As for the masses, they are spared the risks of public humiliation as categorical "targets" of one campaign or another and allowed to pursue their vocations in more orderly fashion without the constant intrusion of "criticism," "self-criticism," "study," and various other digressions. The traditional distinction between public and private, though always relatively tenuous in Chinese political culture, resurfaces in the form of an increasingly autonomous civil society. This civil society is based upon a reinvigorated family network, as well as (more tentatively) upon the emergence of a congeries of voluntary associations that are based either on professional, occupational, or avocational interests, and a media market in which useful and reasonably varied information and entertainment is purveyed.

The distinction between revolution and reform should not be too sharply drawn, for in practice the two patterns intermingle. There were attempts during the Maoist era to introduce the rule of law, more institutionalized political procedures, and other features now associated with reform. And the reform era has been characterized by the recurrent resurgence of the revolutionary animus, both in the form of "non-campaigns" such as the recurrent (1981, 1983, 1987, 1989) drives against bourgeois liberalization or spiritual pollution, and in the eruption of elite strife (1987, 1989) over the line of succession. Thus the attitude of the Deng regime toward its revolutionary ancestry has been ambivalent and compromise-ridden, sometimes seeking to repress the past (as in the official attitude toward the antirightist movement, or the Cultural Revolution), sometimes turning to the past in search of reinforcement to cope with the problems of the present (as in the post-Tiananmen revival of the Mao cult).

The reforms launched by Deng Xiaoping and his supporters at the Third Plenum of the Eleventh CC in December 1978 betokened an effort to reconcile the "contradiction" between revolutionary principles and reformist practice, between politics and economics, by redefining the former in much more modest terms and subordinating it to the latter ("the only criterion of truth is practice"). From being "in command" of the march into the glorious Communist utopia, politics was demoted to the role of midwife and custodian of rapid economic growth. Deng promised a trade-off, on the one hand providing a more conducive climate for business—a younger and more professionally competent officialdom, a rational division of labor between political leaders and functional experts, more tolerance for inequality (rationalized as material incentives), somewhat greater latitude for intellectuals to make their contributions without worrying about ideological taboos, an opening to the outside world—and, on the other hand, demanding in return state autonomy: A set of restraints (usually referred to as the Four Cardinal Principles) was invoked against political activities deemed disruptive to the Four Modernizations. With the exception of the Four Cardinal Principles, the political objectives of reform bore no visible relationship to the old ideological code, whereas the economic growth strategy seemed to ignore, if not contradict, it. The tension between a reformist approach to economic development and revolutionary legitimating principles, redolent of the conflict between moderate and radical wings of the CCP during the Maoist era, has played itself out in the form of a business cycle that lurches between fiscal (and intellectual) expansiveness and economic (and political) retrenchment.

In short, we emerge with a sort of half-reform, characterized by a relatively sharp break from Maoism accompanied by a reluctance to foreclose a return to it under unforeseen exigencies. This seems to have given rise to various forms of cognitive incongruence. Among the more ideologically orthodox members of the leadership, there is a sense of ideological homelessness and nostalgia incongruously mixed with nightmares of a recurrence of the Cultural Revolution; among the radical reformers, an openness to market thinking and Western technology is ironically mixed with an economic "breakthrough" mentality. Both wings of the Party are different amalgams of a revolutionary past, a reformist present, and a nebulous future, locked in an unresolved, seesawing tug-of-war. Thus collective ownership is abandoned to the extent that collective farmlands were redivided into family plots, but the state retains ownership and has adamantly refused to forswear the possibility of eventual resumption of control, despite the chronic insecurity this arouses among peasants. Since Tiananmen, the regime has also endorsed a "voluntary" movement toward recollectivization, albeit with neither popular response nor great political determination. Class struggle is recanted, but only in its "violent, turbulent" form, with the important caveat that enemy class remnants and the struggle against them will continue indefinitely. Mass movements are renounced, but the regime continues to stage publicity blitzes, such as the criticism of spiritual pollution, or bourgeois liberalization, even if not referred to as campaigns. The departure from antimaterialistic asceticism has been similarly ambivalent, with an emphasis on consumerism and "getting rich first" alternating with campaigns for thrift, self-sacrifice, and the emulation of Lei Feng. Even the shift in emphasis from production relations to production forces and from the superstructure to the base has been muddied by the attempt to float the ideal of "socialist spiritual civilization." The campaign against the residual influence of Confucianism continues, now, however, embraced by the Right (i.e., reformists) rather than the Left, which sees in China's past the origins of feudalism, the personality cult, and a pattern of authoritarian submission; the Left, for its part, seems to have assimilated both Mao and Confucius into the nation's patriotic heritage, tracing the seeds of "bourgeois liberalization," "peaceful evolution," and other unhealthy winds.[1]

Yet these internally contradictory tendencies held together reasonably well through the 1978–1984 period, as common beneficiaries of a tide of unprecedented prosperity that raised all boats. Productivity in the rural sector (including small-scale local industry as well as agriculture) tripled during the 1978–1984 period, and industrial growth achieved

---

1. For a historically extended analysis of the xenophobic impulse in Chinese politics, see Kuang-sheng Liao, *Antiforeignism and Modernization in China, 1860–1980* (Hong Kong: Chinese University Press, 1986).

new records; during the 1979–1989 period, China boasted one of the highest average GNP growth rates in the world. Yet the problems accompanying reform gradually became more nettlesome. Although the heavier reliance on material incentives was more effective in motivating enhanced economic performance, it also resulted in appreciable income discrepancies.[2] The introduction of markets to supplement the plan resulted in a "dual economy" in which a given commodity could have different prices depending on the market; this resulted in a loss of political control over consumption, exacerbated inflation, and permitted the type of arbitrage known as *guan dao*, in which cadres would avail themselves of their positions to buy at the planned price and sell at the higher market price. Decentralization sapped the central government of control over capital investment, foreign trade, tax collection, and other macroeconomic levers, while the dismantling of Maoist ideology weakened efforts at political control.

All of these difficulties were intensified when the "second stage" of the reform program was launched at the Third Plenum of the Twelfth CC in October 1984, shifting focus to the much more complicated urban industrial economy. At this point the system was afflicted by what we may call a "partial reform syndrome." Such a syndrome is triggered when the system, in the course of its transition from command planning to "socialist market economy," encounters difficulties serious enough to consider turning back. The search for solutions begs the question: From which system should these solutions be derived? From the standard repertoire of techniques used to manage centrally planned economies, with which the leadership is experienced and comfortable? Or from the armory of techniques typically used to manage market economies? If the problems are political, whence can the leadership muster sufficient legitimacy to command obedience? From the old doctrines of proletarian dictatorship, the leading role of the Party, and democratic centralism? Or from emergent notions of a political market, consumer sovereignty, and civil society? Amid this uncertainty, there is a tendency for the elite to split, precipitating a crisis. Under crisis conditions, mass constituencies, too, gravitate to elite proponents of either "new" or "old" solutions based on their material and ideal interests, exacerbating tensions and leading to polarization.

A partial reform crisis at the system level is analogous to a succession

---

2. See Peter Nolan, *The Political Economy of Collective Farms: An Analysis of China's Post-Mao Rural Reforms* (Boulder: Westview Press, 1988). To be sure, the first to protest about this were not denizens of the poverty pockets left behind (many of whom, however, seem to have abandoned their stricken regions to make unauthorized migrations to urban centers) but members of the old middle classes who felt threatened by relative deprivation as peasants and urban entrepreneurs closed the gap between them. These urbanites fueled the political protests against inflation in 1988–1989.

crisis at the level of leadership. A succession crisis tends to paralyze the decisionmaking capacity of the system by raising the prior issue of who decides. Succession is perhaps an even more serious problem in China than in other Leninist systems due to the tendency of incumbents to play with the issue long before it occurs, partly in order to resolve it premortem but partly also as a way of manipulating the ambitions of other would-be successors to rearrange the elite lineup. Thus the situation becomes doubly complicated if these two crises happen to coincide—if, in the context of relatively severe transitional difficulties en route to market socialism, a succession crisis flares up to further bedevil the situation.

We might term such a compounding of quandaries a "transition crisis." A transition crisis tends to be characterized by power struggle and either a sudden lurch forward or temporary retrogression to an earlier phase. Transition crises arose repeatedly in the 1980s. In a typical scenario, economic expansion is encouraged beyond the system's capacity, triggering inflation ("overheating"), which causes recriminations to ricochet among the elite, which in turn arouses anxieties and second thoughts among "retired" veteran leaders about their succession arrangements, and everything is soon in flux. Since Tiananmen, the economic recovery has hitherto remained under tighter control, and elimination of much of the radical reform wing and the stabilization of elite turnover seem to have allowed the current successors to consolidate their prospects. Yet a recurrence of transition crises cannot be precluded.

There are two main reasons for the tendency to retrogress during crises of transition. The first is that the pattern of structural reform, unlike the previous ideologically based pattern, lacks any clear vision or "map" of the future toward which change is presumed to be moving. This is, to be sure, not officially admitted—change is still said to be moving toward socialism, and any public disagreement with this is effectively precluded—but there is no discernible relationship between the *end* of communism (from each according to one's abilities and to each according to one's needs) and reformist *means* (viz., marketization, privatization, opening to the outside world). Yet it is not deemed valid to reject any given means because it appears inconsistent with the end, so long as it increases production. Under normal circumstances, when the economy is operating efficiently and living standards are rising, the procedural rules of the game suffice to enable the leadership to reach consensus on practical solutions to whatever problems arise. During a situation of crisis, however, when standard operating procedures no longer apply, metacriteria are needed to point in the direction of a "correct" solution.[3]

---

3. Of course, the history of factionalism in the revolutionary era indicates that the existence of a general end toward which political means ought to be oriented was never a guarantee against disagreement. But the range of disagreement was narrowed.

Without them, crises tend to "deepen," raising issues of general direction. In that context there is a tendency to retrogress to previously established criteria and tactics, if not to old ideological dogmas.

The second reason for the tendency to retrogress is that the reform regime has been, in effect, politically stuck in a Leninist organizational structure by Deng's taboo on political reform, making it difficult to resolve new problems with which the existing structure was not designed to deal. For example, it lacks any provision for the articulation of legitimate opposition; the situation is perhaps even worse than during the Maoist era, when opposition and struggle were at least rhetorically affirmed, although no practical measures were undertaken to permit them to be vented constructively. Despite a somewhat more tolerant view of intellectual discussion, the regime remains a single-party system in which opposition is driven underground, erupting unpredictably when the system is weakest rather than on prescribed occasions in arenas built to contain it. Having forfeited its claim to own and manage all "means of production," the Party-state has yet to articulate adequate mechanisms to regulate money supply, credit, and other market variables. Given a political apparatus that does not fit the economic landscape, obstacles are often encountered requiring a rethinking about how to proceed.

For these two reasons, the PRC has, since the death of its most distinguished revolutionary hero-leader, been characterized by a stop-and-go pattern: reform under routine circumstances, with a tendency to revert to "revolutionary" behavior (e.g., spontaneous mass movements, factional struggle, purge) during systemic crises. The "first front" of the leadership is allowed to cope with reform; the gerontocratic "second front" returns during crises. Although activity by the first front is deemed by both participants and outside observers to be "normal," action taken by the second front engenders anxiety due to the uncertainty about when it may suddenly intrude as well as about the capability of a crisis to reset the paradigms of normality.

This "two steps forward, one step back" waltz might be remedied in one of at least three ways. One would be to decide that the era of reform was basically complete and that the status quo should be consolidated "as is." This would reduce the danger of retrogression by eliminating the uncertainties of transition to an unknown destination. The problem is that it is difficult, perhaps economically disastrous, for a partially reformed system—part-market and part-plan—to halt in equipoise.

A second possibility would be to correct the political flaws in the existing reform regime. The problem with this cure (about which more below) is that from the perspective of the Left it would be worse than the disease, requiring reforms violating both the Four Cardinal Principles and the political interests of the incumbent leadership. At least until a generational transition has been completed, political restructuring will encounter fierce resistance.

A third solution would be to adumbrate a new ideological road map setting forth general goals toward which the system is moving and delineating possible routes whereby those goals might be approached. Whereas the first two solutions would aim to eliminate crises of the type that precipitate retrogression, the third, somewhat more modestly, would merely try to equip the system with a compass to navigate crises while staying the course.

This would also be a tall order, however. Taboos against the revision of existing dogma would have to be overcome (i.e., breaching Deng's Four Cardinal Principles), and a new doctrine elaborated that could satisfy both the functional imperatives of the economic system and the ideal interests of elites, masses, and various special interests (e.g., national minorities, intellectuals). It is unclear after the most recent crisis whether Marxism–Leninism–Mao Zedong Thought retains sufficient credibility to serve as the framework on which such a belief system might be built.

And what might such an ideological road map look like? The country seems to be moving in two different directions at once: on the one hand, toward the normative goal of the communist utopia, and, on the other, toward the economic goal of modernization. Yet the former has been increasingly eclipsed by the latter, gravitating into the position of "heaven" in Christian theocracy, a sort of compensatory utopia that fades from the foreseeable future (Jesus clearly expected to see it in his lifetime)[4] to the millennium. Yet unless the Party-state is redefined convincingly in terms of its historical mission—which will necessarily involve fundamental rethinking and probably controversy—it will lose its idealistic appeal to the nation's intellectuals and youth and undergo decay,[5] perhaps even following its European confreres into extinction.

The realistic goal of economic modernization lacks any specific model to which one could point; the implicit models are the United States and Japan, whose iniquities are well known by now to all Chinese and are in any case frequently rehearsed. Even the East Asian NICs—the most recent object of Deng Xiaoping's emulatory enthusiasm—have shown a dismaying interest in democracy. To emulate without being infected, the CCP leadership has, in effect, resuscitated Zhang Zhidong's formula as a criterion for screening out "pollution."[6] Whether it proves more work-

---

4. See Karl Jaspers, *Socrates, Buddha, Confucius, Jesus: The Paradigmatic Individuals*, trans. Ralph Manheim (New York: Harcourt, Brace and World, 1962).

5. For the still-classic description, see Robert Michels, *Political Parties: A Sociological Study of the Oligarchical Tendencies of Modern Democracy* (New York: Dover, 1959).

6. I.e., "*zhongxue wei ti, xixue wei yung*" (Chinese learning as the essence, Western learning of techniques).

able in the twenty-first century than it was in the nineteenth remains to be seen.

Not every ill wind can be traced to the West, but it should be conceded that the market is no political panacea. Whereas economists recorded a net decline in income inequality during the early years of reform, since 1984 it has been on the increase; the introduction of price reforms has repeatedly unleashed inflation; the introduction of a multiprice market has exacerbated corruption; the opening to the outside world has let in spiritual pollution; and privatization seems apt to increase inequality and introduce insecurity to employment, and even to housing and medical care. For a number of years it may not be entirely clear to many Chinese whether the process they are undergoing is socialist reform or "peaceful evolution."

How this all will work out is of course hard to fathom.[7] From the present perspective it appears likely that reform socialism in China will evolve from its present half-reformed, amphibian form toward a corporatist form of market socialism, initially under authoritarian but nontotalitarian political auspices. China may realistically hope to take the same road to political reform as Taiwan or South Korea. The Eastern European route of instantaneous democracy after spontaneous mass upheaval can probably be precluded in China, due to an indigenous revolutionary tradition, the presence of a strong, pro-Communist army, and the absence of partisan or religious traditions around which opposition forces might coalesce. Should reform socialism collapse, it would probably be followed by a less coherent alternative (than, say, Hungary).

Should it survive, China may (with luck) undergo an evolutionary, nonviolent form of change. Over time and amid periodic crises and retrogressions, so long as rapid growth of GNP and per capita income continues, the tension between elites and masses will gradually be contained, as the masses' sense of political efficacy rises with their living standards and the role of elites changes from command to coordination as their legitimating competence shifts from ideology to various economically useful secular vocations. The role of ideology will continue to ebb, to the extent that "domestic policy disputes no longer involve ideology, but conflict between the goal of economic modernization and the tendency toward bureaucratic stagnation."[8] Finally, with the shift from "extensive" to "intensive" development, implying greater reliance on sci-

---

7. See Andrew C. Janos, *Politics and Paradigms: Changing Theories of Change in Social Science* (Stanford: Stanford University Press, 1986), pp. 97–127.
8. Richard Löwenthal, "The Ruling Party in a Mature Society," in Mark G. Fields, ed., *Social Consequences of Modernization in Communist Societies* (Baltimore, Md.: Johns Hopkins University Press, 1976), pp. 81–118.

ence and technology to improve productivity and less reliance on forced-draft mobilization of the primary factors of production (land, capital, and particularly labor), an increasingly intricate functional division of labor may be anticipated, as well as a shift of investment priorities from primary to secondary and tertiary sectors.[9] What is distinctive about the Chinese case is that the imperative for such a shift does not arise from factor shortages, as in the former Soviet Union or Eastern Europe (which face labor and possibly material supply and energy shortfalls), but rather from consumer quality demands in Western markets—given the PRC's intention to pursue an export-oriented growth strategy à la the Asian NICs.

Having arrived at this cautiously optimistic forecast, we should note that it includes a number of lacunae and unresolved tensions. Among these, perhaps the largest general issue concerns the relationship between political and economic reform. Most discussions of change in Communist systems focus on economic developmental strategies and their impact on society, either ignoring politics or relegating it to the status of a dependent variable.[10] Certainly that approximates the current CCP vision of the country's "modernized" future—unruly protests having been forbidden, advocates of the "fifth modernization" driven abroad. After Tiananmen, it also seems to jibe with the mood of a politically anesthetized and commercially vibrant public sector, for whom the old saw "Heaven is high and the emperor far away" (*tian gao huangdi yuan*) finds new appeal.

Yet this seems unlikely. It seems safe to predict that the Chinese will continue to have "politics"—struggles for power and policy—for some time to come. Throughout both the Mao and Deng reigns, the Chinese people have placed great store in political solutions to all manner of problems, and, although in the course of time they have become more locally self-reliant, it seems unlikely that past habits will dissipate quickly. The pattern of deferral of political restructuring and avoidance of any public discussion of national policy issues that we have witnessed throughout the reform era implies that "politics" has meanwhile become overburdened with suppressed demands and grievances and is apt to leap to the top of the agenda when these are legitimated. Among them, the following issues will loom large:

---

9. Bill Brugger, "Undeveloped Socialism and Intensive Development," in Brugger, ed., *Chinese Marxism in Flux, 1978–84: Essays on Epistemology, Ideology, and Political Economy* (Armonk, N.Y.: M. E. Sharpe, 1985), pp. 102–111.

10. Compare, for example, George Fisher, *The Soviet System and Modern Society* (New York: Atherton, 1968); Peter C. Ludz, *Parteielite im Wandel* (Koeln: Westdeutscher Verlag, 1968).

1. How to routinize charismatic leadership (entailing depersonalization as well as institutionalization) without eviscerating it. Leadership has long been the strong suit of Chinese politics, but it could become considerably more stable and effective if balanced by institutionalized countervailing powers (e.g., a strengthened legislative apparatus) and if reliable succession procedures and a functioning political retirement hiatus ban the specter of protracted succession crisis while the system hangs suspended by one flickering life.

2. How to determine the proper role of the Communist Party. As our review of Liu Shaoqi's theories of party-building indicated, it has always been deemed essential for the Party to insulate itself from its social environment in order to preserve its own subculture and organizational integrity. The problem has been that this tends to create a sense of alienation between elites and masses. Reform exacerbates this cleavage: The value system being propagated among the masses—"getting rich quick" through hard work and shrewd business practices—is utterly incongruent with the Party ethos of selfless sacrifice for the public interest. As the command economy goes the way of the sabertooth, Party cadres must redefine their functional relationship to the economy without relinquishing ethical claims. This is a hard line to toe in a market context. If they take advantage of their positions to engage in business or render services in exchange for favors ("rent-seeking behavior"), that is of course viewed as corruption. Yet if cadres strictly avoid involvement in economic activities, they risk becoming irrelevant to the modernization effort (*bao chan dao hu, bu yong ganbu*, or, with family responsibility plots, who needs cadres?)—or so resentful of nouveaux riches entrepreneurs that they stymie reform. Party cadres must be "in" the world but not "of" the world, a sort of secular priesthood—is this feasible?

3. How to foster mass input into the political process without either risking disruption of normal work routines or raising expectations to unrealistic levels. The mass line and its attendant devices for channeling mass participation have not functioned effectively since the 1950s; neither elite-sponsored nor mass-initiated mobilization has proved entirely satisfactory. The fact that the Deng leadership has been so timid in broaching this question (and tends to overreact to any disturbance) does not mean it is not an issue. Yet a refusal to talk is no answer and simply allows resentments to fester invisibly until the situation becomes explosive. Can some constructive synthesis between a Western-style civil society and CCP-style top-down mobilization and control be achieved? There are likely to be experiments along these lines in the future.

4. How to determine China's proper role in a post–Cold War world, where the prospects of international communism seem bright only by comparison with the plight of some of the post-Communist transitions.

From any conventional perspective China's foreign policy under Deng has been highly successful. In the course of reform, Beijing had successfully reversed the economically disastrous "garrison state" priorities of the Maoist era and integrated itself into the world's most thriving regional economy. For the first time since the Opium War, China sees a vista without threats to its national security on the horizon, unfettered by alliance networks inhibiting its diplomatic mobility. Until Tiananmen prompted an adjustment of its agenda, the country seemed well on the way to becoming Asia's fifth (and largest) NIC, and a regional hegemon to boot.

And what of Tiananmen? The crackdown did not reverse as many domestic reforms as its supporters hoped and its victims feared. It has contributed to a healthy caution among both elites and masses that should, ceteris paribus, diminish the likelihood of another such tragedy during succession. In the international arena it has contributed to a certain slippage, a loss of moral self-assurance. China's national identity is less secure without the accustomed international reference groups to set its course by, and the regime has resorted to accelerated armament efforts in the absence of any visible security threat and rigidified its position on certain sensitive issues, such as Hong Kong and the Spratleys. Although understandable under the circumstances, this policy has been the source of some unease among China's regional neighbors and may prove hard to square with Beijing's still-ambitious diplomatic and developmental objectives. All things considered, however, these difficulties seem relatively manageable—twists and bumps in the road toward a future that can be viewed with cautious optimism.

Acronyms and Abbreviations

AP	Associated Press
APSR	*American Political Science Review*
ASEAN	Association of Southeast Asian Nations
BBC	British Broadcasting Corporation
CAC	Central Advisory Commission
CC	Central Committee
CCP	Chinese Communist Party
CDIC	Central Disciplinary Inspection Commission
CFE	Conventional Forces Treaty
CIS	Commonwealth of Independent States
CMC	Central Military Commission
CPPCC	Chinese People's Political Consultative Conference
CPSU	Communist Party of the Soviet Union
CQ	*China Quarterly*
FBIS	*Foreign Broadcast Information Service*
FDI	foreign direct investment
GDP	gross domestic product
GNP	gross national product
IGCC	Institute on Global Conflict and Cooperation
IGO	international governmental organization
IMF	International Monetary Fund
INF	Intermediate-range Nuclear Forces
INGO	international nongovernmental organization
JETRO	Japanese External Trade Organization
JFRB	*Jiefang ribao* (Liberation Daily [Shanghai])
JFJB	*Jiefang junbao* (Liberation Army Daily [Beijing])

KMT	Kuomintang	
LDC	less-developed country	
MST	Mutual Security Treaty	
NCNA	New China News Agency	
NIC	newly industrialized country	
NIEO	new international economic order	
NPC	National People's Congress	
OPEC	Organization of Petroleum Exporting Countries	
PL	Paramount Leader	
PLA	People's Liberation Army	
PRC	People's Republic of China	
RR	*Renmin ribao*	
SAR	Special Administrative Region	
SCMP	*South China Morning Post*	
SDF	self-defense force	
SEC	State of Emergency Committee	
SEZ	Special Economic Zone	
START	Strategic Arms Reduction Treaty	
UN	United Nations	
UPI	United Press International	
USSR	Union of Soviet Socialist Republics or Soviet Union	
VOA	Voice of America	

About the Book and Author

Western images of China have changed throughout the twentieth century, but perhaps never more dramatically than in 1989, when the CCP regime's massacre of student protesters at Tiananmen Square electrified world public opinion and dissipated much of the goodwill built up during a decade of highly successful economic reform. Yet after a temporary pause following the crackdown, economic reform seems to have resumed with undiminished vigor.

Despite the regime's best efforts to put international and domestic fears to rest through a rotation of cadres at the Fourteenth Party Congress and other leadership forums, the political system remains essentially Leninist, leaving it susceptible to factional splits, purges, mass movements, and other forms of politically inspired instability. Although China's unique combination of economic reform and political dictatorship has so far kept it from the fate of the former Soviet Union, the question raised here is whether its fragile structure will be able to withstand future tremors.

Lowell Dittmer reconsiders the progress and pitfalls of Chinese reform socialism at this crucial juncture. Tracing reform momentum back to the radical initiatives and subsequent pragmatic adaptations of the 1950s and 1960s, he focuses on the three central policy arenas of the reform era: political leadership, the mass public, and foreign policy. In each category, he highlights the vivid contrast between the universal revolutionary impulses that laid the foundation for the Chinese Communist Party and the various piecemeal compromises or reversals that have been adopted to sustain both momentum and control.

Dittmer finds that in the leadership arena, the CCP has followed a strategy of institutionalizing and depersonalizing charisma in the wake of Mao's disastrous campaigns. In dealing with mass publics, the post-Mao regime has engaged in an ambivalent effort to coopt and to repress popular participation. In the arena of foreign affairs, a tug-of-war exists between the effort to convince the world of the uniqueness and validity of the Chinese experience and the need to satisfy the specific material and ideal interests of the Chinese state. In each instance, although the revolutionary impulse has been transcended and indeed often forgotten, Dittmer finds that its lingering influence continues to disrupt, inspire, and otherwise shape the progress of the continuing Chinese reform effort.

Lowell Dittmer is professor of political science at the University of California–Berkeley.

Index

A-B conspiracy prosecution, 83
Academy of Social Sciences, 119
Agreement on Strengthening Trust in the Military Realm as a Guiding Principle, 174
Agricultural output, gross value of (1978–1984), 34
Agriculture
  collectivization of, 63
  household responsibility system in, 20
  reforms of (1979–1983), 38
Akihito, Emperor
  visit to China (fall 1992), 196
American values, Chinese convergence with, 188
Andropov, Yuri, 67(n43)
Antagonistic contradiction, 65, 112
Antirightist movement (or campaign), 11, 65, 86
An Zhiwen, 152
April 26 editorial (*People's Daily*), 147
Arbitrage (*guan dao*), 36, 202
ASEAN. *See* Association of Southeast Asian Nations
Asian Pacific, 197
  quadrangle, 182
Association of Southeast Asian Nations (ASEAN), 181–182
August–September 1971 tour. *See* Mao
Autonomous Student Union of Beijing Universities, 157(n98)

Bai Hua, public criticism of, 120(n26)
Bankruptcy package, 43
Baoshan iron and steel plant, 90, 192

Bao Tong, 152
Basic units (*jiben danwei*), 121
Battle of Huaihai (1949), 84
Battle of the Hundred Regiments (August–October 1940), 84
BBC. *See* British Broadcasting Corporation
Be a Good Party Member and Build a Good Party (Liu Shaoqi), 23
Beidaiho, 87
Beijing-Jakarta-Hanoi-Pyongyang axis, 162
Beijing Spring (1978–1979), 27, 41
Beijing University Students' Group for Dialogue, 157(n98)
Berlin, Isaiah, 155
Big-character posters, 111, 123, 128, 134, 136(n63), 137, 139, 142. *See also* Nie Yuanzi
"Blind floating population," 180
Bo Gu, 60
Book of Changes, 110
Border clash at Zhenbao (Damansky) Island (1969), 168
Bourgeois democratic parties, 120
Bourgeois liberal and counterrevolutionary influences, campaign against, 189
Bourgeois liberalization, 129, 143
  campaign against, in 1981, 1987, and 1989, 28; post-Tiananmen, 132
  crackdown on (in early 1987), 33
  denunciation of, 98
Bourgeois privacy, 112
Bourgeois reactionary line, 51, 75
Bourgeois reactionary nation-states, 159
Bourgeois reactionary road, 71

Bourgeois values
  of liberty, fraternity, and equality, 113
  "reactionary," 3
Bo Yibo
  in the Cultural Revolution, 21
  reaction to the August 1991 Soviet coup, 178
Brezhnev, Leonid, 67(n43)
Brezhnev Doctrine, 172
British Broadcasting Corporation (BBC), 148, 153
Bunce, Valerie, 67–68
Bureaucratic capitalism, 44(n60)
Bureaucratic class, 16
Bureau of Information and Publication, 119
Bu zheng zhi feng (ill wind, e.g., bribes and corruption), 43–44

CAC. *See* Central Advisory Commission
Cadre corruption, campaign against, 28
Campaign against Lin Biao and Confucius (pi-Lin pi-Kong) (1974), 76, 122
Campaign against "peaceful evolution" (*heping yanbian*), 186
Campaign criticizing Confucius, 122
Campaign to study dictatorship of the proletariat and to criticize "bourgeois rights" (1975), 76
Cancun conference (October 1981), 163
Capitalist road, 14
  criticism of, 132(n55)
"Cat theory," 19
CCP. *See* Chinese Communist Party
CDIC. *See* Central Disciplinary Inspection Commission
Ceausescus, execution of, 173
Central Advisory Commission (CAC), 26, 32, 94
Central Cultural Revolutionary Group, 134
Central Disciplinary Inspection Commission (CDIC), 26, 32
Central People's Government Council, 84
Central Propaganda Department of the CCP, 120
Central Soviet of Jiangxi, 83
Chaos (*luan*), 29–30, 116
Charismatic leadership, 3, 54–55
  Christ as charismatic leader, 54
  routinization of, 54, 55, 208
Chen Boda, 133–134
  Lin Biao's supporter, 77
  Mao's personal confidant, 38, 65

Chen Yi, 113
  in the Cultural Revolution, 21
  Nanchang Uprising, 83
Chen Yun, 46
  commenting on Mao's reputation, 106
  economic retrenchment, 90
  "Eight Opinions," 145(n85)
  endorsing Pudong (1992), 123
  as leftist, 39
  during 1950s, 36
  reactions to August 1991 Soviet coup, 178
  and Tiananmen crackdown, 96
  and veterans' retirement, 93
  and Zhao Ziyang's case, 100, 151
Chernenko, Konstantin, 67(n43)
Chiang Kai-shek, 71, 85
Chi Haotian (PLA chief of staff), visit to the Soviet Union, 177, 177(n37)
China
  aid from, 162
  annual growth rate for farm output (in the 1970s), 34(n48)
  arms sales, 198(n60)
  complaints about Japanese investment, 194
  debt service, 166–167
  foreign policy (1971), 75, 164; during the era of continuous revolution (1949–1978), 3, 6
  gross domestic product (GDP), 1, 1(n1), 34
  gross national product (GNP), 33(n44), 35(n49), 166
  military modernization, 174–175
  national identity, 209
  political structure, 120
  rearmament program, 185, 185(n54)
  revolutionary foreign policy, 3–4 (*see also* China's foreign policy)
  share in world trade (1978–1988), 33(n44)
  trade imbalance, 1984, 138(n72); with Japan, 193
China-India-Egypt alignment, 162
Chinese Communist Party (CCP), 49
  leadership, 2
  "revisionist" episode, 10
Chinese Democracy Federation, 151
Chinese People's Political Consultative Conference (CPPCC), 26
Chinese Socialist Youth League, 82
Chinese Third World policy, 162
CIS. *See* Commonwealth of Independent States
Civic Forum, 109
Civil culture, 154

Index

Civil society, 5, 109, 153–155, 158, 199, 202, 208
Class collaboration, 162
Class struggle, 87, 123, 160, 201
  extinction of, 72
  renunciation of, 28
  revival since Tiananmen demonstrations, 28
Clean official (*qing guan*), 115
Cold War
  revival of, 169
  termination of, 6
Collective leadership, 12, 53, 67, 125, 201
Commonwealth of Independent States (CIS), 178
Communes, dissolution of, 44(n64)
Communist bloc, 39, 161
  China's identification with, 167
Communist utopia, 44
Contradiction, 65
  between advanced productive relations and underdeveloped productive forces, 11
  between economic and revolutionary objectives, 4
  between the people and the enemies of the people, 112
Conventional Forces (CFE) Treaty (December 1990), 170
Corruption, 44(n59). *See also* Cadre corruption
Counterrevolutionary values and interests, 3
CPPCC. *See* Chinese People's Political Consultative Conference
Crisis, sense of (*weiji gan*), 179
Criterion of truth, 125
  debate on, 90
Crossing the River by Groping for Stones, 125
Cuba, China's aid to, 179
Cultural Revolution (1966–1976), 4, 10, 12–13, 17, 21–22, 36, 45, 51, 71–73, 73(n55), 74–75, 79, 87, 113, 131–133, 132(n55), 154, 156
  criticism of, 38
  egalitarian rhetoric of, 44(n60)
  image of, 30
  legacy of, 37
  Mao's Thought about, 25
  1984–1985 campaign to negate, 30(n38)
  in post-Mao China, 24
  reversal of, 26–29
  revival of, 28
  springboard for reform era, 37
  tactics, 155
Cultural Revolution Group, 135
Cultural superstructure, 51

Da gong, wu si. See "Great public, nothing private"
Dangan. See Personnel files
Dang quan pai. See Faction in power in Socialist Education Movement
Decollectivization, de facto, 38
"Deepen the Reforms, Improve the Economic Environment, and Restore Economic Order," 100
Democracy Movement, 150
Democracy Wall movement, 28, 30, 41, 90, 137–138, 157
Democratic centralism, 17
Demonstrations
  December 1986, 131
  April–May 1989, 109, 131
Deng Liqun, 173
  "advisory" role in the propaganda system, 120
  leftist, 39
Deng-Li-Yang troika, 150
Deng Nan (Deng Xiaoping's daughter), 106
Deng Rong (Deng Xiaoping's daughter), 106
Deng Tuo (vice-mayor of Beijing), 135(n62)
  rehabilitation of, 23
Deng Wenming (Deng Xiaoping's father), 81
Deng Xiaoping, 4–5, 7, 10, 39, 45, 54, 67(n43), 68, 74, 76, 78, 78(n62), 84–85, 103, 118, 123, 135, 155, 200
  accused of setting up an "independent kingdom" by Mao, 87
  antirightist movement (1957), 13, 86
  April 26 editorial (*People's Daily*) (1989), 147
  attacking Gorbachev's "new thinking," 172
  attitude toward spontaneous mass participation, 92
  ban of "four big," 128
  call for new international political and economic order (October 1988), 163
  case against Gao Gang and Rao Shushi, 85
  "cat theory," 19
  in CCP Central Organization in Shanghai (1930s), 83
  charismatic leadership, 55
  China's foreign policy, 164
  coalition with Liu Shaoqi, 85–86
  concern with "responsibility," 32(n41)

creation of a five-power socialist alliance, 175
criticism of Japanese militarism, 196
in Cultural Revolution, 21
defense of Maoist foreign policy, 168(n19)
Democracy Wall movement, 90, 137
denunciation of bourgeois liberalization, 98
divorce, 84
emancipation of intellectuals, 27
family life, 91
Four Cardinal Principles, 34, 41, 128
Four Modernizations (1975), 88
in France, 82
Gang of Four, 89–90
and Gorbachev, 171, 173
heirs apparent of, 97
and Hua Guofeng, 24, 90
Hundred Flowers, 86
industrial relocation, 85
and Jiang Zemin, 152
at Jinggangshan (a red area in Jiangxi Province), 83
leadership, 91–92
upon liberation, 84
Long March, 84
and Mao Zedong thought, 80–81
martial law (Beijing, May 19, 1989), 149
materialism, 38
and Nie Yuanzi, 135(n61)
opening to the outside world, 38
opponent of the cult, 25
personal succession, 94
political reform, 98(n104), 141
political transparency, 125
price reforms, 100, 100(n109)
purged, 88
purge of Hu Yaobang, 101
purge in the military, 103
reactions to the Soviet coup (August 19, 1991), 177
reforms, 22
rehabilitating about three million cadres and party members (July 1977), 39
relationship with his father, 81–82
repression of intellectuals (1979), 33
restoration of collective leadership, 26
retirement of, 95–97
reversal of just verdicts, 89
revisionism, 13
revisionist pragmatism, 46
rise of, 31, 72
routinization, 107
self-criticism, 87–88

shifting support from Zhao to Li Peng, 100
in Soviet Union, 83
succession crisis, 93
superiority of the socialist system, 38(n54), 186
support of the Great Leap Forward, 65, 86
suspending prosecution of Zhao Ziyang, 151
theory of "building socialism with Chinese characteristics," 106(n119)
theory of Three Worlds, 162
Tiananmen Incident (1976), 137
Tiananmen Square demonstrations (1989), 102, 104, 109, 150
trip south (1992), 96, 186
"two fronts" arrangement, 65
"two whatevers," 25
ultimate veto power, 156
work teams, 76
Zunyi conference, 84
Deng Xiaoping solution, 180
Deng Xiaoping Thought (*Deng Xiaoping sixiang*), 91
Deng Xixian (Deng Xiaoping), 81
Deng Yingchao, 99
Deng Zihui
resistance to hasty collectivization, 12(n6)
responsibility for field system (in mid-1950s), 12
Depersonalization, 55, 107
Deradicalization, 129
De-Stalinization, 63
Development, Chinese (Maoist) approach to, 3. *See also* Stalinist model, departure from
Dictatorship of the proletariat, 115
Di er qudao. *See* Second channel
Ding Guangen, 120
Direct foreign investment (1979–1987), 33(n45)
Division of labor, 107
Dongluan. *See* Turmoil
Double Hundred policy, 151
revival of, 27
See also Hundred Flowers movement
Double standard ("value rationality" within, "purpose rationality" without), 17
Dual communication network, 119
Dual economy, 202
Dual price structure, 36
Du Rensheng, 152
East Asian newly industrialized countries (NICs), 38, 205

Index

Economic Affairs Committee of the Central Administration Council (antecedent of State Council), 85
Economic base, 51
Economic "breakthrough" mentality, 201
Educational credentials, 27
Egalitarianism, 73
Eighth Five-Year Plan (1991–1995), 96(n100)
Eighth National People's Congress (March 1993), 2
Eighth Party Congress (1958), 11, 65, 85
  Eleventh Plenum of, 134
  Mao's speech at, 69
Eisenhower, Julie Nixon, 79
Electoral campaign (1980–1981), 132. *See also* Multicandidate district elections
Emancipation of Mind, 27, 30, 33, 125, 129
Employment in rural township enterprises (1978–1988), 34(n48)
Erikson, Erik H., 65
European Enlightenment, 112–113
Evening Chats at Yanshan, 23
Existentialism, 130
Existentialist thinkers, 55
Expanded meeting, 129
Expanded session, 118

Factionalism, 157(n98)
Faction in power (*dang quan pai*) in Socialist Education Movement, 20
Fairbank, John King, 56
Falklands War, 186
Fang Lizhi, 145, 191(n62)
  democratic reform, 141(n80), 142
  Deng's commentary on, 99(n106)
Feng Yuxiang, 83
Fen qi fen pi (stage by stage), 40
Fetishism, 125
Feudal succession, 106
Fifth Commandment, 54
Fifth modernization, 207
Fifth Plenum of Eleventh Central Committee (CC) (February 1980), 23, 23(n26), 40, 93
Fifth Plenum of Seventh Central Committee (April 1955), 85
"Fifty Days," 136(n63)
First echelon, 94
First Five-Year Plan, 11
First front, 61, 64(n36), 65–66, 204
First intermediate zone, 162
First World, 162–163
Five black classes, 22

Five-power socialist alliance (Soviet Union, North Korea, Mongolia, Vietnam, and China), 175–176
Five Principles of Peaceful Coexistence, 161, 187
Five Stresses (civilized behavior, decorum, hygiene, discipline, and morals), 41. *See also* Four Points of Beauty; Three Deep Loves
Five upholds and five oppositions, 178
Floating population, 36
Foreign investment, 1
Foreign Leap Forward, Hua Guofeng's, 192. *See also* Great Leap Westward
Foreign policy under Deng Xiaoping, 209
Formalization, 127
"Four big" (big-character posters, the rights to speak out freely, air views fully, and hold great debates), 128
Four Cardinal Principles (*si xiang jiben yuanzi*), 27, 34, 38, 41, 81, 128, 137, 143, 200, 204–205
Four cleans. *See* Socialist Education Movement
Four Modernizations, 76
Four old, 71
Four Points of Beauty (the mind, language, behavior, and the environment), 41
Fourteenth Party Congress (October 1992), 91, 96
  rotation of elites, 2
Fourth "encirclement" campaign, 83
Fourth Plenum of the Thirteenth Central Committee, 103, 151
French Revolution, 113
"From each according to his abilities, to each according to his work," 31
"From the bottom up," 76
"From the top down," 76
Fujio, Masayuki (Minister of Education of Japan), 194
Functional division of labor between two fronts, 62

Gang of Four, 4, 25, 75
  arrest of, 89
  crimes of, 30
  criticism of remnants of, 90
  fall of, 114(n12)
  February Adverse Current, 29, 30(n37)
  proletarian revolutionary line, 38
  trial of, 38
Gang of Ten, public trial of, 90

Gao Gang, 12(n6), 62
General Mirror for the Aid of Government (*zi zhi tong jian*), 56
General Political Department of Red Army in Ruijing, 83
German reunification, 172
"Gerontocratic" tendencies, 53
"Getting rich first," 201
"Getting rich quick," 208
Goddess of Democracy, 155, 188
Golden age (1950s), 10, 13, 36
Golden Fifties. *See* Golden age
Gong. *See* Public
Gongkai. *See* Publicity
Gongkaixing. *See* Transparent
Gorbachev, Mikhail S., 67(n43)
  "new thinking," 184
  political reform hero, 171
  and popular discontent with perestroika, 174
  visit to Beijing (May 1989), 148, 170
  "voluntary" resignation, 178
Gorbachev-style reform, 179
Grachev, Pavel (Russian defense minister), meeting with Qin Jiwei, 183
Great Depression, 43
"Greater China" policy, 182
Greatest famine in the world, 3(n4). *See also* Great Leap Forward
Great Leap Forward (1958), 3, 3(n4), 4, 10, 13, 37, 46, 63–65, 87
Great Leap Westward (*yang yao jin*), 90. *See also* Foreign Leap Forward, Hua Guofeng's
Great Proletarian Cultural Revolution. *See* Cultural Revolution
"Great public, nothing private" (*da gong, wu si*), 112
"Groping for stones to cross the river," 36
Group of 5, 135
Group of 7, 192
Group of 24, 165
Group of 77, 163, 165
Growth during Maoist period, 35
Growth in post-Mao period, 35
Guan dao. *See* Arbitrage
"Guiding principles for inner-party political life," 40
Gulf crisis, 175
Gulf War, 186

Hai rui ba guan. *See* Hai Rui's Dismissal
Hai Rui's Dismissal, 133(n58), 135(n62)

"Half-feudal, half-colonial," 49
Hai sha she ying ("holding sand and throwing shadows"), 122
Hand Copied Documents, 121
Hard-liners, 149–150
Headquarters for Defending the Square, 157(n98)
Hebrew norms of filial piety, 54
Hegel, G.W.F., 111
hei qi lei. *See* Seven black classes
hei wu lei. *See* Five black classes
Ho Long, 84
  Nanchang Uprising, 83
Honecker, Erich, 67(n42)
  trial of, 179
Hong Kong, incorporation into China in 1997, 34
How Steel Is Tempered, 176
How to Be a Good Communist (Liu Shaoqi), 15, 23, 51(n6)
Hua Guofeng, 30, 42(n58), 125
  and Deng Xiaoping, 24–25
  foreword to fifth volume of Mao's *Selected Works*, 25
  first attempt to modulate Maoist radicalism, 4
  foreign leap forward, 192
  1979 projections, 2(n1)
  political downfall, 24–25, 90, 90(n87)
  succession, 90
  and Tiananmen Incident (1976), 137(n66)
  "two whatevers" (February 1977), 25
Huangfu Ping, 96(n100)
Hu Hao (former ambassador to Japan), sent on an "appeasement mission" to Xi'an (October 1985), 139
Human feeling (*renqing wei*), 113
Human rights, 165
Human targets, 3
Hundred Flowers movement (1957), 13, 30, 49, 63–65, 128–129
  Deng delaying implementation of, 86
  reblooming of (summer 1985), 38
Hunger strikes (from May 13, 1989), 148, 155
Hu Qiaomu, advisory role in the propaganda system, 120
Hu Qili, 100
  dismissed, 103
  purged from Politburo, 152
  and students protesting Japan (1985), 139
Hu Yaobang, 95, 120, 138, 157
  asking Deng to give up his power, 98(n103)
  death of, 101, 146

Index

demotion of, 143
fall of, 38
purge of, 93(n92)
resignation of (January 1987), 99, 99(n105), 129
revival of Double Hundred policy, 140
secretary general of the party secretariat, 26
state funeral of, 156
and veterans' retirement, 93

Ideological secularization, 130
Imperial Kwantung Army, 138
Indo-Pakistani tensions, 182
Industrial output, gross value of, 35
Industrial relocation, 85
Inflation, 36
Institutionalization, 55, 107
Institutionalized personalism, 5. *See also* Leadership succession
Intellectual blooming (summer 1986), 33
Intermediate-range Nuclear Forces (INF) Treaty (December 1987), 170
Intermediate zone theory, 162
Internal (*neibu*) printed media, 120
"Internal Reference" (*Neibu cankao*), 121
International Atomic Energy Agency, 190
International class solidarity, 159
International Communist movement, 180
International demonstration effect, 164
International Monetary Fund (IMF), 163
Iron rice bowl, 35

Japan
 aid to China by, 192(n65)
 foreign direct investment in China by, 193, 193(n66)
 major financial power, 193(n67)
 "northern territories," 174
Japanese-American Mutual Security Treaty (MST), Chinese attitudes toward, 195–196
Japanese commercial invasion (fall 1985), 28, 131, 194
Japanese External Trade Organization (JETRO), 167
Japanese textbooks issue, 194
Jiang Qing, 4, 65, 78, 105
 after Lushan confrontation, 87
Jiang Zemin
 appointment of, 94
 and Deng Xiaoping Thought, 106(n119)
 denouncing Gorbachev, 173
 leadership core, 95

 low-profile suppression of Shanghai's democracy movement, 152
 successorship, 103
 visit to Moscow, 176
 visit to Pyongyang (spring 1990), 173
Jiben danwei. *See* Basic units
Jinggangshan, 83
Jin-Ji-Lu-Yu military region (Shanxi-Hebei-Shandong-Henan), 84
Joint ventures, 33(n45)

Kaifang zhengce. *See* Open-door policy
Kaifu, Toshiki, visit to China, 196
Kang Sheng
 and *Hai Rui's Dismissal*, 133(n58), 134
 Mao's personal confidant, 65
 and Nie Yuanzi, 135(n61)
 proletarian revolutionary line, 38
Kang Youwei, 125
Khmer Rouge in Cambodia, 182
Khrushchev, Nikita, 67(n42–43)
 1956 critique of the cult of personality, 65
 peaceful evolution, 162
 secret speech denouncing Stalin (1956), 86
Kirilenko, Andrei, 67(n43)
Kissinger, Henry, 56, 80
"Kitchen cabinet" of radical intellectuals, 87
KMT. *See* Kuomingtang
Kokaryo, ownership dispute between Taiwan and PRC, 194, 195(n71)
Korea, Democratic People's Republic of, 49
Kuai Dafu (Red Guard leader), 74, 136
Kuomingtang (KMT), 58, 160

LDCs. *See* Less-developed countries
Leadership efficacy, 49
Leadership succession
 Deng's solution, 5
 Mao's solution, 5
Lei Feng, 129, 201
Lenin, V. I., last testament of, 67(n43)
Less-developed countries (LDCs), 161–162
Let a Hundred Flowers Bloom, 33. *See also* Hundred Flowers movement
Liao Mosha, 135(n62)
 rehabilitation of, 23
Ligachev, Egor, 176
Lin Biao, 64(n36), 76
 after Second Plenum of Ninth Party Congress, 117–118
 confrontation with Mao, 77
 death of (September 13, 1972), 72
 Mao's closest comrade-in-arms, 77

Nanchang Uprising, 83
September 13 [1972] Incident, 88
Li Peng, 100, 103, 145, 147, 156
    call for closer economic cooperation with socialist countries, 172
    denouncing Gorbachev, 173
    leading role in June crackdown after Tiananmen Square demonstrations (1989), 150
    rise of, 99
    and students protesting Japan (1985), 139
    visit to Moscow (April 23–26, 1990), 174, 177
    visit to Southeast Asian countries after June crackdown, 164
    Zhao Ziyang's indictment, 151
Li Rui, 146
Li Ruihuan, 103–104, 152
Liu Binyan
    against the Four Cardinal Principles, 141
    expelled from party, 142(n81)
Liu Bocheng, 84
    and Nanchang Uprising, 83
Liu-Deng alignment, 86
Liu-Deng Army, 84
Liu Huaqing, 103
Liu Shaoqi, 10, 45–46, 78, 85, 91
    bureaucratic institutionalization, 92
    chief of state, 64(n35)
    "China's Khrushchev," 88
    and Chinese interpretation of Marxism, 161(n4)
    and cult of personality, 86
    and Cultural Revolution, 21, 71
    on *dang quan pai,* 21(n23)
    and Deng Xiaoping, 22–23, 85
    distinction between politics and economics, 17–18
    on division of labor, 19(n20)
    elitism, 16
    first front, 62
    Great Leap Forward, support of, 65
    inner-party mechanisms of self-cultivation, 22
    Mao's criticism target, 134
    Mao's heir apparent (1959), 64, 67(n42)
    on the masses (1942), 18
    material incentives, 38
    and Nie Yuanzi, 135(n61)
    and principle of collective leadership, 86
    published works, 23, 23(n29)
    purged, 88
    rehabilitation of, 23, 40

    revisionism, 13, 15
    in Socialist Education Movement, 20, 20(n21)
    "two fronts" arrangement, 65
    in "White" area, 17
    work teams, 76, 136(n63)
Li Xiannian, 151
    chief of state, 26
    in Cultural Revolution, 21
    secret consultations with Deng before fall of Gang of Four, 145
Liyi. See Self-interest
Local rumors (*xiaodao xiaoxi*), 123
Long March, 56, 84, 102
Long-Term Trade Agreement (with Japan), 191
Love-them-and-leave-them pattern (succession pattern), 94
Luan. See Chaos
Lu Dingyi
    bourgeois liberalization, 141
    in Cultural Revolution, 21
Luo Fu, 60
Luo Ruiqing, 62
Lu Ping, 135(n61)

Ma Ding, 141. *See also* Song Longxiang
Malenkov, Georgi, 67(n43)
Mandate of heaven, 115
Many roads to socialism, 13
Mao Zedong, 2, 6–7, 15, 42, 44(n60), 54, 56, 79, 91, 104–105, 120, 122, 126, 133
    absolute and monolithic conception of truth, 17–18
    against bureaucracy, 92
    age and youth, political implication of, 55
    August–September 1971 tour, 78
    Bohemian life style, 92
    big-character posters (July 1957), 128(n50)
    Cankao xiaoxi ("Reference News"), 121(n29)
    and Central Cultural Revolutionary Group, 134
    charismatic leadership, 55
    "class struggle," revival of (1962), 87
    communist utopia, 4
    continuous revolution, theory of, 162
    on contradictions, 111–112
    cult of personality, 25
    Cultural Revolution, 21, 71, 74, 87
    and Deng Xiaoping, 86
    father, relationship with, 56–58
    favorites of, 97
    and Gao Gang, 61

Hai Rui's Dismissal, 133(n58), 135(n62)
Hundred Flowers and the Great Leap Forward, 13
  on iconoclasm, 16
  on intellectuals, 19–60
  and Jiang Qing, 84
  Jinggangshan, 83
  Korean War, 85
  lifelong radical commitments, 73
  and Lin Biao, 66(n41), 77–78
  and Liu Shaoqi, 62, 66(n41)
  love-them-and-leave-them pattern, 94
  Lushan, 11
  Marxism, superficial acquaintance with, 56(n18)
  mass line, 15, 76
  May 1966 comment, 31
  meeting of 7,000 cadres (January 1962), 87
  mother, relationship with, 56–58
  and Nie Yuanzi, 134
  Oedipal complex, 56, 58(n22), 60
  Peng Zhen, complaints against, 117(n17)
  poetry by, 69–70
  premortem succession, 68
  proletarian revolutionary line, 38
  public criticism of, 129
  purge during the Cultural Revolution, 73(n55)
  Red Guards, 51, 156
  rehabilitation of veteran cadres, 72
  resignation from "first front," 62, 63–64, 64(n35)
  on revolution, 16
  "second front," 86
  Selected Works, fifth volume of, 25
  Snow, Edgar, conversation with (1965), 70
  Socialist Education Movement, 20, 20(n21)
  Soviet Union as model for China, 167
  succession problems, 65–66, 77
  Three Worlds, theory of, 88, 162
  visit to his birthplace, 65
  and Wang Hongwen, 78
  Wu Han, criticism campaign of, 135(n62)
  on youth, 59–61, 70
  and Zhou Enlai, 62
Mao Zedong Thought, 45, 63, 71, 154
  achievements of, 39
  deleted from CCP Constitution, 11
  fallibility of, 26–27
  revival of, 31
  "schoolhouse" of, 15
Market economics, 130
Marketization (1960s), 14

Market reforms (1960s), 31
Martial law (May 19, 1989), 103, 129, 149, 158
Martial law imposed by China on Tibet, 144, 144(n84)
Marx, Karl, 111
  denigration of "bourgeois privacy," 112
  on division of labor, 19(n20)
Marxism, Chinese, 50
Marxism-Leninism, goals of, 3
Mass criticism or purge, 20. *See also* Socialist Education Movement
Mass culture, 154
Masses, 15–16, 51, 112
Masses' interests, 18
Mass line, 15, 208
Mass media, 119
Mass mobilization, 21–22, 76, 123, 131
Mass movements, 3, 5, 123–124, 153, 201
  renunciation of by Cultural Revolution policies, 27–28
Mass participation, 76
Mass struggle, 27
May Fourth Movement (1915–1924), 55, 58
May 16 Circular, 135
Means of production, 204
Meritocratic Confucian bureaucracy, 111
Meritocratic pluralism, 32
Military cutbacks, 184
Ministry of Broadcasting, Television, and Movies (China), 119
Ministry of Culture (China), 119
Missile Technology Control Regime, 190
"Money is everything" (*wang qian kan*) mentality, 130
Monocratic nature of CCP leadership, 53
Monument to People's Heroes, 138
Mukden Incident, 138
Multicandidate district elections (1980–1981), 30
Multiple-candidacy county-level elections, 41
Multiple-candidacy elections to local people's congresses, 29
Multiprice market, 206

Nanchang Uprising, 83
National liberation wars, 162
National output (GNP) growth, 34
National Students' Federation Preparatory Committee, 147
NCNA. *See* New China News Agency
Nehru, Pandit, pacifism of, 162
New China News Agency (NCNA), 42
New Democracy, 11

New international economic order (NIEO), 163
"New Order for the Socialist Commodity Economy," 100
"New thinking" (Gorbachev), 184
"New world order," 175
  China's role in, 181
NICs. *See* East Asian newly industrialized countries
Nie Yuanzi, 135(n61)
  defiance of the work team, 134
Ninth Party Congress (April 1969), 77
Nixon, Richard, February 1972 visit to China, 169
Nixon opening, 188
Nomenclature, 40
Nonaligned Movement, 161–162, 165
Nonantagonistic contradiction, 65, 112
Normalization of Sino-American relations (1979), 39
North Expedition (*beifa*) (1926–1927), 83
Nuclear Non-Proliferation Treaty, 190
Nuclear proliferation to regional powers, 189

On Cultivation, 23
"One country, two systems," 34
On Inner-Party Struggle, 23
On Liberty, 111
On the Correct Handling of Contradictions Among the People, 111
On the Party, 161(n4)
OPEC. *See* Organization of Petroleum Exporting Countries
Open-door policy (*kaifang zhengce*), 33, 39
"Open-door" system in education, 75
Opening to the outside world, 141
Opinions of the masses (*renmin qunzhong de yijian*), 111
Organization Department of the CCP, 85
Organization of Petroleum Exporting Countries (OPEC), 165
Outer Space Treaty, 190

Pacific Fleet (Russia), 184
Pacificism, 162
Paramount leader (PL), 52–54, 92, 108
Paris Communes, 72
Parliamentary road, 72
Partial reform syndrome, 202
Party elite, 16
Party rectification campaign (1982), 40–41, 42
Party's legitimacy, 44

Peace and Friendship Treaty (Sino-Japan) (1978), 191
Peaceful evolution, 162, 186, 188, 206
Peng Dehuai
  adhering to the principle of collective leadership and combatting the cult of personality, 86
  Battle of the Hundred Regiments, 84
  and Gao Gang, 62
  "military club," 117
  purge of, 86
Peng Zhen, 26, 117(n17), 151
  chairman of "group of five," 135(n62)
  in Cultural Revolution, 21
  Mao's criticism target, 134
  member of Cultural Revolution Group, 135
  rehabilitation in 1979, 23
People's Daily, 119, 126, 140, 143
People's democratic dictatorship, 115
"People's publications" (*min kan*), 138
Per capita national product (China) (1977–1985), 34
Perkins, Dwight, 73
Personality, cult of, 51, 129, 134
  critique of, 65
Personnel files (*dangan*) (of unit membership), 121
Petofi Club, 109
PL. *See* Paramount leader
Plaza Accord, 193
Politburo members, power bases of, 52
Political reform, 98, 98(n104), 144, 204
"Politics in command," 42, 46
Polozkov, Ivan, visit to Beijing, 176–177
Populism, 50–51
Post-Leap experiments, 13
Post-Leap revisionist period, 36
Post-Mao Left, 39
Postmortem political succession, 66–67
Power seizures by Red Guards (1967), 74, 136
Practice as the Sole Criterion of Truth, 33, 125
Premortem political succession, 66, 68, 93
Price reform, 100, 206
  arbitrage (*guan dao*), 36
  dual price structure, 36
"Primary stage of socialism," 11, 37
Princes and princesses (*taizi*), 138
"Princes' party" (*taizi dang*), 94
Privatization, 14, 117, 206
Productivity in the rural sector, 201–202
Profit-maximizing (*liji zhuyi*), 112
Proletarian dictatorship, 202
Proletarian hegemony, 50

Index

Proletarian revolutionary line, 38, 51
"Proletarian revolutionary" nation-states, 159
"Proletarian road," 71
Propaganda system, 119–120
Protest against Japanese commercial imperialism, 138–139
Protest movement in favor of democracy and reform (fall 1986), 28
Protests of the intellectuals (1986), 101
"Provisional Regulations on Safeguarding National Secrets," 121
Psychoanalysis, 130
Public (*gong*), 110
Publications in China, 127
Publicity (*gongkai*), concept of, 110, 115
Public opinion (*yulun*), 111
Public sphere, 5, 114, 124, 157–158
Pye, Lucian, 56

Qian Qichen (foreign minister), visit to African countries after Tiananmen crackdown, 164
Qiao Shi, 100, 104
  and Ceausescu, 172
  "Chinese solution," 173
Qin Benli, 152
Qing guan. *See* Clean official
Qingming festival (Chinese memorial day), 89
Qiu shi (official journal), 119–120

Radical policy line, 14
Rao Shushi, 12(n6), 62
Realpolitik, 117
Records of the Historian (*shi ji*), 56
Red Army, 83
Red Chamber Dream, 122
"Red-eyed disease," 44(n60)
Red Flag, 140
Red Guard, 113, 134, 156
  demobilization, 73, 77
  faction fight, 74
  Mao's blessing, 71
"Red head reference" (*hong tou cankao*), 121
Red Star (army newspaper), 84
"Reference Information" (*Cankao ziliao*), 121
"Reference News" (*Cankao xiaoxi*), 120, 120(n29)
Reform
  demonstrations in support of (December 1986), 131
  post-Mao movement, 9

second stage, 202
three different pedigrees, 10
Renqing wei. *See* Human feeling
Republic of Russia, 182
"Resolution of the CCPCC on the Guiding Principles for Building a Socialist Society with an Advanced Culture and Ideology," 98, 141
"Resolution on Some Historical Questions in Our Party since the Eleventh Party Congress," 126
Responsibility field system (mid-1950s), 12
Responsibility plots (before 1962), 38
Responsibility system, 31, 44(n60)
Returned student faction, 60
Reversal of just verdicts, 89
Revisionism, 40
  critique of, 21, 22
  Deng Xiaoping, 13
  Liu Shaoqi, 13
Revisionist policy line, 5, 14
Revolution
  continuing, early stage of, 14; under dictatorship of proletariat, 2
  continuous, 3
Revolutionary approach to modernization, 3
Revolutionary Committees, 72, 74
Revolutionary masses, 22, 76
Revolutionary Military Council, 84
Revolutionary revivalism, 64
Revolutionary successors, 94
Rich peasant line, 83
Romantic triangle, 169
Routinization, 107
Rui Xingwen, 103, 152
Rural township and village enterprises, 35
Rustication of Red Guard (summer 1968), 136

Salisbury, Harrison, 56
Samizdat, 124(n37)
Sanctions against China for human rights violations, 166
San jia cun. *See* Three family village
SARs. *See* Special Administrative Regions
Schmidt, Helmut, 80
SDF. *See* Self-defense force (Japan)
Second channel (*di er qudao*), 127
Second Cold War, 181
Second echelon, 94
Second Field Army (129th Division), 84
Second front, 61, 64(n36), 65–66, 86, 204
Second "Great Leap Forward," 140
Second intermediate zone, 102

Second line, 64(n35). *See also* Second front
Second Plenum of Ninth Party Congress, 118
Second World, 162
Secularization, 125
Seek truth through facts, 23, 33
Selected Works of Deng Xiaoping (1975–1982), 106(n119)
Self-censorship by mass media, 119
Self-defense force (SDF) (Japan), 196
Self-interest (*liyi*), 112
Self-reliance, 73, 166
  reversal of, 33
September 13 [1972] Incident, 88
Seven black classes (*hei qi lei*), 22
Seventh Red Army, 83
SEZs. *See* Special Economic Zones
Shanghai People's Council, 52
Shao Quanlin, 135(n62)
Shenzhen Youth Daily, 131(n54)
Shi shi qiu shi. See Seek truth through facts
Sino-American contacts (early 1970s), 162
Sino-American relations (since Tiananmen), 188
Sino-Japanese trade, 191–192
Sino-Russian relations, 186–187
Sino-Soviet antagonism, 169
Sino-Soviet dispute, 85
Sino-Soviet normalization talks (1982), 170
Sino-Soviet relations (1980s), 169, 188
Sino-Soviet trade, 175
Sit-in, 146
Sixth Plenum of Eleventh Party Congress, 126
Sixth Plenum of Twelfth CC, 98, 141
Small gang of four, 30, 93(n92)
Smith, Adam, 43, 111
Snow, Edgar, 70
Socialist camp, 162
Socialist Education Movement (1962–1966), 14, 20
Socialist fraternity, 187
Socialist imperialism, 162
Socialist market economy, 202
Socialist spiritual civilization, 41, 129, 132, 141, 201
Socialization of means of communication, 115
Socialization of means of production, 3, 11, 36, 44, 51, 84–85, 115
Social monolithicity (*yiyuanhua*), 42
Soft science, 141
Solidarity (Poland), 109
Song Jiang, 122
Song Longxiang, 141
Song Ping, 151–152

South Pacific Nuclear Free Zone, 190
Soviet-American détente, 6, 170
Soviet-American relations, 188
Soviet coup (August 19, 1991), 177, 180
Soviet crackdowns on Czechoslovakia (1968), 153
Soviet crackdowns on Hungary (1956), 153
Soviet military cutbacks, 171(n24)
Soviet model, CCP rejection of, 14
Soviets (*suweiai*), 83
Soviet Union, 73, 124, 160–162
  disintegrated, 178
  electoral deposal of Khrushchev, 108
  preemptive nuclear strike against China, 168
  succession crisis, 68
Special Administrative Regions (SARs), 34
Special Economic Zones (SEZs), 38
Specialized households, 32
Spiritual pollution, 129
  campaign against, 28, 42, 99, 132
Stage of primitive socialism, 12
Stalin, Joseph, 67(n43)
  after Khrushchev's repudiation of (1956), 13
  political violence, 73, 73(n55)
Stalinist model, departure from, 14
State Council's Education Commission, 145
State enterprises (1991), 45(n61)
Stone Corporation, 158
Strategic Arms Limitations Talks, 39
Strategic Arms Reduction Treaties, 170
Strategic triangle, 169
  dissolved, 6
Structuralism, 130
"Struggle between two lines," 65, 75
Student protests (December 1986), 27, 98, 142–143
Succession arrangements, 65–66, 80
Succession crisis, 30, 66–67, 93, 95, 102, 107, 191, 203, 208
Sun Tzu, 116
Sun Yatsen University, 83
Su Shaozhi, 144

Taiwan
  dollar diplomacy, 174
  membership in the Asian Pacific Economic Community, 182
Taizi dang. See "Princes' party"
Tan Zhenlin, 21
Tenth Party Congress, 78, 88
Tenth Plenum of Eighth CC, 87

Index

Ten-Year Plan (1991–1999), 96(n100)
Ten years of catastrophe, 29, 36
Textbook crisis (Japan), 195
Theory of continuing the revolution under dictatorship of proletariat, 126
Theory of continuous revolution (1950s), 162
Theory of Three Worlds, 162–163, 165
Third echelon, 94
Third Plenum of Eleventh CC (December 1978), 90, 101, 128, 131
Third Plenum of Thirteenth CC, 100
Third Plenum of Twelfth CC (October 1984), 139–140, 202
Third World, 161–163
   Beijing's return to, 164
   China's competition with, 166
   China's flexible stance toward, 165
   China's identification with, 169, 179, 181
Thirteenth Party Congress (November 1987), 11, 37, 95, 99, 102
Three bad years (1959–1962), 65
Three crises of faith, 36
Three Deep Loves (motherland, socialism, party), 41
Three economic development zones (May 1992), 183
Three family village (*san jia cun*), 135(n62)
Three Obstacles to normalization (with Soviet Union), 170
Three Red Flags (Great Leap Forward, people's commune, and General Line), 3, 49
Three types of person, 40, 44(n60)
Tiananmen Incident (April 5, 1976), 30, 76, 136–137
Tiananmen Square demonstrations (1989), 109, 116, 122, 143, 156, 158, 171, 190, 197, 209
   consequences of, 6, 10
   June crackdown after, 1, 46, 96, 150, 196
   retrenchment after, 180
Tian Han (playwright), 135(n62)
Tong Dalin, 144
Trade deficit (1985), 140
Transition crisis, 203
Transparent (*gongkaixing*), 128
Treasury of Deng Xiaoping's Thought, 106(n119)
Trip south (*nanxun*), 96, 186
Tukhachevsky, Mikhail, 73
Turmoil (*dongluan*), 147
Twelfth Party Congress (September 1982), 40, 42, 93(n92)
"Two-camps" model, 161

Two fronts, 61, 65. *See also* First front; Second front
Two-tiered foreign policy, 160
"Two whatevers," 125, 125(n39)

Ulbricht, Walter, 67(n42)
Underground railroad (after Tiananmen crackdown), 151
United front, 58
United Nations, China's entry into, 163
United States, 162
   China's largest single export market in 1989, 189
   imposition of sanctions by, in aftermath of Tiananmen, 188–189
   Japan-bashing by, 196
Unity and consensus (*yu lun yi zhi*), 114
University of Science and Technology in Hefei, 142
University of Toilers of the East in Moscow, 60
Urban reforms, 42(n57)

Veterans' retirement, 93, 93(n92)
Vietnam, China's border war with (1979), 186
Vietnam War, 168–169
VOA. *See* Voice of America
Voice of America, 148, 153

Wang Guangmei, Taoyuan (peach) Garden Brigade, 20
Wang Hongwen, 78, 78(n62), 92
Wang Meng, 152
Wang Ming, 60
Wang qian kan. *See* Money is everything
Wang Ruoshui, 144
Wang Ruowang, 142(n81)
Wang Zhen, 151
Wan Li, 141
War of Resistance Against Japan Museum, 195
Warsaw Pact, 172
Water Margins, 122
Weber, Max, 16, 54
Weiji gan. *See* Sense of crisis
Wei Jingsheng, petitions for release of, 144
Western concept of the "private," 111
Western concept of the "public," 112, 114
Western democratic theory, 130
Western Marxism, 130
"Whateverists," 38
Wolf, Markus, trial of, 179

Work teams, 134, 134(n60), 136(n63), 139, 145
  in Cultural Revolution, 22
  in Socialist Education Movement, 20
World Bank, 163
World Economic Herald, 131(n54), 152, 158
World trade, China's share of, 166(n16)
Worldwide proletarian revolution, 160–161
Wu De, 137(n66)
Wu Han (vice-mayor of Beijing and playwright), 122, 135(n62)
  critique of, 21
  rehabilitation of, 23
Wu Xun (film), criticism of, 122

Xiaodao xiaoxi. See Local rumors
Xinhua News Agency, 119
Xu Jiatun, 42
Xu Xiangqian, 118

Yang Baibing, 103
Yang Fucheng, 164
Yang Shangkun, 83, 103, 147, 178
  leading role in the Tiananmen crackdown, 150
  visit to Arab countries and Latin America, 165
Yangtze Gorge dam project, 119
Yang Xianzhen (philosopher), 135(n62)
Yang yao jing. See Great Leap Westward
Yan Jiaqi, 144
Yan Mingfu, 103, 152
Yan Xishan (Shanxi warlord), 17
Yao Wenyuan's critique of *Hai Rui's Dismissal*, 135(n62)
Yao Yilin, 100, 145
  call for closer economic cooperation with socialist countries, 172
Yasukuni Shrine issue, 138–139, 194
Ye Jiangying, 118
Yeltsin, Boris, 176–178
  visit to China (December 1992), 183
Yiyuanhua. See Social monolithicity

Youth League, 61
Youth League faction, 140
Yu Guangyuan, 144
Yulun. See Public opinion
Yulun yi zhi. See Unity and consensus
Yu Pingbo, 122

Zhang Zhidong, 43, 205
Zhang Zhixin, 29(n36)
Zhao Ziyang, 26, 99, 145, 146–147, 155–157, 171
  and April 26 editorial, 147
  and Chen Yun's Eight Opinions, 145(n86)
  confrontation with Li Peng, 149
  fall of, 38, 95, 103–104, 143, 151
  political reform, 42(n58), 144
  price reform, 100
  proposal for creation of a new international economic order (NIEO), 163
  rendezvous with hunger strikers, 156
  three functions for the media, 130(n53)
  and Tiananmen demonstrations, 102
  ultimate power of Deng Xiaoping, 101
Zhengfeng (rectification) movement, 52(n8)
Zhengzhi jichu. See Power bases
Zhou Enlai, 4, 67(n43), 74, 78, 82, 85, 120, 168
  in Cultural Revolution, 21
  and mass media, 120(n26)
  Nanchang Uprising, 83
  and Nie Yuanzi, 135(n61)
  Ninth Party Congress, 77
Zhou Jiahua, 145
Zhu De, 17
  in the Cultural Revolution, 21
  and Gao Gang, 62
  Jinggangshan, 83
  Nanchang Uprising, 83
  and Twentieth Party Congress of the Soviet Union in Moscow, 86
Zhugo Liang, 50
Zhu Rongji, 96(n100), 103
Zunyi conference (1935), 84